The Sattler's Diary

998

A Love Story
Between a Store and Its Community

by Mary Ann Siuta Voorhees

SATTLER'S SHOE STORE
1000

The Sattler's Diary

A Love Story Between a Store and Its Community

Copyright © 2021 Mary Ann Siuta Voorhees

ISBN:978-1-945423-31-4

PUBLISHED BY: Five Stones Publishing
A DIVISION OF: The International Localization Network
randy2905@gmail.com ILNcenter.com

Without limiting the rights under copyright reserved above, no part of this publication may be reproduced, stored in or introduced into a retrieval system, or transmitted, in any form, or by any means (electronic, mechanical, photocopying, recording, or otherwise), without the prior written permission of the publisher.

The picture on the front cover is of the opening ceremony of Sattler's Golden Jubilee in 1939. Pictured from left to right are John G. Sattler, Charles Hahn and Buffalo Mayor Thomas L. Holling. Photograph courtesy of the Archives and Special Collections Department, E. H. Butler Library, SUNY Buffalo State.

The picture on the back cover is from October 1935. A crowd gathered outside Sattler's for the first of four weekly drawings to win a 1936 Graham Sedan. Photograph courtesy of the Voorhees Family.

Contents

Dedication

This book would not have been possible without the stories and memories of Julian Rabow, Bob Cornelius, Jack Hahn and Jill Hahn Russo, as well as the hundreds of people who kindly shared their family stories, photographs and experiences at Sattler's. That is what inspired me to write this book. I dedicate *The Sattler's Diary* to them and their families.

Introduction

What really made Sattler's unique for its customers were its employees, the advertising, the promotions, the contests, the giveaways, the grand openings and the celebrities who visited the store. Let's not forget all the merchandise, the bargain prices and the large range of services the store had to offer everyone. There are so many categories of events and happenings at the store over the years that I have found it hard to group them. As a result, I thought it best to put this book in chronological order. See what made Sattler's that "Hellzapoppin'" place for its customers and its employees!

I would like to offer anyone who has memories, photographs, or stories of Sattler's to share them on "***The Sattler's Diary***" Facebook page. As you read this book you will notice many of the photographs have unnamed faces. Please help me bring their contributions to Sattler's to light - and let them not be forgotten - by adding a name to an unknown face in a photograph. Thank You!

\- Mary Ann Siuta Voorhees

Photograph courtesy of the Voorhees Family.

John G. Sattler

John G. Sattler was born in East Aurora, New York on July 29, 1871 to German immigrants, George Adam and Elizabeth Geise Sattler. John added the "G" as a middle initial, for his father's name, George, so people would not confuse him with his cousin, John Sattler.

John had three siblings: a sister, Lizzie, who married Franz Herber and who was believed to have died during childbirth at the age of 22; another sister, Katherine, who died at age 6 (1); and a brother Adam, who is believed to have died as a young child. (2)

First living in East Aurora, the Sattler family moved to Buffalo, NY when John was three. He attended Public School 31 in Buffalo, and then Bryant & Stratton Business School for one year. (3)

John's father, George, was in the grocery business. He had shops at the corner of Broadway and Fox, as well as on Clinton, Howard, Smith Streets and Fillmore Avenue - all in the city of Buffalo. He was also involved in home construction, along with other family members on Buffalo's East Side.

Being exposed to the family businesses, John obtained a personal understanding of the business world in both grocery and real estate. This would become a key to his successful business career.

At the age of 15, John started working at Eckhardt's Department Store on Broadway and Fillmore. The store was owned by John H. Eckhardt and his wife Catherine L. Haberman Eckhardt. Catherine was John's first cousin. It must have been an enlightening experience to work for John H. Eckhardt, who became known as the "father" of the Broadway Fillmore Business District.

John Sattler was ambitious and started working at Eckhardt's for a salary of $3 per week. He received a .25 raise each week until he became manager of the shoe department, for which he earned a weekly salary of $12.

The year was 1889, and John was 17 years old when this young entrepreneur started his own store on a piece of property that his mother owned. John's mother gave him the money to start his store, which he called "The Broadway Market Shoe House." John was finally his own boss. He was also the only employee, so his jobs included salesperson, buyer and janitor. He lived above the store with his mother. When the store was slow or when he went upstairs for dinner, a bell attached to the door would alert him to a new customer. At first John only sold ladies' and gentlemen's shoes. However, with the Broadway Market open directly across the street from the fledgling shoe store, John saw an opportunity and began to market his shoes to the area's workmen and farmers. (4)

The farmers and vendors would bring their produce, honey and animals to sell. At the end of the day when their wares were gone and their pockets were full, they would come over and buy pairs of boots. All boots and shoes were only 98 cents. Mr. Sattler made sure to keep the shoes at a bargain price below $1.00 and he marketed them as "Nothing Fancy." Later in life he once recounted that "I used to tie the pairs together by their strings and put them all in tray-like counters, nothing fancy you see."(5)

In 1900, Broadway was still a street made of cobblestone, with wooden planks for sidewalks. But it was time for "The Broadway Market Shoe House" to be replaced with a larger and more modern building! This was the first of many major expansions for the store. (5)

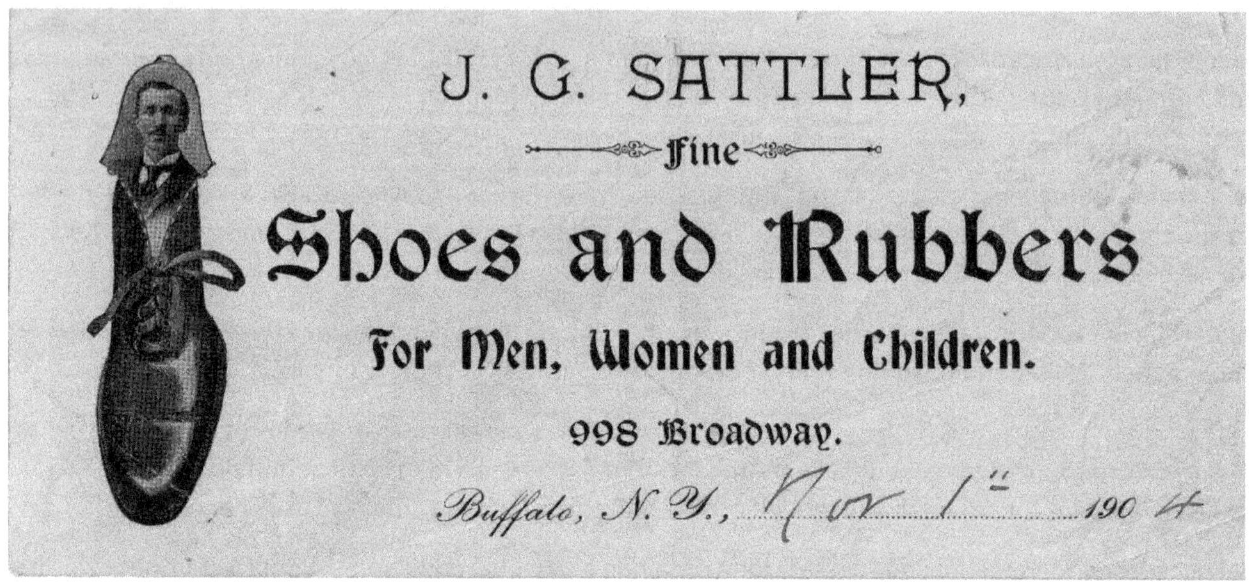
J. G. SATTLER,
Fine
Shoes and Rubbers
For Men, Women and Children.
998 Broadway.
Buffalo, N. Y., Nov 1st 1904

A Cherished Photo for a Granddaughter

While I was visiting my mother-in-law just a few years ago, we began talking about her family. She showed me pictures of her paternal relatives. In due course we began to talk about the Sattler family, and she lamented that she never knew what her grandmother, Alma Sattler, looked like. I thought that was rather odd, as my mother-in-law came from a prominent family. The only pictures of the Sattler family that I found were in the archives of the Sattler's building at 998 Broadway. It was then, with many tears that the story came out that a small fire had destroyed all of the known Sattler family pictures.

Of course I told my dear mother-in-law that I would do my utmost to find a picture of her Grandma Sattler. But where to look? I had been unsuccessful for over 20 years asking relatives. Where else could I turn? Then I looked up her name on the internet and I couldn't believe my eyes! There was information on "Gen Forum" from a gentleman who posted: "I purchased the subject studio portrait of a young woman taken by William B. Todd, Buffalo, NY. It is identified on the back of the mount in period handwriting: 'Alma Otto Sattler, January-1903'."

Wow! I was blown away. The posting on the computer was dated October 10, 2009, about 6 years before I discovered the inquiry. I contacted the owner of the portrait of Alma Otto Sattler and he lived hundreds of miles out of town. He told me that he had done some research on Alma and found out that she was the wife of a shoe dealer.

I bought the portrait for $20.00 and mailed the original to my mother-in-law. Once she opened the unexpected gift there were tears of joy. We spoke on the phone about how quickly I was able to find and obtain a picture of her grandmother through internet connections. We were so grateful that this kind Midwestern gentlemen cared enough about an unknown family that he did his own research and posted the portrait of Alma Otto Sattler online.

Photograph courtesy of Jill Hahn Russo.

Alma Otto

Alma Otto was the daughter of Charles Otto, a foundry worker at the Howard Iron Works, and Ida Drewelow, a homemaker. Alma's parents, as well as 5 of her siblings, her widowed maternal grandmother, 3 aunts, and 3 uncles all emigrated together from Hanover, Germany. They moved to the United States in 1872 and made homes on the East Side of Buffalo. A family quote from Alma's Grandma, Wilhelmina Drewelow, stated that "I brought my children here to be industrious men and women and worthy citizens."(6) Alma became a model for this family creed.

Alma was born August 16, 1877 and was the first of her siblings to be born in the United States. She had sisters Emma and Elsie born after her. Alma attended the most populated Buffalo Public School, PS 31 located on Emslie Street near William. Her older sister, Mary M. Otto, was one of the 5th grade teachers there. Alma graduated from PS 31 in 1893 and remained very involved with its alumni association, being elected to the position of vice-president in 1898. (7, 8) In the 1900 census Alma is said to be a "bookkeeper." (9)

Alma and her younger sister Emma were instrumental in helping to form a new social and dramatic club known as The Othello Club, in December of 1899. The sisters held the offices of secretary and vice-president, respectively, in the Ladies Auxiliary of The Othello Club. (10)

The Othello Club was wildly popular. The first year, the Club held an Othello Day event at "Buffalo's Coney Island," Crystal Beach. The Club provided the festivities of the day for a ticket cost of 25 cents. The ticket included a boat ride to and from the event, as well as an all-day packed program, starting at 10:30 A.M. with a ballgame between the "Othello's" and the "Buffalo Stars." The day included water polo games and swimming races, potato, three leg, sack, shoe, tub and boat races with prizes, dinner, supper and music. There were musicians from The Othello Club who performed as a quartet. Shows included a buck and wing dancer, tambourine dancer, comedians, acrobats, solo singers and solo musicians. There were bands playing for dancing throughout the afternoon and evening, with a huge fireworks display ending the event.

"Othello Day" at Crystal Beach and its resort area had the largest crowd of the 1900 season with 8,000 people crossing the lake to enjoy the performances and sporting events. The well-respected Club's actors also kept The Othello Club busy with performances throughout the years, with shows such as *Millions for a Wife*, *Married Life* and *What is Love?* The Club's *Masquerade Dances, Mistletoe Parties and The Othello Club Circus* were performed at weddings, schools, church events and private parties. (11-17, 18-22)

John and Alma

None of the descendants of John and Alma seem to know how the couple met. Since Alma's family had been living at 320 Sherman Street in the city of Buffalo for several decades, it has been suggested that John and Alma met when John Sattler had been visiting his family members on Sherman Street. (His grandparents George and Katherine Sattler lived in a home on Sherman Street, as did his Uncle Caspar and Aunt Catherine Haberman.) The couple also attended the same school, PS 31, and it has been suggested that Alma may have been an employee at The Broadway Market Shoe House. Whatever the fortune that brought the happy couple together, an early June wedding was planned in the summer of 1902.

The couple was married in the bride's sycamore-shaded family home on Sherman Street. It was a modest city home with a small front porch and an even smaller front lawn. The weather was fair during the day, with moderate temperatures and southerly winds. But, by the time the marriage ceremony was performed in the evening, it was raining. It is said that when there is rain on your wedding day, it is good luck for the couple. But truly, did anyone care? There was Alma in her blue traveling gown with her sister Emma as her attendant. John's best man was Frank Beckman. The marriage was performed by

Reverend F. A. Kahler of Holy Trinity Lutheran Church. The wedding was a small private affair, as the remaining immediate family members of the bride and groom consisted only of the bride and groom's mothers and Alma's remaining siblings.

On June 8, 1902 a marriage announcement appeared in the *Buffalo New York Morning Express*:

Sattler-Otto.

The marriage of Miss Alma Otto to Mr. John G. Sattler was quietly solemnized at the home of the bride on Monday evening, June 2d, the Reverend F. A. Kahler officiating. The bride wore her traveling gown of blue cloth. She was attended by her sister, Miss Emma R. Otto, and the best man was Mr. Frank Beckman. Mr. and Mrs. Sattler will be at home after July 20th at No. 1615 Fillmore avenue. (23)

Alma and John G. Sattler. Photograph courtesy of the Voorhees Family.

Purchase of a Home at 80 North Parade

After John's marriage and a brief move to a home on Fillmore Avenue, the Sattler family bought a double located at 80 North Parade Avenue. John's mother, Elizabeth Sattler, joined them at this address. **Photograph courtesy of the Voorhees Family.**

August 1903

Marion Sattler Is Born

August 19, 1903 was a "fair" weather day according to *The Buffalo Courier*. There were stories out of Oyster Bay, NY that President Roosevelt would not be attending the international yacht race, known as The America's Cup, which would be starting the next day. The two hot contenders for The America's Cup were the challenger *Reliance* and the defender *Shamrock III*. Another big story featured Jack W. Glenister swimming the rapids at Devil's Hole. However, at the Sattler household the joyful news was that Marion Sattler, the first child of John and Alma, was born. A healthy, strong child who would grow to be a Buffalo beauty. (24)

Photographs courtesy of the Voorhees Family.

June 1906

Katherine Sattler

June 28, the second of the Sattler girls would be born: a delicate daughter, Katherine Alma. Katherine was the apple of John Sattler's eye. She suffered from a congenital heart condition and would spend much of her life in bed.

Katherine and Marion Sattler
80 North Parade Street, Buffalo.
Photograph courtesy of the Voorhees Family.

1908

Real Estate Business

Along with Sattler's Shoe Store, John Sattler had an additional lucrative business career in real estate. (25, 26)

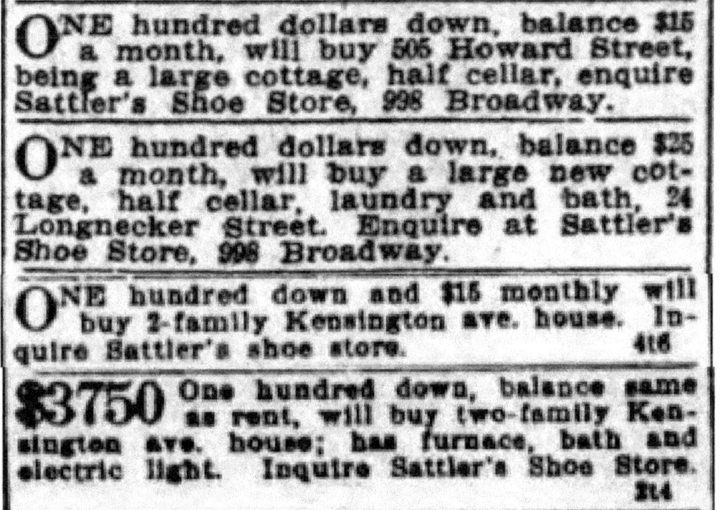

ONE hundred dollars down, balance $15 a month, will buy 505 Howard Street, being a large cottage, half cellar, enquire Sattler's Shoe Store, 998 Broadway.

ONE hundred dollars down, balance $25 a month, will buy a large new cottage, half cellar, laundry and bath, 24 Longnecker Street. Enquire at Sattler's Shoe Store, 998 Broadway.

ONE hundred down and $15 monthly will buy 2-family Kensington ave. house. Inquire Sattler's shoe store. 416

$3750 One hundred down, balance same as rent, will buy two-family Kensington ave. house; has furnace, bath and electric light. Inquire Sattler's Shoe Store. 2t4

April, 1909

Birth of Doris Sattler

The last of John and Alma's children was Doris Grace. Doris was born on April 5, 1909. She was a large ten-pound baby whose heart had stopped after birth and needed to be resuscitated. Luckily, Doris grew to be a healthy child. (27)

Photograph courtesy of Voorhees Family

December 1911

Gifts for Shoeshine Boys

LETTERS to Santa Claus should be addressed in care of Sattler's shoe store, 998 Broadway; children purchasing a box of 10c shoe polish will receive a handsome present; store open every evening until Xmas. 21122

It is only a guess on my part, but I believe it is very likely that John Sattler took care of the boys who made his business shine. Keeping the shoeshine boys happy was smart for business. The boys could tell him about the durability and quality of Sattler's shoes after they left his store, and the boys were also a source of information about how styles were changing. In addition, Mr. Sattler could get the skinny on other shoe dealers in the area from the shoeshiners. (28)

October 1913

Boy Injured by Auto

BOY INJURED BY AUTO.

John Lens, seven years old, of No. 1004 Humboldt parkway, was knocked down by an automobile in Fillmore avenue near Best street yesterday afternoon. The machine was driven by John G. Statler of No. 80 North Parade avenue in Fillmore avenue. A cut over the left eye was dressed by Dr. Fred Terrasse of No. 878 Sycamore street, after which the boy was driven home by Mr. Statler.

This article was in the *Buffalo Courier* on October 15, 1913. How times have changed. (29) Note that Mr. Sattler's name is incorrectly spelled, but the man driving the car was indeed Mr. John G. Sattler.

August- September 1915

Sattler Enters Race for Buffalo City Council

J. G. SATTLER ENTERS RACE FOR COUNCIL

Friends Obtain More Than Number of Signatures Required.

John G. Sattler, a proprietor of shoe stores at 998 Broadway and William and Shumway streets, announced today he will be a candidate for nomination as councilman. Mr. Sattler's friends have been circulating a petition which contain many more than the required 300 signers.

The committee named in Mr. Sattler's petition comprises Michael Whissell, lumber merchant, residing at 143 Lexington avenue; John Eckhardt, dry goods merchant, at 950 Broadway, and John A. Kloepfer, 166 Jewett avenue, president of the Union Stockyards bank.

"Friends began sending in votes for me to the NEWS in its Preference Primary," said Mr. Sattler today, "and urged me to enter the primary. These friends are all property owners, who are anxious to have a real business administration of city affairs, which, they believe, would result in more real development and public improvement in Buffalo, with lower tax rate because, with business principles applied to municipal management there would be no such extravagance and waste of the city's funds, such as Buffalo has suffered in recent years."

(30)

Councilmanic Candidates and Votes They Received

	Candidate	Votes
1.	Francis G. Ward	19,183
2.	Charles B. Hill	18,846
3.	Knowlton Mixer	16,661
4.	Charles M. Heald	15,943
5.	George B. Burd	15,028
6.	Fred W. Bond	14,776
7.	Arthur W. Kreinheder	13,701
8.	John F. Malone	12,219
	(First eight nominated.)	
9.	Francis T. Coppins	10,043
10.	James Smith	9,864
11.	Louis J. Kenngott	9,595
12.	William J. Burke	8,275
13.	Frederick G. Bagley	6,500
14.	Gustave A. Hitzel	4,855
15.	Elmer E. Harris	4,644
16.	Charles E. McDonald	3,773
17.	Allan I. Holloway	3,495
18.	Arnold T. Armbrust	3,290
19.	John J. Smith	2,592
20.	William J. Coad	2,328
21.	William G. Humphrey	2,135
22.	Otto L. Geyer	1,407
23.	Vincent Roth	1,398
24.	Frederick P. Kull	1,353
25.	Frederick Haller	1,350
26.	Charles Robilfs	1,217
27.	Frank J. Eberle	1,101
28.	Michael J. Burke	998
29.	John G. Sattler	933
30.	James Battistoni	847
31.	Vincent Tuero	818
32.	Patrick O'Brien	811
33.	Harry Wurff	670
34.	Nicholas J. Mock	572
35.	James L. Nixon	469
36.	Alvin J. Marsch	379
37.	Harry Fisher	349
38.	John Purcell	304
39.	Leander A. Armstrong	238
40.	Edward C. Franklin	217
41.	William A. Bean	181
42.	Benjamin Lade	166
43.	Emanuel Hauk	163
44.	Anthony P. Schaeck	135
45.	William A. Rohloff	129
46.	George Blickensdorfer	120
	Total	314,100

(31)

John Sattler was not to be the candidate of choice for the 1915 election, as he was unable to win the primary with only 933 votes and was off the ballot at the 29th position. However, his cousin Mary's husband, Arthur W. Kreinheder, did win the Buffalo Council seat.

January 1916

Death of Katherine Alma Sattler

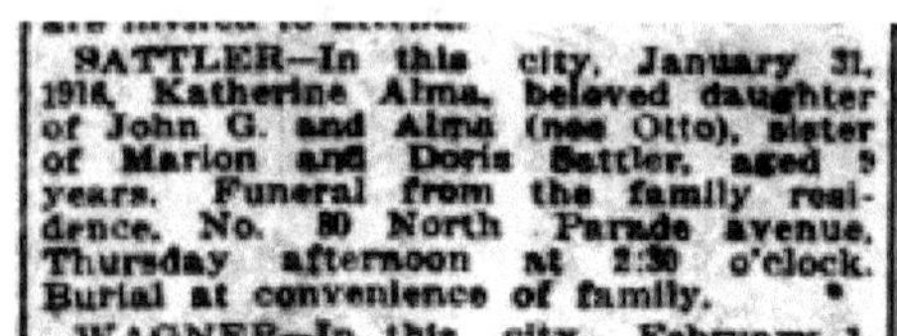

SATTLER—In this city, January 31, 1916, Katherine Alma, beloved daughter of John G. and Alma (nee Otto), sister of Marion and Doris Sattler, aged 9 years. Funeral from the family residence, No. 80 North Parade avenue, Thursday afternoon at 2:30 o'clock. Burial at convenience of family.

(32)

The Sattler's middle child was their darling Katherine. Katherine was a sickly child who suffered from a weak heart and she was often in bed because of weakness. In January of 1916, at the age of 9, Katherine's heart became still. John Sattler had a pocket watch made with the image of his dear little girl on the face of the watch. It was always a reminder of a child who had a sweet smile and a gentle disposition. **Photograph courtesy of the Voorhees Family.**

May 1917

Liberty Gardens

World War I had taken its toll on the European farmlands and fields that were used for battlegrounds. Food shortages were plaguing Europe, and the U.S. government urged the people of the United States to utilize unused lots and land to grow crops. The goal of this effort was to relieve Europe's hunger problem and to prepare the United States in case such devastation occurred in this country upon entering World War I.

In response, "Liberty Gardens" were planted throughout the country. In Buffalo, John Sattler offered 500 lots to be used for gardening. (33)

MERCHANT OFFERS FREE USE OF 500 LOTS FOR GARDENS

John G. Sattler, merchant at No. 998 Broadway, offers free use of 500 lots to home gardeners. They are in Union road, out Geneeee street. He has fifty lots in Genesee street near Bailey avenue, which gardeners may use. He will give use of one lot only to each applicant. Applications must be made at Mr. Sattler's store.

July 1924

Sattler's Expands

Here is a famous picture of John G. Sattler's first store. I am always amused when I look at the 100 + year-old photo. Young John G. Sattler is the clean-shaven man in the center of the photograph, standing next to the doorway. Mrs. Elizabeth Geise Sattler, John's mother, is wearing a white apron. I always wonder who the boy with the bike is, and what is the name of the dog? Signs posted in front of the store advertised shoes for sale at 49 and 59 cents; what a bargain!

The Tiny House at 998 Broadway Undergoes its First Expansion in 1924.

The buildings at 994-998 Broadway were replaced by a new three-story building. The cost for the new structure was estimated at $50,000 - $100,000. (34)

John Sattler (above right) and some of his employees. They are standing in front of his new store in 1925. This is an enlargement of the photograph on the previous page.

All photographs on this page and on page 23 are courtesy of the Voorhees Family.

It was the personal touch of Mr. John Sattler that helped draw in customers. Mr. Sattler would stand at the door and greet his customers daily, knowing many of them by name. More importantly, he would be at the door when the customers left the store. If a customer left without a purchase, Mr. Sattler would ask how he could serve them better in the future. That is how he found out what his customers wanted and needed so that he could modify his inventory by finding those items and adding them to his store. **Photograph courtesy of the Voorhees Family**.

Mr. Sattler was a canny businessman and also a man with a generous heart. He truly had concern for his community. While making those inquiries about what was needed by his customers, he also wanted to make sure that people in the Buffalo community had jobs. Mr. Sattler often would find businessmen in the Buffalo area who would manufacture an item needed for his store. By requesting services and goods from other local businesses, he helped keep the people of Buffalo employed. (35)

October 1925

Courtship and Wedding

One family who were tenants at the North Parade home became very close with the Sattler family. It was the family of Charles L. Hahn Sr., his wife Catherine and their young son Charles Jr.

The Hahn family rented the upstairs apartment on North Parade Ave. from the Sattler family. During that time, Marion Sattler and Charles Hahn became the best of friends. Several years later, the Sattlers - with the exception of John's mother Elizabeth Sattler - moved to a home that was located at 4014 Main Street in Eggertsville, NY and was built on some of John G. Sattler's vast real estate property.

The move out of 80 North Parade was difficult for Marion Sattler. Additional stress was brought on by Alma Sattler, Marion's mother, who was suffering from the effect of a debilitating stroke which left one of her legs partially paralyzed. At this point, Alma also suffered from severe depression which had plagued her since the birth of her last child and was a great source of concern for the Sattler family. In addition, the loss of Katherine, the younger sister of Marion Sattler, from congenital heart disease was still a heartbreaking memory that haunted Alma. None of this made life easy for Marion in her new home.

Marion dearly missed her Grandmother Elizabeth Sattler at her old home and her close friendship with Charles Hahn. It was during this time that Marion ran away and went back to the home where she grew up with her grandmother on North Parade. The circumstances and stress of the family's situation likely added to John and Alma's decision to allow Marion to stay with her grandmother.

Encouraged by the scheming Grandma Sattler, who adored Charles, the relationship between Marion and Charles grew into romance. When the parents of Charles were out, Marion would be a frequent visitor at the Hahns' apartment while Grandma Sattler would keep watch for the return of Charles' parents. Upon their return, Grandma Sattler alarmed the young couple by whacking the radiator with her cane to alert them that Charles' parents were approaching. (36, 37)

Elizabeth Geise Sattler

Marion Sattler

Charles Hahn

Charles Hahn was well liked by the Sattler Family. At the age of 22, he became an employee at Sattler's Shoe Store and his innovative style of business began catapulting Mr. Sattler's business to a very profitable bottom line. Consequently, when the intention of the young couple to marry was brought to John Sattler, he was delighted that Charles would be joining the family. **Photographs courtesy of the Voorhees Family.**

October 1925

Hahn-Sattler

On October 29, 1925, *The Buffalo Evening News* published the following marriage announcement: "Mr. and Mrs. John G. Sattler announce the marriage of their daughter, Marion, to Mr. Charles Hahn of Kenmore, NY Wednesday, October 28, at their home in Eggertsville, N.Y. Mr. and Mrs. Hahn are taking a wedding trip and will be at home on their return in Koster Row, Eggertsville." (38, 39)

A family story has been told about how John Sattler accompanied the young married couple on their honeymoon. He sat in the back seat of the car that Charles was driving and enjoyed munching on apples during their honeymoon trip.

June 1926

Bid for Welfare Shoes
Politics, Politics, Politics

The director of the Welfare Bureau, John J. Aeschbeck, put out a bid for pairs of shoes and rubbers for needy persons to be supplied by the Welfare Bureau. Complaints that Commissioner Perkins disregarded the low bid of $10,000 by John G. Sattler were heard at several Buffalo City Council sessions. The following information is on public record from City Council meetings held from June 1926 to September 1926:

Mr. Sattler's letter was as follows:

Hon. Mayor F. X. Schwab
Buffalo, NY

Buffalo, June 17, 1926

Dear Mayor,

We have submitted samples of shoes and rubbers with prices as per bids advertised for by the Bureau of Public Welfare. Two of our managers were present today when the bids were opened. Our bid was the lowest on shoes, also on first quality rubbers and our competitor bid on second grade rubbers which can be easily determined by name of the rubber. By calling up any rubber footwear dealer you can get this information.

Mr. Hillman, who opened the bids, stated that he was not a judge on footwear and would call in an expert to determine which the lowest bid was. Our price being so much lower than our competitor, we cannot understand his attitude. All we ask, is a fair deal. We are buying stocks from time to time at large discounts. As we have purchased the entire shoe stock from the E. P. Beaumont Mail Order House, Lincoln Building, Washington Street, amounting to about $40,000.00 at a discount of 27 ½ percent from the manufacturers' price on good wearing and up-to-date footwear, makes it possible to sell at prices quoted in our bid.

It is about three years that we bid on shoes and at that time we were the lowest bidder. Mr. Perkins called me up telling me he wanted to divide this business to give one Eastside dealer one West Side dealer and I believe one South Side dealer this business, which was business we were entitled to as the other dealers were not the lowest.

If you can do anything to give us a fair deal, it will be greatly appreciated.

Very truly yours,

JOHN G. SATTLER

Bids were as follows:

Department of Public Affairs
No 332 Ellicott Street,
Buffalo, N. Y.

Buffalo, June 16, 1926

Gentlemen:

We are herewith submitting samples and quote the following prices at which we will supply the Bureau of Public Welfare with shoes and rubbers.

	Shoes	Rubbers Pairs
Children's, age 6 years, sizes 9 to 10	$1.50	.73
Children's, age 7 years, sizes 10 1/2 to 11	1.50	.73
Misses', Youths', age 8 years, sizes 11 ½ to 12	1.50	.73
Misses', Youths', ages 9 years, sizes 12 ½ to 13 ½	1.50	.73
Boys' and girls', age 10 years, sizes 1 to 1 ½	1.50	.73
Boys' and girls', age 11 years, sizes 2 to 2 ½	1.00	.85
Boys' and girls', age 12 years, sizes 3 to 3 ½	1.00	.85
Boys' and girls', age 13 years, sizes 4 to 4 ½	1.00	.85
Boys' and girls', age 14 years, sizes 5 to 5 ½	1.00	.85
Women's sizes 2 1/2 to 8	1.00	.85
Men's sizes 6 to 12	1.00	1.05

Enclosed please find certified check for $200.00, as per requirements.

Very truly yours,

JOHN G. SATTLER

Bureau of Public Welfare,
City of Buffalo

Buffalo, June 16, 1926

Commissioner F. C. Perkins:

I agree to supply the Bureau of Public Welfare with good, serviceable shoes, oxfords and rubbers as per samples submitted or better.

	Shoes, Black or Tan	Oxfords Black or Tan	Rubbers
Age 6 years, 9 to 10	$1.75	$1.75	$ .75
Age 7 years, 10 ½ to 11, child's	1.75	1.75	.75
Age 8 year, 11 ½ to 12 misses'	2.00	2.00	.85
Age 9 years, 12 ½ to 13 ½ youths'	2.00	2.00	.85
Age 10 years, 1 to 1 ½, boys' and girls'	2.50	2.50	.90
Age 11 years, 2 to 2 ½ boys' and girls'	2.50	2.50	.90
Age 12 years, 3 to 3 ½ boys' and girls'	2.50	2.50	1.00
Age 13 years, 4 to 4 ½ boys' and girls'	2.50	2.50	1.00
Age 14 years, 5 to 5 ½ boys' and girls'	2.50	2.50	1.00
Sizes 2 ½ to 8, women's shoes	2.55	2.55	.90
Sizes 2 ½ to 8, women's oxfords	2.50	2.50	.90
Size 6 to 12, men's shoes	2.85	2.85	1.25
Size 6 to 12, men's oxfords	2.85	2.85	1.25

Yours truly,

AUGUST C SMITH & SON

Bureau of Public Welfare,
City of Buffalo

Buffalo, June 16, 1926

Gentlemen:

Complying with your notice for supplying your department with good, serviceable shoes and rubber, we take pleasure in submitting the following samples and prices:

	Shoes
Children's age 6 years, sizes 0-10	$1.79
Children's age 7 years, sizes 10 ½ - 11	.40
Misses' – Youths', age 8, sizes 11 ½ - 12	1.79
Misses', age 9, sizes 12 ½ - 13 ½	1.95
Youths', age 9, sizes 12 ½ - 13 ½	1.89
Boys' and girls', age 10, sizes 1 - 1 ½	1.95
Boys' and girls', age 11, sizes 2 - 2 ½	2.30
Boys' and girls', age 12, sizes 3 - 3 ½	2.30
Boys' and girls', age 13, sizes 4 - 4 ½	2.30
Boys' and girls', age14, sizes 5 - 5 ½	2.30
Women's, sizes 2 ½ to 8	2.90
Men's, sizes 6 to 12	2.90

	Rubbers
Children's age 6 years, sizes 9 to 10	$ .40
Children's age 7 years, sizes 10 ½ - 11	.40
Misses', age 8 years, sizes 11 ½ - 12	.50
Misses', age 9 years, sizes 12 ½ - 13 ½	.50
Girls', age 10 years, sizes 1 – 1 ½	.50
Girls', age 11 years, sizes 2 – 2 ½	.50
Girls', age 12 years, sizes 3 – 3 ½	.50
Girls', age 13 years, sizes 4 - 4 ½	.50
Girls', age 14 years, sizes 5 - 5 ½	.50
Youths', age 8 years, sizes 11 ½ - 12	.65
Youths', age 9 years, sizes 12 ½ - 13 ½	.65
Boys', age 10 years, sizes 1 – 1 ½	.65
Boys', ages 11 years, sizes 2 – 2 ½	.79
Boys', ages 12 years, sizes 3 - 3 ½	.79
Boys', ages 13 years, sizes 4 - 4 ½	.79
Boys', ages 14 years, sizes 5 – 5 ½	.79
Women's rubbers	.50
Men's rubbers	.79

Trusting to receive this valued order, we beg to remain.

Respectfully yours,
LIBERTY SHOE CO.
(Signed) D. ABRAMS

Mr. Sattler asked the City Council for a "fair deal" when the bids for the shoes were voted upon.

Mr. Sattler sent a letter that was read aloud by City Clerk Backman at the City Council meeting. Commissioner Perkins, who had been critical in the past when other Council members disregarded low bids, sat stone-faced as he was questioned by fellow Commissioners Ayer-Love and Moore.

In the letter, Mr. Sattler referred to a telephone conversation he had three years ago with Commissioner Perkins. Mr. Sattler was the low bidder for that contract and he believed that he should have won that contract, but Commissioner Perkins informed Mr. Sattler that the contract for the shoes would be split three ways between shoe dealers from the east, west and south sides.

The saga of the Welfare Shoe Contract became front page news as it dragged on for 5 months. July 1, 1926 news articles informed the public that Commissioner Perkins had not yet received the decision about the award of the shoe contract from Director John J. Aeschbeck's office, and therefore Perkins attempted to discredit Mr. Sattler and his letter.

July 8, 1926 brought more news about the Welfare Shoe Contract. The experts for the inspection of the shoes were two shoe and rubber dealers who volunteered their services to be shoe judges for the City of Buffalo: Mr. Clarence I. Lanich, president of the Buffalo Shoe Dealers Association, and Mr. John J. Ryan of the New York State Shoe Association. They spent 3 ½ hours inspecting the shoe samples and bids. The caption in the newspaper read "SATTLER LIKELY TO LOSE $10,000 SHOE CONTRACT." It was printed that judges chose 8 pairs of shoes from A.C. Smith & Son, 4 pairs of shoes from Liberty Shoes and 3 pairs of shoes from Sattler's, concluding that the award for the contract should be given to A. C. Smith & Son.

However, there was one slight problem with the judging of all the shoes. The shoes were clearly marked as to who submitted them. Both Mr. Sattler and Mr. Abrams complained about the unfair process and lack of impartial judging. The newspapers were having a heyday with the Welfare Shoe Contract proceedings.

The bickering in the City Council chambers was endless. It got so outrageous that Commissioners Moore, Schwartz and Ayes-Love set forth a motion that all the bids for the shoe contract be rejected and materials for making the shoes were to be purchased and brought to Commissioner Perkins' office where he could assemble the shoes himself and make his own judgment.

At a Council meeting on July 7, 1926, Fredrick Becker, former shoe dealer and Deputy Superintendent of Business and Accounts, offered to judge the shoes and the shoe bids and give his opinion as to who should be awarded the welfare shoe contract. He would then report to a committee of five: Commissioners Perkins, Moore, Ayes-Love, Schwab and Schwartz.

In September 1926, the confusion continued as Mr. Fredrick Becker published the following statement:

15 **Sept. 8, 1926**

No. 150. Buffalo, Sept. 8, 1926.

Shoes and Rubbers, Public Welfare Department.

As per your request of July 28, 1926, a committee of three shoe men, including myself, carefully inspected the shoes and prices according to specifications of June 2, 1926.

I beg to report it is impossible to intelligently pass upon these shoes and rubbers as submitted, as sizes do not run according to specifications. I would recommend that the bids be rejected, readvertise, and have sizes run as follows:

Shoes.

Infants'—5 to 8.
Childs'—8½ to 11.
Misses'—11½ to 2.
Women's—2½ to 8.
Youths'—9 to 13½.
Boys'—1 to 5½.
Men's—6 to 12.

First Quality Rubbers.

Children's—5 to 10½.
Misses'—11 to 2.
Women's—2½ to 9.
Youths'—10 to 2.
Boys'—2½ to 6.
Men's—6 to 12.

Respectfully submitted,

FREDERICK BECKER,
Deputy Superintendent.
Business and Accounts.

Received, filed and recommendation adopted.

Ayes—Love, Moore, Perkins, Schwab, Schwartz—5.

Noes—None.

Therefore, a new proposal for the Welfare Shoe Contract was sent out, and this time four shoe dealers responded. Mr. Sattler did not respond. One can only wonder why Mr. Sattler decided not to continue with the catastrophe of the Welfare Shoe Contract. In December 1926, the whole ordeal ended when the Bureau of Public Welfare Shoe Contract was given to the Liberty Shoe Company. (40-54)

March 1927

Death of Elizabeth Sattler

Pictured are Elizabeth Geise Sattler holding her first grandchild, Marion Sattler. Photograph courtesy of the Voorhees Family.

John Sattler's mother Elizabeth had been in poor health for the last few years of her life. Her death at age 83 was not a surprise, but it took its toll on the family. Mrs. Elizabeth Sattler had been John's business partner in Sattler's Shoe Store, known as Sattler's since 1926. When she retired in 1907 at the age of 63, she still owned the property at 994-998 Broadway. Upon her death, the property was willed to her son John.

Charles Hahn, the husband of Marion Sattler, was particularly grieved at having lost a close friend and a confidant. Elizabeth Sattler was well known as a kind soul who was very gentle and a bit mischievous. She was well loved by her family and friends.

Mrs. Sattler came to America in 1852 at the age of 9 from her home of Westfalen, Germany with her father Bernhard, her sister Mina and her two brothers Henry and Phillip Geise. Most of the Geise family and their descendants resided in the Darien, NY area where Elizabeth's family first lived in the United States. (56)

After Elizabeth moved to Buffalo, she became very involved with the churches of Saint Anne and Saint Mary Magdalene. In her later life, she moved to a home in Eggertsville on Westfield Road in order to be nearer to her son John. Her wake was held at her home in Eggertsville, and her funeral mass was said at Saint Benedict Church. Her final resting place is in Forest Lawn Cemetery in Buffalo, New York.

Because of Elizabeth's devotion to the church, in 1929 her son John donated St. Elizabeth's Church to the Catholic Diocese of Buffalo in memory of his mother. St. Elizabeth's Church was a mission church of Lake View Parish and was located at Cloverbank on Shore Road between Wanaka and Mt. Vernon-on-the-Lake. The church was blessed and formally opened on August 4, 1929, with mass and a benediction presided over by Rev. Father Toomey. (55, 57-60)

1929 Struggling with Changes

John Sattler's wife, Alma, was bedridden at home and in need of constant care. She suffered with angry outbursts of temper and debilitating depression. In addition to the daily running of his business, which changed names in 1926 from Sattler's Shoe Store to Sattler's, John became more involved with his real estate and construction business. Overwhelmed with responsibilities, John knew something had to give, and thus in 1929 John Sattler turned over the daily running of the store to his son-in-law, Charles Hahn. Although Mr. Sattler was frequently at Sattler's, the day-to-day business of the store was left to Charles from that point on.

With the crash of the stock market, Sattler's was on solid ground due to its sales policy of cash only. The seriousness of the effects of the depression were constantly on the minds of the new store president, Charles Hahn, as well as the owner, John Sattler. With countless discounts on every product sold, Sattler's became the place to go shopping. In turn, Sattler's gave back to its employees and the community in many ways.

1930 Sattler's Social Club Is Instituted

In 1930, Mr. Sattler initiated the Sattler's Social Club. It was started so that all employees, from stock boys to the store owner, would get to know each other through the promotion of fellowship among all employees.

This photo is from the first Sattler Social Club Masquerade Ball that took place in 1930. It's in two parts. The photo was cut for an unknown reason. Note the lady on the left in the white outfit and hat; she is also in the photo below. **Photographs courtesy of Michael Stark's Family**.

April 1931

As a Result of a Fire

A passing patrolman from the Fillmore Station, Henry Pike, noticed a fire at 998 Broadway and called in the alarm. The sprinkler system got a workout in the early morning of April 3rd at the store. The Sattler's building sustained only about $100 damage as result of a fire in the stockroom located in the basement at 994-998 Broadway. However, there was extensive water, fire and smoke damage to merchandise that led to $25,000 in losses. (61)

May 1931

Death of Alma Otto Sattler

Alma's health continued to decline and on the morning of May 4, 1931, Alma died at the age of 53. John and Alma Sattler had been married almost 29 years, and because of Alma's long-lasting illness, her death was not unexpected. The recently built Sattler home on Ivyhurst and Main Street in Eggertsville was the site of the funeral, which was held in the afternoon on May 7th. The afternoon was clear and mildly warm as the funeral procession was led to Forest Lawn Cemetery on Delaware Avenue. Alma Sattler was laid to rest where her daughter Katherine Alma is interred in the Sattler family mausoleum. (62) **Photograph courtesy of the Voorhees Family**.

August 1931

450 Employees Enjoy Outing

Sattler's Social Club sponsored their second annual outing. Approximately 450 store employees and their families attended a picnic at Bennett Beach in Angola-on-the-Lake. Sattler's employees were to be in front of the store at 998 Broadway at 9 A.M., as a total of 8 buses were chartered by Sattler's Social Club. The outing included a picnic lunch and a wiener roast in the evening. Refreshments were served throughout the day.

One of the many highlights of the day was a Sattler's employee baseball game. The 998 furniture department was captained by Walter Young. The opposing team was composed of employees from the first and second floor; they were called "the first and the second floor 9" and were led by enthusiastic Aaron Rabow. As fate or perhaps skill would have it, "the first and second floor 9" out-teamed those burly furniture foes by a score of 19-9.

Several other events took place at that picnic, including a wrestling match between Stephen Solar and Jesse Smalley, with Smalley winning the fall. An array of sporting matches was enjoyed in friendly competition by children and adults alike, including: 15-yard dash for 6 and under, 35-yard dash for 10 and under, 60-yard dash, 150-yard dash and 75-yard peanut race. (63, 64)

September 1931

Majestic Radio Show

When I saw this ad, I thought that it was advertising an old radio show that took place in the mezzanine of the Lafayette Theatre. The Radio Show featured actors and stories that were broadcast over the radio waves. After reading the fine print - and a little research - I discovered that this was just a show to display Majestic Radios at the Lafayette Theatre, with a little bit of that Sattler razzle-dazzle. The fine print reads: "The Radio show of the year starts with a BANG tomorrow. The new Lafayette Theatre will be the scene of Sattler's Majestic Radio Show! All the newest 1932 Majestic models will be displayed in decorative surroundings - in keeping with the beauty and scientific advances of the New Majestics. Don't miss this show – Sattler's have *[sic]* spared no expense for your enjoyment – be there when the curtain goes up!"

Continuing on the right side, the fine print is as follows: "A BIG SURPRISE EVERY DAY OF THE SHOW Determined to measure up to the public's expectations of Buffalo's largest radio dealers, Sattler's has planned a real party for its hundreds of friends. Every day of the show a big surprise – something that you can't afford to miss – awaits you! These daily surprises are possible only through a great expense on the part of Sattler's – but we want you to reap the fullest benefit! GRAND SURPRISE! On Wednesday, September 30th, Sattler's Radio Show will present the grand surprise of the week! No matter what day of the week you attend the show – no matter whether or not you're in the audience at this time – you will be eligible for this grand surprise! May we repeat – you can't afford to miss Sattler's Majestic radio show! Call the Sattler's store or the new Lafayette Theatre for details." (65)

1932

Free Rides To Sattler's

This ad reads: "Every car and bus listed below will bring you right to the door of Sattler's without transfer of any kind. Nobody will ask you for money, transfers or tokens of any kind. Just get on and ride. " (66)

Find Your Street Car on This Schedule

And Ride to Sattler's Free Tomorrow

Every car and bus listed below will bring you right to the door of Sattler's without transfer of any kind. Nobody will ask you for money, transfers or tokens of any kind. Just get on and ride.

Watch for Sattler's Signs on the Street Cars

BROADWAY CAR leaves city line 10 A. M.; leaves Broadway and Washington 10:41 A. M.

GENESEE CAR leaves city line 10 A. M.

SENECA CAR leaves city line 10 A. M. Another car leaves Washington and Seneca 10:48 A. M.

SOUTH PARK CAR leaves city line 10 A. M. Will be at Seneca and Fillmore 10:20 A. M.

MAIN STREET CAR leaves city line 10 A. M.

NIAGARA CAR leaves city line 10 A. M.

FILLMORE CAR leaves city line at Hertel, 10 A. M.

BAILEY AVENUE BUS leaves Bailey and Winspear 10 A. M. Will be at Bailey and Broadway 10:17 A. M.

July 12, 1932

SATTLER'S TO CLOSE EVERY WEDNESDAY IN JULY AND AUGUST

Employees Who Will Benefit by Sattler's Plan

A recent photo of Sattler's employees taken in front of the store at 998 Broadway. These are the hundreds whose welfare was considered when Sattler's decided to continue the custom of closing all day every Wednesday during July and August.

650 Employees Get Full Day Off

For many years it has been the policy of Sattler's and other stores in the Broadway-Fillmore business section to remain closed on each Wednesday throughout July and August. This year Sattler's are justly proud to announce that its 650 employees, supporting or helping to support a total of 2,860 persons, will find no change in this old Sattler custom. All Sattler's regular employees get full day off with pay!

Believing that this policy means more to the employees and to the store in good will and contentment than the extra dollars the store might take in on those days, Sattler's have opposed the move to abolish the custom, from the very first. We feel that you, the customer, will see and enjoy a reflection of this plan in the cheerful and courteous service accorded you by a group of salespeople whose wishes and well-being have not been thrust aside in a mad rush for dollars.

Policy of Regular Vacations With Pay Also to be Continued

Besides each Wednesday during July and August, every regular Sattler employe will be given his or her usual vacation with full pay. After a year's work serving the greatest crowds of any store in the city, our employees, we feel, have earned this rest and recreation.

We have cut no wages or salaries. Instead we have increased them. In the past six years we have never laid off an employee because of general business depression. And in the same time we have increased our personnel 500 per cent. A large proportion of this phenomenal increase has taken place in the past two years.

Such a record is largely responsible for the atmosphere of security enjoyed by Sattler employees . . . unharried by fears of wage slashes and layoffs.

Hundreds of Members Enjoy Sattler's Social Club

All work and no play have no place in the Sattler program. Sattler's Social Club, an employees' organization, sponsors regular outings that cost its members only a few cents a week. For every dollar paid the treasury of Sattler's Social Club by its members, an equal amount is contributed by the Sattler Store! On Wednesday, July 27, Sattler's annual picnic will be held at Buffalo Municipal Beach near Angola. Approximately 2100 employees and members of their families will enjoy this outing.

Among the other activities of Sattler's Social Club are monthly dances, dinners, card parties, wiener roasts, entertainments, etc.

SATTLER'S Store will be CLOSED TOMORROW

. . . But Don't Miss Our Ad in Tomorrow's News

This ad appeared in *The Buffalo Evening News* (67)

September 2, 1932

Fall Fashion Show

"The most brilliant fashions of the new season will be modeled all day tomorrow in Sattler's Window Fashion Show! And you'll never believe your eyes when you see the low prices! Here is something you really should see! " (68)

This Fashion show was for both men and women. Models would sometimes stay as still as a mannequin in order to surprise a passer-by.

September 23, 1932

Sattler's Bargain Fair

Sattler's 1932 Bargain Fair! There was "sawdust on the floor, a barker out in front of the store, lively calliope music, rollicking clowns throughout the store passing candy out.

"All you need to participate in the other 'free' attractions are 'free tickets' given to you with every purchase of .10 or more. With 2 free tickets you can receive delicious and wholesome lemonade made fresh every hour in the store. If you hand the popcorn man 1 free ticket you get a bag of the tastiest popcorn you ever ate! A gaily colored balloon, all yours for 2 'free tickets.' There are cooling and refreshing orange, grape or cherry flavored ices for 2 'free tickets.' An honest-to-goodness merry-go-round in front of Sattler's, only 3 'free tickets' for a ride. And great big candied apples on a stick for 3 'free tickets.' "

A ticket gave you a chance to guess how many beans were in a jar. If you were the lucky winner, you would win a handsome occasional chair. There was a $25 prize for your church, and how did your church win that? You would take your free ticket and write the name of your favorite church on the back of that ticket. Every ticket you dropped into the ballot box would represent 25 votes! (69, 70)

Winners of the Guessing Contest and Church Voting Contest featured in Sattler's Bargain Fair were: Miss Dorothy Sehnert of 34 Gold Street won the handsome occasional chair with her guess of 37,198 beans in the jar. Corpus Christi Church won the first prize of $25.00 with a total of 33,900 votes, and St. Stanislaus and St. Ann's churches received honorable mention with 15,900 and 7,700 votes respectively. (71)

March 5, 1933

President Roosevelt Declares a Bank Holiday

Just 36 hours after President Franklin D. Roosevelt took office, he issued Proclamation 2039 ordering the suspension of all banking transactions, effective immediately. The presidential proclamation stated "No such banking institution or branch shall pay out, export, earmark, or permit the withdrawal or transfer in any manner or by any device whatsoever, of any gold or silver coin or bullion or currency or take any other action which might facilitate the hoarding thereof; nor shall any such banking institution or branch pay out deposits, make loans or discounts, deal in foreign exchange, transfer credits from the United States to any place abroad, or transact any other banking business whatsoever." (72)

Of course, this proclamation caused panic in the business world. With a depression in full swing, this was the fuel that could cause employers to close up shop. There was no money to pay employees, no money for raw materials to run a manufacturing business, and Sattler's was the outlet for those manufacturers to sell their wares. No products to sell could cause the closing of Sattler's and further drive the people of Buffalo into more economic chaos.

As always with Sattler's management, they were concerned about their employees and their suppliers. However, Sattler's was run by ingenious, innovative and creative fellows. Charles Hahn, president of Sattler's, met with his management team and instituted a brilliant business plan.

"Our sales were all in cash, so consequently we had a tremendous amount of money. With this accumulated money, we had built-in cash and we sent our buyers to every market to tell the manufacturers that we could loan them money too, so they could meet their payroll because of course they were getting no checks; no money was coming in to them," explained Charles Hahn. (73)

It has been said that Charles Hahn also filled a suitcase full of money and headed out on a train to New York City where he met with Sattler's out-of-town suppliers. He paid any outstanding balances owed to them by Sattler's, as well as some loans, in cash. (73)

"We gave out thousands and thousands of dollars," said Charles Hahn. "We loaned (money) to our people who were supplying us with merchandise. And they in turn, of course, they appreciated it and in future times would compensate with good bargains to us." (73)

Mr. Hahn also stated, "My store in Buffalo was a forerunner of the so-called discount stores. We never heard of a discount store. We just ran a low-price bargain-oriented store, so at this time during the Depression it was a very opportune time for us. At that time there were no ads whatsoever in the newspaper in Buffalo, with the exception of Sattler's. And consequently, anyone who did want to buy anything looked in the newspaper and saw our ads and we got tremendous response. As far as in my instance, it was the beginning of the making of my business; it is quite unique, but it just so happened that way. "(73)

Although the Hahns and Sattlers prospered financially during this time, it was quite clear that this was not the case for many. In a Dictaphone recording that Charles Hahn made in the 1970's, he describes the Depression: "People were selling apples for a nickel apiece on the street to try to get money. There were lines, bread lines, food lines. It was the most, well, I would say, 'depressing,' that's the only word I could use to describe it, era that I've ever seen in my life; it was pitiful. And it covered not only one little locale but the country as a whole." (74)

There was a dark side to being wealthy when others were in such desperate straits. The management's families had to be on guard for their safety. It was Charles Hahn's daughter Jill who told me of the frequent phone calls with threats of kidnapping. When such threats were made, the Hahn children would be taken to school by a driver and then walk with the driver to the door of the school. When the times were not so threatening, Jill remembers a period of personal fear. She would be afraid that she would be recognized as she walked to school, and therefore she would wrap her arms around her lunch box so no one would notice her name that was written on the outside of the box. (75)

March 1933

Minstrel Show

Even though tough times were apparent, Sattler's Social Club continued to uplift the store employees. The Club presented a minstrel show at the Elk's Temple Auditorium on Delaware Avenue. Over 1,000 people attended the two-hour show featuring a cast of 50 people performing humorous monologues, zany skits, songs and dances. (76, 77) This type of show would now be considered offensive, as it often depicted people using negative stereotypes. Please consider the era in which this event took place. I would like to report the actual happenings of those times. Today this type of show would not be acceptable.

April 1933

Social Club 1933

Seen below is a Sattler Social Club gathering from April 1933. These stills are taken from a film found in a family archive. In the early part of the film, there were skits performed by two men dressed up in tutus, a clown act, singers and a skit in which a man was holding a broom and saluting. Below are pictures of the Sattlerites who were in the skits and others who performed. Unfortunately, the films are silent. It is my hope that you may recognize a family member or friend.

When the skits were completed, the film featured a group of Polish dancers in costume entertaining the crowd as they whirled about the huge dance floor. The remainder of the film showed an orchestra and scenes of hundreds of people dancing and celebrating. Pictured in the second row from the bottom are only a few of the Polish dancers.

1933

Welcome Whale

This promotion is from 1933. Over the store, Sattler's is flying a large balloon that is shaped like a whale sporting a big toothy grin. The balloon has the word "welcome" printed on its underbelly. The pictures on this page were taken from a family film. (78)

Three Fine Fellows

When John Sattler was entering his later years in life, he wanted to spend more time with his real estate business, travel across the United States, and visit his relatives in Europe. Knowing that he had an amazing staff at Sattler's, Mr. Sattler felt assured that his store was in good, capable hands and thus he was able to do what he wanted.

John Sattler's confidence was inspired by Sattler's Vice President Charles Hahn, Sattler's Store Manager Aaron Rabow and Marketing Manager Robert S. Cornelius. If it weren't for these three fine fellows with their innate marketing genius and eccentric, charming, charismatic and industrious personalities - along with just a bit of out-there-craziness and a dash of luck - Sattler's certainly would have never become the "Hellzapoppin' " store it was.

How I would have loved to have been a fly on the wall when these 3 chums sat around having a brew at the local watering hole! They were not just work partners; they were friends and they stayed that way throughout their lives. Most of the information for this chapter of the book was given to me in interviews with: Jack Hahn and Jill Hahn Russo, who are the children of Charles Hahn and grandchildren of John Sattler; Julian Rabow, son of Aaron Rabow; and Bob Cornelius, son of Robert S. Cornelius.

From left to right Robert S. Cornelius, Charles Hahn,
Ernie Watson (director of the Shea's Buffalo Orchestra), Aaron Rabow
Photograph courtesy of the Voorhees Family.

Charles Hahn

Photograph taken by Luedeke Studio
Printed with permission from Gretchen DeBartolo

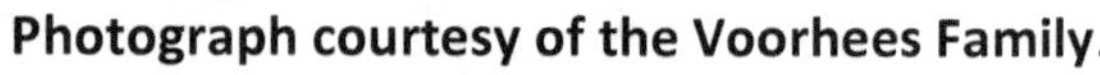

Photograph courtesy of the Voorhees Family.

Charles Hahn started working at The Broadway Market Shoe House at the age of 22, and Mr. Sattler soon found that Charles was a young man who possessed incredible marketing skills. Charles had a keen sense for seeking out extremely talented people and convincing them to come work for Sattler's. He was given the nickname "The Prize Boy" as a youngster and indeed, he was in the center of the ring his entire life, surrounded by handpicked skillful employees and people.

When Charles was vice president of Sattler's (even though he was sometimes called president before he actually became president of Sattler's in 1941), he was given free rein by John Sattler. This enabled Charles to mold a company with extraordinarily talented people, some of whom were called "the boys." In addition, Charles was a master at inventory, as he always knew what he had in stock and what was needed. He walked the floors of the store chatting with customers and found out what they wanted or wished they could buy. It could be anything from coal to heat your home, or the home itself. Eventually Sattler's sold it ALL! It truly became the one-stop shopping store.

Charles and Marion Hahn with their children Jack and Jill
Photograph courtesy of the Hahn Family.

There was also a silent partner in "The Prize Boy's" corner. That was his wife and silent store partner Marion Sattler Hahn. Charles developed a national reputation for being able to get any product he wanted and having that product shipped to Sattler's with flawless expert ability. That ability was not unnoticed by the United States government; as a result, Charles was recruited by the military during World War II. He was offered a commission in the United States Army, and it was Marion who ran Sattler's in his absence.

Aaron Rabow

Aaron Rabow was born in Massachusetts, the son of Russian immigrants. He was the middle child of five boys. The family lived in NYC at the time that Aaron's father, Julius Rabow, passed away. Aaron's mother, Celia, was left with five young boys to raise. (79, 80)

Celia Rabow was a milliner by trade. She decided to move her boys to Toronto, and it was there that she opened a millinery shop in her rented house. Celia's talents were sought after, and her millinery business flourished. Celia soon opened a store in downtown Toronto, and later she added another store in St. Catharines, Ontario.

Celia decided it would be good for her business to open a store in Buffalo, NY. Her son Aaron moved to Buffalo to manage the new shop that was located on Chippewa Street. Aaron was living at the local YMCA during this time, and in the evenings he would play badminton with a man he became friends with named Charlie Hahn, who was managing The Broadway Market Shoe House for his father-in-law, John G. Sattler.

Aaron Rabow and Charles Hahn in their later years.
Photographs courtesy of the Voorhees Family.

In 1926 the store changed its name to Sattler's and sold $400,000 worth of shoes a year. By 1927, Sattler's was the largest retail shoe store between New York and Chicago. (81) It was time for bigger and better things for the store, and Charles Hahn was a savvy and persuasive businessman who recognized the retail talent in Aaron Rabow. Charles proposed that Aaron leave his mother's millinery store and come work at Sattler's to add a line of ladies' daytime dresses.

Mr. Rabow had no knowledge of the dress business, but Charles assured him that Sattler's would send him to New York City to meet dress manufacturers who would explain all he would need to know to get started. Aaron decided to accept Charles Hahn's proposal and he went to work at Sattler's.

Aaron Rabow at the Sattler's Stand at what was known as the Hamburg Fair in the 1930's Photograph courtesy of the Voorhees Family.

Mr. Rabow's innate marketing sense came to good use at Sattler's as he introduced a line of ready-to-wear dresses. The new dress department thrived, and new departments and more employees were added. The store was quickly growing. Both Charles Hahn and John Sattler were aware of the keen, confident gentlemanly nature of Aaron's leadership as manager of his department. His input of ideas for the store was one of the catalysts for the store's prosperity. He understood what the public wanted and he knew how to present that merchandise so that it was appealing to the customers.

Over the course of many years and numerous store expansions, Aaron was named store manager, then vice president and ultimately president of Sattler's. But it is in the course of conversations with former Sattler's employees that the true gift of Aaron Rabow's talents and personality is brought to light.

Aaron was the "proud father" in the store. He knew the names of almost all the "Sattlerites" and he knew about their families. He ate at the restaurant in the store, and as one former waitress told me, "He was a pleasure to wait on." He had the ability to make employees comfortable, which made them happy to come to work. He truly cared about the employees and they knew he had an open door policy to his office. If you needed to talk, he was available.

It was Aaron's custom to walk through the store every morning and greet as many of the "Sattler family members" as he could before the workday began. He encouraged employees to take pride in their work and he recognized a job well done. Aaron was quick to give praise and reward good work with a promotion when he could.

As many past Sattlerites have told me, they loved to go to work at the 998 store. It was a family; it was a happy place. Sattler's was like going home when you came to work. People who were offered jobs at other companies turned them down because they could not imagine leaving their Sattler's family.

"You never knew if you would be in an employee parade or win a prize that day for having the best answer to a random question posed to you by Aaron Rabow," said Mary Ann, a former worker in Accommodations. "And when I worked at Sattler's, I looked forward to going in every day; I couldn't imagine working anywhere else. My friends would always say, "Let's meet at Sattler's."

Robert S. Cornelius

East Eden Rd, Hamburg 1938

Picture courtesy of the Robert Cornelius Family

Probably the most unsung hero of the three fine fellows was Robert S. Cornelius. Bob, as his friends called him, was born in the South. He and his wife, Sadie Belle, grew up in Birmingham, Alabama. At the age of 19, Bob submitted material to *The Buffalo News* and the newspaper offered him a job. So, he and Miss Sadie Bell came up to New York and were married in New York City at the age of 19, and then moved to Buffalo where Sadie Bell had an aunt living.

Bob started working at *The Buffalo News* a few weeks before the stock market crash of 1929. At this time, Sattler's did not have an advertising department, *so The Buffalo News* would use Bob to prepare the ads for Sattler's. With Sattler's continually expanding its market on Buffalo's East Side, management became aware that it needed an in-house advertising manager. Sattler's loved Bob's advertising work at *The Buffalo News,* so they hired him as Sattler's Marketing Manager.

Alex Osborn, another advertising genius, then offered Bob a job at his advertising firm named Barton, Durstine and Osborn. Bob left Sattler's for about one year, but he did not like working at his new job, and thus returned to Sattler's and remained there until 1958.

Bob Cornelius' Ads for Sattler's

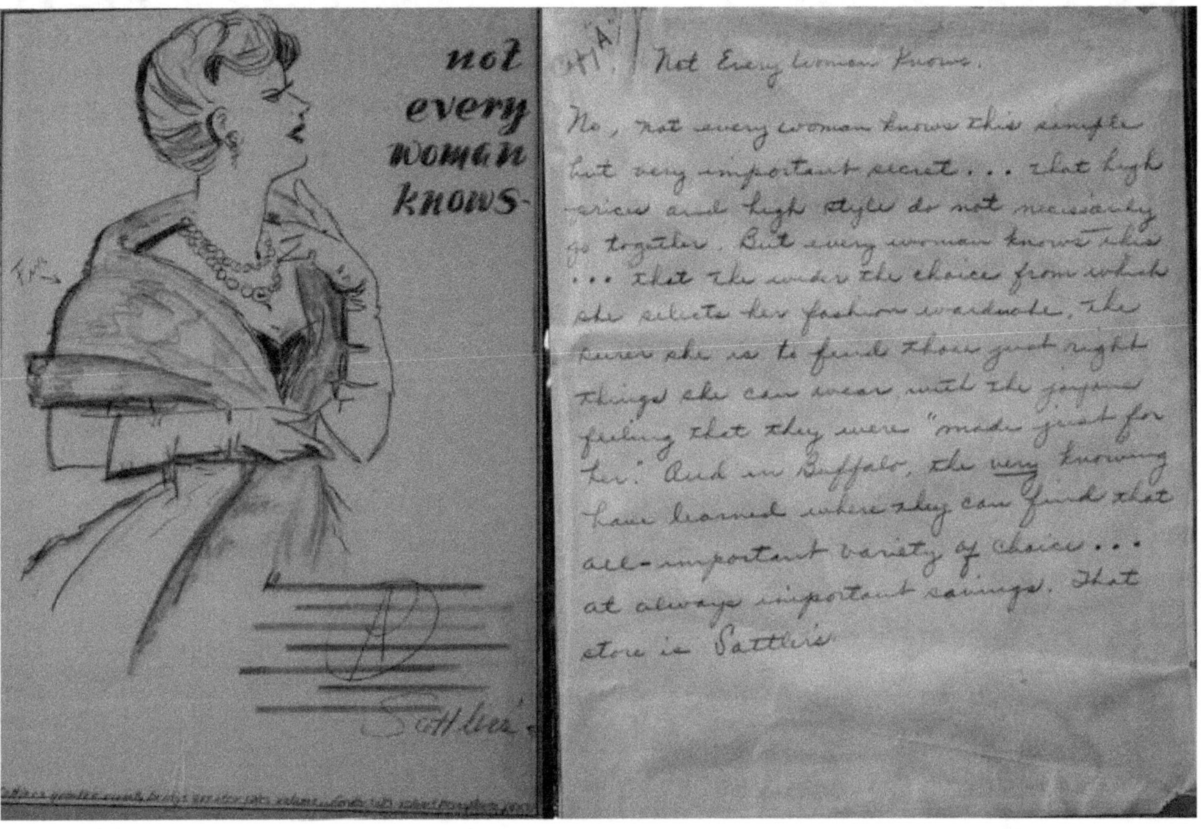

Courtesy of the Robert Cornelius Family.

Some of Bob's original work still remains. In the above pictures you will see the front and back of a framed original advertisement that Bob Cornelius created for Sattler's. The Cornelius family is proud to display Bob's work and share it with us in this book.

Not Every Woman Knows.

No, not every woman knows this simple but very important secret…that high prices and high style do not necessarily go together. But every woman knows this… that the wider the choice from which she selects her fashion wardrobe, the surer she is to find those just right things she can wear with the joyous feeling that they were "made just for her." And in Buffalo, the <u>very</u> knowing have learned where they can find that all-important variety of choice…at always important savings. That store is Sattler's.

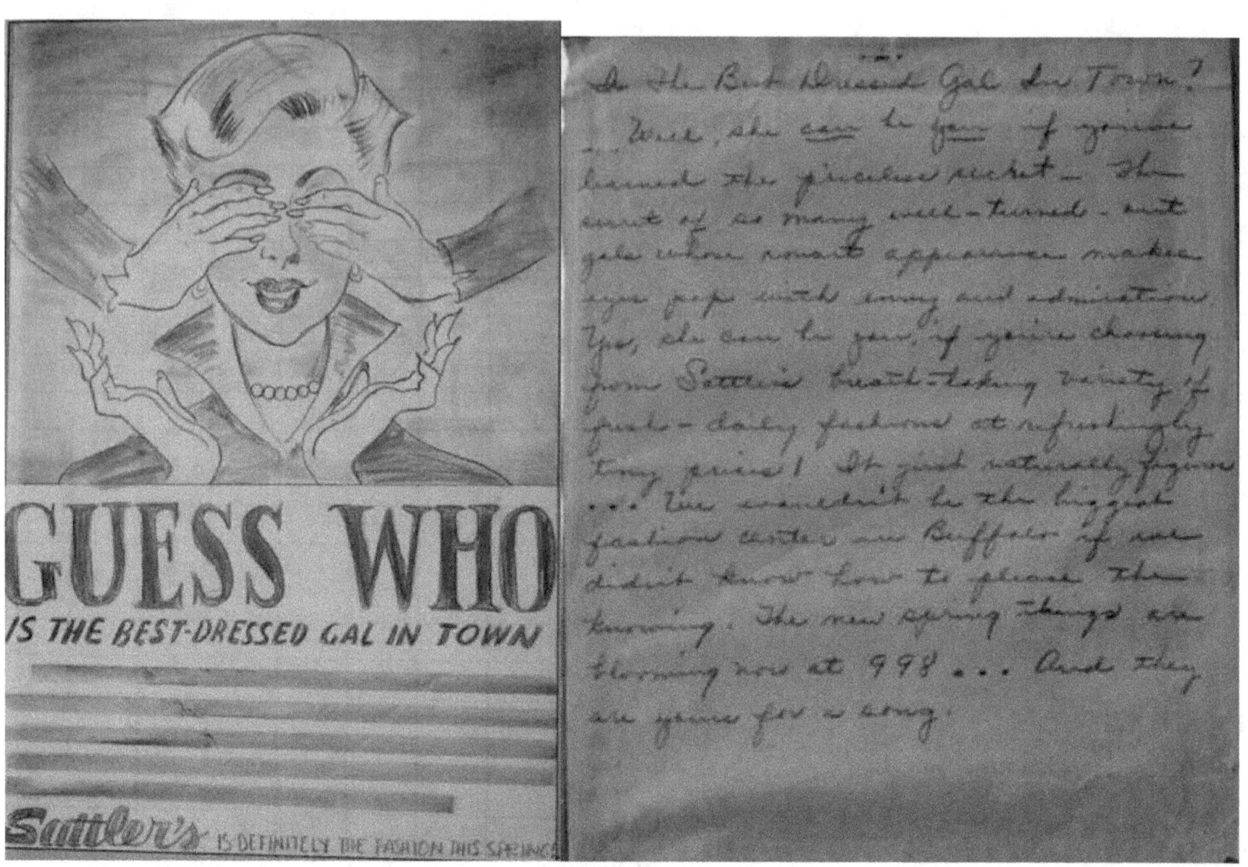

Courtesy of the Robert Cornelius Family.

Another framed original shared by the Cornelius Family:

Guess Who Is The Best Dressed Gal In Town?

... Well, she <u>can</u> be <u>you</u> if you've learned the priceless secret - The secret of so many well-turned-out gals whose smart appearance makes eyes pop with envy and admiration. Yes, she can be you, if you're choosing from Sattler's breath-taking variety of fresh-daily fashions at refreshingly tiny prices! It just naturally figures... We wouldn't be the biggest fashion center in Buffalo if we didn't know how to please the knowing. The new spring things are blooming now at 998... And they are yours for a song.

The three masterminds of Hahn, Rabow and Cornelius ran the show at Sattler's 998 for the next few decades with the blessing of John G. Sattler. They were brainstorming ideas before the term "brainstorming" was popular, and they knew that if you really wanted something to work - don't tell the boss (Mr. Sattler) ......at least don't tell him too much.

December 1933

Let's Get Ready To Party!

(82)

February 1934

Coloring Contest Winners

Sattler's had a George Washington coloring contest and the kids were ready to win some cash!

As always, there were hundreds of entries to the coloring contest. Sattler's often sent out letters of thanks for entering a contest, when children were involved, thanking them for their efforts and recognizing them for their work. An exhibit of the children's artwork for the George Washington Coloring Contest was shown on the second floor at 998. (83)

May 1934

A Wedding in Sattler's Window

Here Comes the Bride!

Not to mention the groom—Yes siree! There's going to be a wedding at Sattler's pretty soon . . . and you're invited!

The blushing bride to be is Miss Catherine Schmidt of 59 Verplank Street. The lucky groom is Mr. Norman Harran of 1392 Amherst Street.

Everybody's busy getting ready for the big event—and what an event that's going to be! There'll be beautifully gowned bridesmaids, organ music, flowers, rice, old shoes and all the trimmings!

WATCH SATTLER'S ADS FOR THE DATE—Then come out and help us launch Catherine and Norman on a happy voyage over the sea of matrimony—The whole town will be here!

One of the best promotions for Sattler's happened in 1934. A wedding. Yes, a wedding at Sattler's! Sattler's had advertised a contest to have a couple marry at their store at 998 Broadway. The contest was won by a couple who were both 21 years old: Norman Harran and Katherine Schmidt, who met while they were in grammar school together.

The anticipation of this wonderful event had Sattler's employees buzzing as piles of letters came in, as well as a myriad of phone calls asking about the arrangements and about the couple who won the contest to be the first to have their wedding take place at Sattler's.

It was a Thursday evening on May 24, 1934, at 6:30 to be exact. It was a clear cool evening with the temperature at 52 degrees as the crowds gathered in the street in front of 998 Broadway. Ten uniformed police officers from the Jefferson Police station were on hand for crowd control, as the street was abuzz and humming with anticipation for the wedding of Katherine Schmidt and Norman Harran. The store aisles inside Sattler's were teeming with friends, relatives and well-wishers. Flowers decorated the store, soft organ music played, and the clergy was ready as the couple appeared in the store window at Sattler's to exchange their vows. The bride, groom and all their attendants, who were employees of the store, were outfitted from head to foot in the latest of fashions courtesy of Sattler's. It was during the Depression, and all the wedding expenses and details were totally covered by Sattler's, right down to the rice and the old shoes to be tied to the back of the newlyweds' transport vehicle. A final gift for the bride and groom was $50 for the honeymoon trip. The wonderful wedding that took place at Sattler's back in 1934 carried Norman and Katherine to 67 year of marriage. (84- 92)

Mr. & Mrs. Norman Harran
Picture courtesy of Linda Chludzinski

(93)

May, 1934

Sattler's Smile Contest

Beautiful Evelyn Frank, just 16 years old and daughter of John G. and Elizabeth Frank of Choate Avenue in South Buffalo, became the winner of Sattler's May Smile Contest.

Picture courtesy of Mary Chase Connors.

Evelyn became one of the finalists in a "screen and voice test in conjunction with the Metro-Goldwyn-Mayer Motion Pictures Studio's search for new screen personalities that was conducted by the *Buffalo Courier-Express* and the Shea Theatres." (94-96)

The Benefits of Working at Sattler's

Year after year, Sattler's enticed more people to work for them through advertising, and it paid off. Sattler's had wonderful fringe benefits and a close caring family atmosphere at the store. (97)

National Industrial Recovery Act (1933)

The National Industrial Recovery Act (NIRA) was enacted by Congress in June 1933 and was one of the measures by which President Franklin D. Roosevelt sought to assist the nation's economic recovery during the Great Depression. (98)

As a response to the NIRA Act of 1933, Sattler's announced that, "The entire staff of 675 employees has been notified of wage increases of 10 to 15 percent."(99) And in 1935 the store announced that, "There will be no change in the hours or wages of 600 employees. All regular employees will get vacation with pay this summer."(100, 101)

August 1934

Treasure Hunt at Sattler's

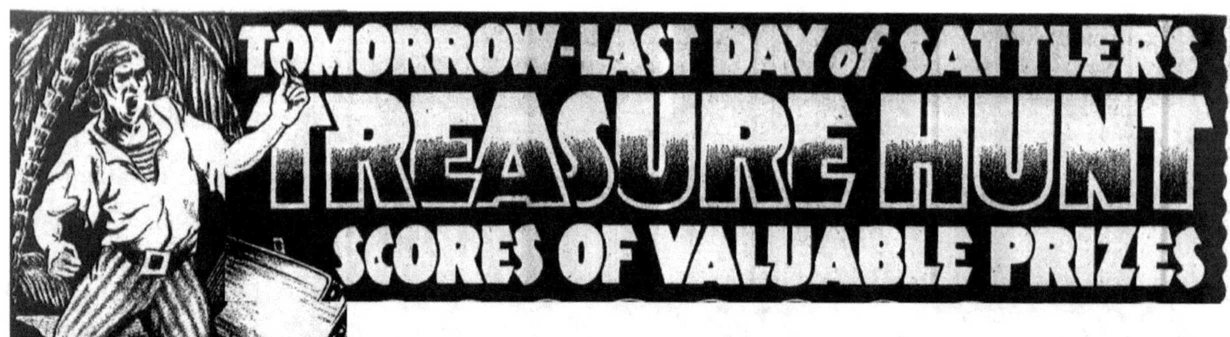

Yo, ho, ho and a boatload of booty to be had at Sattler's! Pirates will be greeting you at the main entrance of Sattler's. They'll be handing out treasure maps that may lead you to one of four valuable cash prizes and 350 merchandise prizes.

It was August of 1934 when the movie *Treasure Island* was being shown in the local movie theaters, and Sattler's took every advantage of the pirate craze. A copy of a picture with Wallace Beery and Jackie Cooper, the stars of the movie *Treasure Island*, appeared in a Sattler's ad. The ad announced a coloring contest that children, up to age 14, could enter. They were to color the picture, write their names and addresses in the margin of the paper, and bring it into Sattler's. First prize $5 cash. Second and third prizes were a pair of new school shoes. (102)

(103) 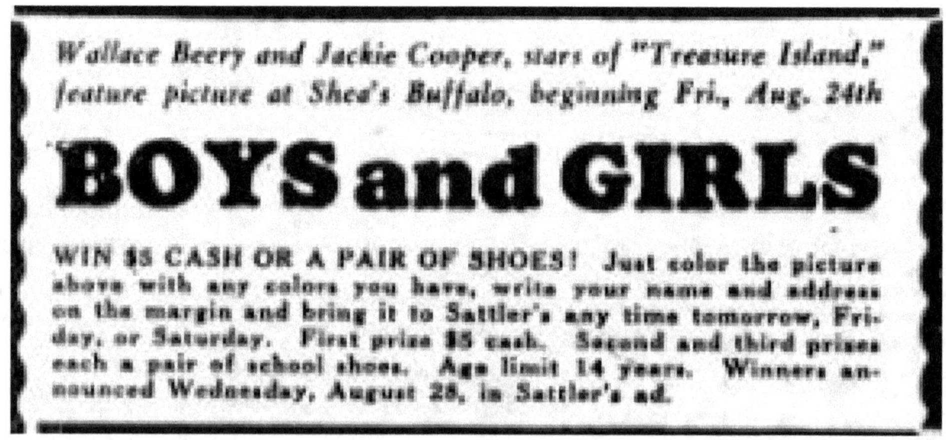

Wallace Beery and Jackie Cooper, stars of "Treasure Island," feature picture at Shea's Buffalo, beginning Fri., Aug. 24th

BOYS and GIRLS

WIN $5 CASH OR A PAIR OF SHOES! Just color the picture above with any colors you have, write your name and address on the margin and bring it to Sattler's any time tomorrow, Friday, or Saturday. First prize $5 cash. Second and third prizes each a pair of school shoes. Age limit 14 years. Winners announced Wednesday, August 28, in Sattler's ad.

The drawings from the coloring contest were on display at Sattler's. The first prize was changed from a $5 prize to a $10 prize. The $10 cash for first place went to Mary Skarbek, 452 Sweet Avenue. Second prize of a new pair of school shoes was won by B. Kohler, 87 Phyllis Avenue. The third prize was another pair of school shoes, which was won by Mildred Dankowski, 12 Hoerner. (104)

January 1935 **Sattler's Social Club Celebrates 5 years**

Sattler's Social Club had its 5th annual dinner dance at the Hotel Buffalo. Speeches were given by John G. Sattler and Aaron Rabow, Sattler's general manager. Election of officers for the Social Club took place, resulting in the election of: Arthur Varga, president; Leo S. Stanek, vice president; Miss Marie Pfieger, treasurer and Miss Mary G. Smith as secretary. (105)

January 1935 **Sattler's Follies**

The Vaudeville Show of 1935 called "Sattler's Follies" took place at St. John Kanty's lyceum, just down the street from Sattler's at the corner of Broadway and Swinburne. A huge audience of 2,500 people attended the event. The entertainment included hula girls, "Café Rouge" (a continental skit with gay Parisians), a "Down South Jubilee," and "Dutch Blues." Other performances included choral singers, comedy skits, specialty dances and two female dancing choral groups. Refreshments were provided. (106)

March 1935 **Life of Christ Display**

Brochure given out at Sattler's for the Gauci Brothers display.
Photographs courtesy of Scheerer McCulloch Auctioneers.

This exhibit traveled extensively throughout Canada and the United States. It was brought to Sattler's in sections and assembled on site by the Gauci brothers, who made the exhibit. It took the Gauci brothers many days to prepare for the exhibit, which was displayed on the second floor of the store. Even though there was a moderate fee to view the quadorama, thousands of people lined up to see the masterpiece. In addition, Sattler's covered the expense for many school children and religious organizations to view the model of the Holy Land.

Joseph and Salvatore Gauci made the model of the Holy Land to depict the time of Christ. It took the brothers 11 years to build this labor of love, which was finished in 1925. The model was a staggering 18' deep x 46' wide. It included over 12,000 stationary figures and 730 miniature animated figures that moved by electricity and clockwork. The model was reported to have over 6 million pieces, some of which were so small that a microscope had to be used to assemble the pieces correctly.

The model reproduced 124 scenes over the 33-year life of Christ, from Jesus' birth at the stable in Bethlehem to his crucifixion on Mount Calvary. The depictions represented the areas of Galilee, Samaria and Judea. The lighting on the scenes was cleverly executed so that various scenes were shown as sunrise, daytime, evening or night, and each scene was also marked with a number that correlated to an informational brochure that every viewer received.

Photograph is courtesy of the *Boston Herald.*

The Gauci brothers, from the isle of Malta, had pursued the dream of making an unforgettable piece of art. While still living in Europe, they began their quest for knowledge that would help them achieve their desire. Salvatore acquired a background both in mechanical and electrical engineering during his days working in a shipyard in Malta during World War I. He also spent a great deal of time in the study of puppetry and marionettes while in Europe.

Joseph spent 5 years in Palestine studying with an archeologist to learn about the vegetation, roads, mountain paths and streams that no longer existed in modern Palestine. He learned how the terrain of the land was different now and about the crops that the people of Jesus' time planted. He needed to know about the clothing and customs of both the people of that day and the Roman soldiers.

There also was the problem of the Bible itself, as the translation they had was not exact enough to have all the information that was needed. The two men sought information in museums, churches and in manuscripts throughout Asia and Europe to acquire more insight into the scriptures.

The Gauci family moved to Edmonton, Alberta. Salvatore was unable to find a job in carpentry as he wanted, but he did find a job in a blacksmith shop. Joseph was hired as a sign painter and these jobs enabled the brothers to learn new skills which they needed to build their model. By day the two brothers worked their jobs-for-pay, and by night the brothers built their dream model of the life of Christ. (107-112, 590-599)

June 1935 Wedding Bells Ring Again at Sattler's

Sattler's did have another wedding in its store during June of 1935. Miss Beatrice Pim and Mr. George Benson tied the knot at Sattler's. The matron of honor was Katherine Harran, and the best man was Norman Harran. (The Harrans were the first couple to be married at Sattler's in May of 1934.) This was indeed another great event at the store.

YOU'RE INVITED to the Wedding

TOMORROW EVENING AT 6:30 SHARP AT SATTLER'S

Only a few more short hours and Beatrice Pim will be George Benson's blushing bride.

The beautiful ceremony will take place in Sattler's big show window tomorrow—Thursday Nite—at 6:30 P. M.

There'll be organ music, beautiful bridesmaids, beautiful flowers (supplied by Dreyer's Flower Shop) and everything it takes to make a wedding complete.

A loud speaker system will be installed and a platform will be built so everyone can see and hear. We'll even furnish you with a little bag of rice to throw at the "Honeymooners" as they dash to their Packard car. (Furnished by Buffalo Packard, Inc.)

It was another beautiful rain-free day in Buffalo and the temperatures reached a high of only 60 degrees. Sattler's second store wedding was better organized, and the improvements enabled the well-wishers to see and hear the lovely couple's vows more clearly. Sattler's had a platform built so that viewing the couple in the window would be easier, and a loudspeaker was installed for the enjoyment of all. Now, not only the vows but the music could be heard by the crowds that came to enjoy the happy couple's nuptials. The crowd was enormous - it teemed not only into Broadway, but stretched from the Broadway Market across the street, down to the corner of Gibson Street.

When Wagner's *Bridal Chorus* began, the huge crowd witnessing the wedding fell silent and the men reverently removed their hats. The minister approached the decorated arches built in front of the store window, followed by: Mrs. Katherine Harran (the matron of honor), then the bridesmaids Betty Naber and Mrs. George F. Volk, the twin sister of the bride. Next was the groom George Benson with his best man, Norman Harran. Lastly came the bride, Miss Beatrice Pim, arrayed in white and carrying a massive bouquet of lily-of-the-valley.

Once the last of the vows were said, the crowd erupted in noisy celebrations as Mr. and Mrs. Benson had their first kiss as a married couple and were introduced as husband and wife.

The ceremony was followed by a reception at 908 Lovejoy, the home of Mrs. Joseph Workoff, who was the bride's sister. About 100 people attended the reception to celebrate the Bensons' nuptials.

This Sattler's wedding resulted in 59 years of wedded bliss. (113-120)

July 1935 Victorious Bean Counter

Mrs. Mary Meier was the winner of a month-long contest at Sattler's to guess how many beans were held in a jar. Her winning guess of 128,688 won her a new Norge refrigerator. (121)

August, 1935 Sattler's Employee Summer Picnic

Sattler's summer picnic at Green Lake in Orchard Park was a whopping success, with over 500 people attending the day-filled event. The Social Club provided food, games with prizes, and dancing. There was no time to be shy for the husband-calling contest that was won by Mrs. Al L. Wells. And even the littlest of participants, Lottie Matuszak, won the peanut scramble. The Fruit Department was the champion team of the tug of war. Other games included: ladies' races, men's newspaper-swatting contest, boys' shoe race, ladies' nail-driving contest, baseball throwing, egg and spoon race, girls' skipping contest, ladies' and men's taking off and putting on a shirt contest, and boys' cracker-eating contest. (122)

September 1935

The Bargain Fair of 1935 was run in a similar way as the previous Bargain Fair of 1932. With each 10 cents you spent at Sattler's, you received a certain number of "free" tickets you could use on "free" items and "free" rides. However, this year's Bargain Fair was a bit different in that there were sideshow attractions and entertainers where no "free" tickets were needed to see the entertainment. (123)

Big Yank

Big Yank paid a visit to Sattler's for the 1935 Bargain Fair. Harold Anderson (with the stage name of "Big Yank") was originally from Jamestown, New York and stood at 6 feet 5 inches tall, weighing 448 pounds with a size 27 shirt, size 66 union suit and a size 8 1/4 hat. He carried a cigar and walked with a cane the size of a baseball bat. He would often be invited to stores to help promote "Big Yank Clothing" for large men. He was a popular entertainer at the Chicago World's Fair in 1933. (124-128)

Moro the "Human Iceberg"

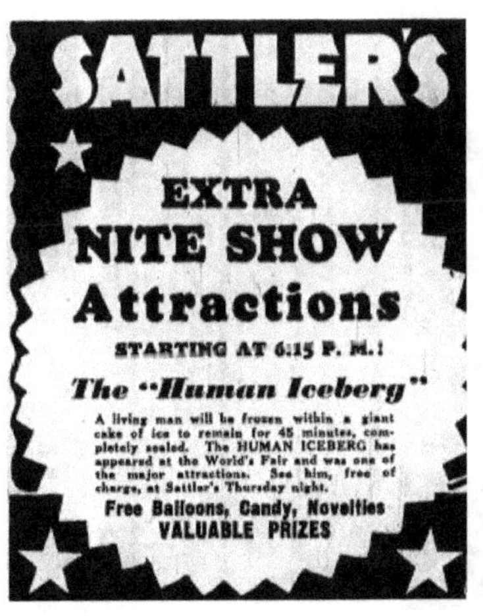

Also appearing at Sattler's was Moro the "Human Iceberg." His real name was William Aspinwall of Portland, Oregon. On Thursday, September 19, 1935 at 6:15 P.M., Moro the" Human Iceberg" was encapsulated in a block of ice for about 45 minutes at Sattler's Bargain Fair. For this performance, a 12,000-pound piece of ice was carved out like a coffin. Moro reclined in the lower half of the Ice tomb and the tomb's cover was placed over him. Then the ice was melted around the seams so no air would be able to pass through the cracks of the ice block. After the required time of entombment, the ice was chopped open and Moro emerged unharmed and unaffected - except for being a bit chilled. Moro was a very popular attraction, having performed at the Chicago World's Fair of 1933. (129-132)

Other performers were "The Man with the Iron Stomach" who could eat iron, fire, glass, steel and razor blades and the "Master Mind Reader" who could tell guests what they were thinking. (133)

Churches and Prize Winners

"Free tickets can also be used in any of the guessing contests and as a vote for your favorite church. The church receiving the most votes will be given $25.

Corpus Christi Church won the most popular church and wins $25. Mrs. M. Finkblener of 75 Grape Street wins a 9 x 11 Congoleum rug and C. Moiel of 124 Victoria Avenue wins 6 x 3 Congoleum rug. Rita Ball of 5 Court Street, Lancaster wins a beautiful table lamp. William Petrillo of 266 Broadway wins a comfortable occasional chair." (357)

FREE TICKETS

WITH EVERY PURCHASE

With every purchase of 10c or more you will be given a ticket which will enable you to participate in any and all of the numerous attractions. Tickets can be used to obtain BALLOONS, LEMONADE, CANDY and NOVELTIES FREE! Tickets can also be used in any of the guessing contests and as a vote for your favorite church. THE CHURCH RECEIVING THE MOST VOTES WILL BE GIVEN $25.

Bring in the kiddies. There will be clowns and entertainment galore for them.

CIRCUS ACTS TAKING PLACE ALL DAY *and* EVENING!

October 1935

Graham Sedan Give Away

Sattler's was well known to have massive crowds waiting outside before the store opened. The store was also famous for their generous giveaways. At 6:45 P.M. on October 24, 1935, Sattler's drew quite a crowd as it held a drawing for the first of four new 1936 model Graham Sedans.

Photograph courtesy of the Voorhees Family.

The first Graham Sedan was won by Ignatius Olejniczak of 93 Lombard Street. The next Graham Sedan giveaway was held on October 31st, and due to the large crowds it had to be moved across the street to the Broadway Market Plaza. That car was won by Mrs. William Bates of 224 Lewis Street, and the following Thursday, November 7, the car was won by Miss Helen Ziobro of 124 Player Street. The last Graham Sedan on November 14th was won by Rose Hylasek, 235 Lord Street. (135-139)

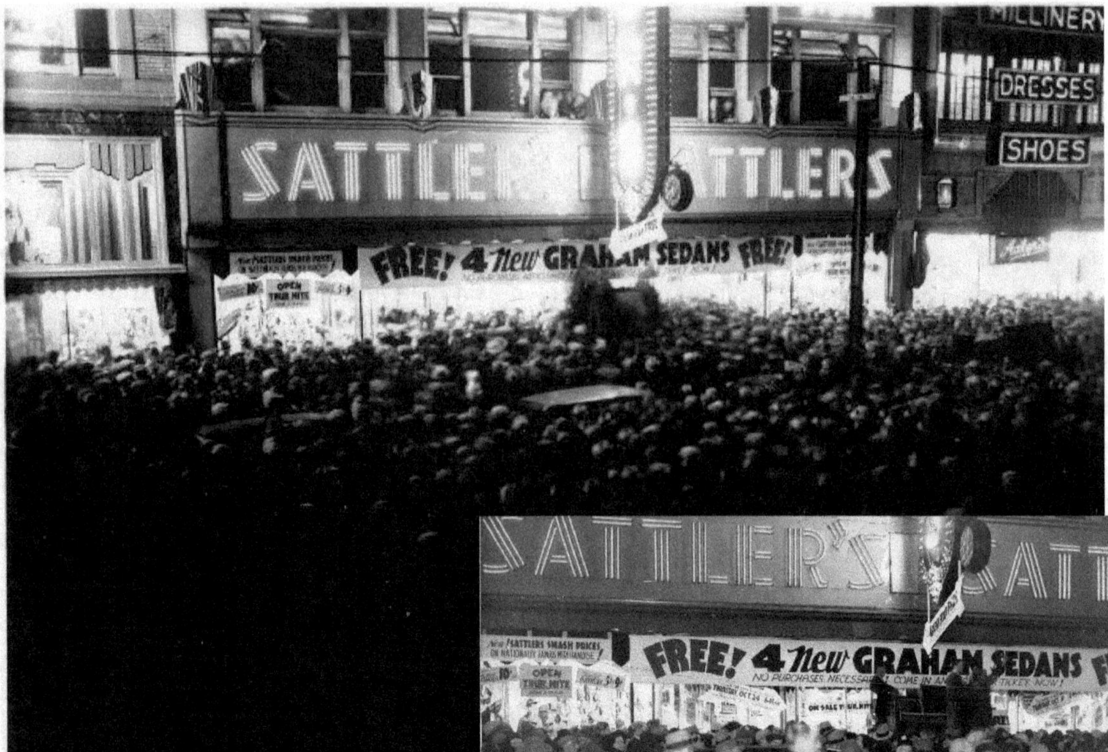

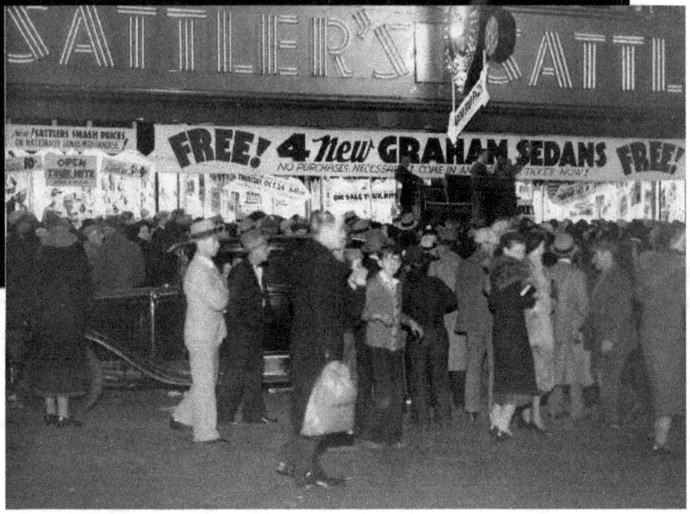

Photographs courtesy of the Voorhees Family.

November 1935

Sattler's Knitting Contest

YOU STILL HAVE TIME TO ENTER SATTLER'S

Knitting CONTEST

$30 in PRIZES

ASK FOR DETAILS IN OUR YARN DEPARTMENT

4 OZ. KNITTING YARN

A fine quality yarn at today's actual cost. A wide range of colors to choose from. You may be the winner of a valuable prize.

36c SKEIN

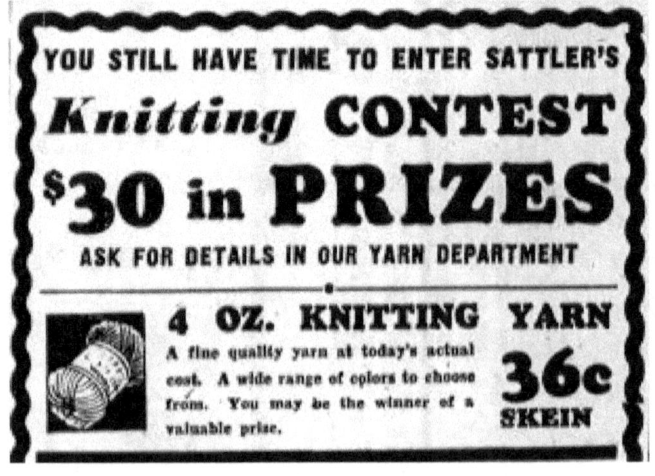

What a great way to get your customers in to buy your product! The judges of the knitting contest were Miss Sarah Lewis, feature writer of *The Buffalo Evening News* and Dorothy Winthrop, a shopping columnist for the *Buffalo Times*. The winner of the first prize of $15 was Mrs. Barne, 571 Niagara. Second prize of $10 went to Julia Randolph of 505 Ashland, and third prize of $5 went to Violet Noble of 147 Fordham. However, the best prize of all was bragging rights! This went to all the winners, as their knitted articles were on display in Sattler's Yarn Department. (140, 141)

November 1935

A Little Sattler's Shopper is Born! Welcome Patricia Ann Harran Born on November 9, 1935

CONGRATULATIONS

Are Now in Order

Mr. and Mrs. Norman Harran

(Sattler's Bride and Groom of 1934)

ARE THE PROUD PARENTS OF A BABY GIRL!

Patricia Ann—Born Nov. 9th

Yes, mother and daughter are both doing nicely. It won't be long before Patricia Ann will be joining mother on her shopping tours to Sattler's. And it won't be long before Patricia Ann will be convinced that Sattler's certainly do give you more for your money.

"**CONGRATULATIONS** Are Now in Order. **Mr. and Mrs. Norman Harran** (Sattler's Bride and Groom of 1934) **ARE THE PROUD PARENTS OF A BABY GIRL!** Patricia Ann – Born Nov.9th. Yes, mother and daughter are both doing nicely. It won't be long before Patricia Ann will be joining mother on her shopping tours to Sattler's. And it won't be long before Patricia Ann will be convinced that Sattler's certainly do *[sic]* give you more for your money." (142)

December 1935

Yule Baskets

Sattler employees decided to forgo their large company Christmas party and make sure less fortunate families had a merry Christmas. 200 yule baskets of food were made and given to the Council of Social Agencies, which saw to it they were placed in deserving homes. (143)

January 1936

Employee Dinner Dance

Over 400 employees attended Sattler's annual dinner dance held at the Buffalo Hilton. Mr. Sattler was the main speaker at the event, and he praised the employees for their thoughtful decision to forgo a Christmas party in December and donate the funds from that party so others might have a merry Christmas. He also spoke about the value of good fellowship in business. Mr. Sattler received a standing ovation. The speeches were followed by the yearly election of officers for the Sattler's Social Club, with entertainment and dancing rounding out the evening. (144)

February 1936

Air Conditioning at Sattler's

In February of 1936, an air-conditioning system was installed at Sattler's in its own brick building on the roof. There were 39 individual automatically-operating units throughout the store and every hour 10,000,000 cubic feet of air was dehumidified, cooled and filtered to clean out pollen and dust. The system was operated 365 days a year. (145)

Pictured from left to right are Aaron Rabow, Charles Hahn and John G. Sattler. They are standing in front of the newly installed refrigeration plant made by the Mollenberg-Betz Machine Co. of Buffalo, NY. (146)

Photograph taken by Bob Bros. Studio courtesy of Jeff Bob.

"Ten million cubic feet of cool filtered air pour into Sattler's department store every hour. That makes it possible for you to shop in healthful comfort at all times. Sattler's is the only department store in Western New York that has installed a modern air cooling system." (590)

March 1936

Kit Klein

Buffalo has always been a sports town, and when speed skater Kit Klein came to Sattler's Department Store the crowds were there to greet her. This hometown hero lived on Northampton Street in Buffalo. She skated at the Humboldt Park ice rink just a few blocks away from where she lived. Who would have guessed that this dark-haired smiling youngster would become a world champion speed skater?

Kit competed in speed skating as a demonstration sport in 1932 at the Lake Placid Olympic Games. In the 1936 Olympic Games in Garmisch-Partenkirchen, Germany, Kit Klein took first place in speed skating.

In March of 1936, Kit returned from competitions in Norway, Sweden, France and Germany and was greeted by hundreds of fans as her train from New York City arrived at Buffalo's Central Terminal. She was soon whisked away by an awaiting limousine. When her motorcade reached Broadway and Michigan Street, the Lafayette Republican Women's Club fife and drum corps led the hero's homecoming parade through the downtown streets of Buffalo. It was a four-mile parade route that led from the train terminal to the steps of City Hall, and it was packed with crowds of cheering fans that delighted the city's "Ice Queen." Kit was greeted by Mayor Zimmerman, politicians, reporters and a lively throng of well-wishers on the steps of Buffalo's City Hall. (147-154)

This Photograph of Kit Klein is on dispay at City Honors High School. Kit Klein attended the former Fosdick-Masten Park High School in Buffalo, where her roller skates and skate box are kept as mementos of her time at the school.

Picture courtesy of City Honors High School, Buffalo, NY.

April 1936

Let's Go

In April of 1936, a cast of 40 employees put on a musical show at St. John Kanty's lyceum called *Let's Go*. The evening was sponsored by the Sattler's Social Club. The show included a snake dance in an African village setting, and a couple in a musical song and whistling performance. (155, 156)

July 1936

Celebrating Tonawanda Centennial

There were celebrations of every kind to commemorate the centennial year of the Town of Tonawanda during July of 1936. There were fireworks and parades as Governor Herbert H. Lehman rode through the streets of Tonawanda. There were bike races, doll shows, a Girl Scout pageant, marching bands, military pageantry... and even a swarm of 70,000 bees who decided to cluster near the Tonawanda Administration building during the celebrations.

On the afternoon of July 8, 1936, Sattler's brought the big featured acts that were performing at the Tonawanda Centennial Exhibition to 998 Broadway. These included Palmer's Famous Performing Dogs and a group of 5 dancing accordionists known as the Balabanow Family. The father and manager of the group was Taras Balabanoff. Balabanoff was not just any musician; he was a former musician for Emperor Nicholas II of Russia. In the year 1903, Taras fell out of favor with the Czar. Most of Taras' possessions were confiscated by the Czar, and Taras fled with his wife, Catarina, and his young son John. The Balabanoffs fled Russia aboard the ship *Noorden* and arrived in Philadelphia on June 7, 1903. From there, the young family moved to Newark, New Jersey, where they changed their surname to Balabanow. The family quickly grew with the addition of 2 more sons, Leonid and Valentine, as well as 2 daughters, Marie and Olga. Taras opened and operated the Balabanow Accordion Factory in Newark, New Jersey. He produced exquisite accordions, which were renowned for their quality the world over. In 1933, Taras and his 5 children performed throughout the USA, Canada, and Europe. "Their show used a variety of accordions - including 3 of the smallest accordions in the world and one of the most costly instruments ever produced. This large accordion is played virtuoso; it required more than a year and an expense of more than $2,000 to make."

The day after the Balabanow Family performed at Sattler's, they were scheduled to play at the Tonawanda Centennial celebration. The performance of many of the acts continued into the evening. Taras was enjoying watching the other performers while sitting off stage. At 10:30 in the evening, he suddenly began to complain of indigestion, fell off his chair, and died. (157-161, 596-602)

Nicholas II of Russia and Alexandra Fyodorovna (Alix of Hesse)

Photograph from Wikimedia Commons, the free media repository

July 1936

How Times Have Changed

One of the major characters that Bob Cornelius created for Sattler's was the old Scotsman, Sandy B. Thrifty. Another was created in 1936 when Sattler's became the first major building in Buffalo that was fully air conditioned. That promotional figure was Coolie Cucumber. Today the stereotyped cartoons would not be socially acceptable, especially Coolie Cucumber who had a Chinese face and a Chinese coolie hat. Also, note the Native American further down the page. Although these images would be very hurtful today, this kind of depiction was common for the times in 1936. (162, 163)

The above ad is from 1938; it is one of the few advertisements in which I found Coolie Cucumber.

"COME ON IN-----THE WEATHER'S FINE!

"Save cash and perspiration at Sattler's the only Air-Conditioned department store in Western New York! Shop comfortably in the coolest, cleanest, freshest air you ever breathed." (164)

"It's Cool as a CUCUMBER at SATTLER'S!

"--Fact is, it's a good deal cooler than a cucumber at Sattler's. For the ONLY department store Air-Conditioning plant in this neck of the woods is busy keeping it that way, even on hottest days.

"No more sweltering discomfort, but plenty of clean, cool fresh air. Come in and enjoy real spring weather while you shop and save." (165)

" YOU'RE MONEY AHEAD SHOPPING AT AIR-COOLED SATTLER'S

"When it means money in your pocket as well as fresh air in your lungs, it's just the sensible thing to do to shop at Sattler's. Plan a trip to Sattler's tomorrow. See what a real difference Air-Conditioning makes." (166)

"Shop And Save In Buffalo's FRESH-AIR STORE Fresh Air!

"Ten million cubic feet of it are poured into Sattler's department store every hour of the day! And the air isn't only **FRESH.** It's cooled and dehumidified for real shopping comfort. Remember-Sattler's is the only Air-Conditioned department store in this part of the state. **Come** in and **COOL OFF!** "(167)

"TRY A COOL STORE!

"The good old summer time isn't so good if it means roasting alive every time you shop. Keep cool! Shop at Sattler's, Buffalo's only Air-Conditioned Department Store.

"And Remember---no matter what it is, you can get it for less at Sattler's." (168)

"It's the Talk of the Town

"When folks say, 'Let's go inside and cool off,' that's news. But that's just what they're saying out at Sattler's. And Sattler's is really cool these days, thanks to the $150,000 Air-Conditioning system that pours ten million cubic feet of cool, filtered, de-humidified air into the store every hour. Come in and cool off!" (169)

August and September 1936 **Four Ford V-8's Given Away**

During two weeks in August and two weeks in September of 1936, Sattler's was giving away brand new Ford V-8's. During the last week, the additional prizes listed below were given away. If you wanted a chance to win the Ford V-8 cars, you would have to visit Sattler's. When you entered the store you were given an entry form, and you had to be present when the car drawing took place to win. (170-173)

GET YOUR FREE CHANCES NOW! NOTHING TO BUY!

Thursday night, this week, Sattler's give away the last of four brand new 1936 Ford V-8's. But that isn't all . . . five other big prizes will also be given away at the same time. See the list of additional prizes below. Then plan now to do all your shopping at Sattler's. Remember, every time you enter the store up until 5:30 o'clock Thursday night, you will be given another chance on these splendid prizes. Ticket holders must be present at drawing to win. No tickets to children.

1ST PRIZE: A brand new 1936 Ford V-8 Sedan. Worth $650.

2ND PRIZE: A brand new 1937 Norge Gas Range. Worth $79.50.

3RD PRIZE: A handsome "Palmer" Inner Spring Mattress. Worth $39.50.

4TH PRIZE: A handsome 5-piece Breakfast Set (table and 4 chairs). Worth $37.50.

5TH PRIZE: A good looking 9x12 Wool Rug. Worth $37.50.

6TH PRIZE: A luxurious Pillow Back Chair. Worth $29.95.

DRAWING FOR THE ABOVE PRIZES WILL BE HELD THURSDAY NIGHT OF THIS WEEK. THE TIME: 6:45 P. M. THE PLACE: BROADWAY MARKET PLAZA, ACROSS THE STREET FROM SATTLER'S STORE. BE THERE!

The crowds for the car giveaways were so huge that the prize drawings took place in the evening at the Broadway Market Plaza across the street from Sattler's.

September 1936

Bargain Fair

"Everyone has oodles of fun at Sattler's famous 'Bargain Fair.' Music! Clowns! Sawdust on the floor! A barker out front and everything! With every purchase of 10c or more, you'll be given a free ticket. Use these tickets as cash in participating in any and all of the scores of free attractions. Watch for the clowns to distribute free merchandise. Each clown carries a sign telling how many free tickets are required for his particular free attraction." (174)

Hiram Thistlebottom

On display at the Bargain Fair was a mechanical hillbilly by the name of Hiram Thistlebottom. This mechanical man was invented by Albert Hedden of Decatur, Illinois. Albert Hedden, a telegraph operator for over 50 years, made this life-size robot that sang, talked and answered questions. He spoke by use of a phonograph record and a radio speaker in his throat. He even was once rigged to smoke a pipe. (175-178) **Photograph courtesy of the South Bend Tribune.**

October 1936

See and Hear the World Series

In 1936 the World Series between the New York Giants and the New York Yankees could be experienced at Sattler's, where *The Buffalo Evening News* play-o-graph could be seen in front of the store.

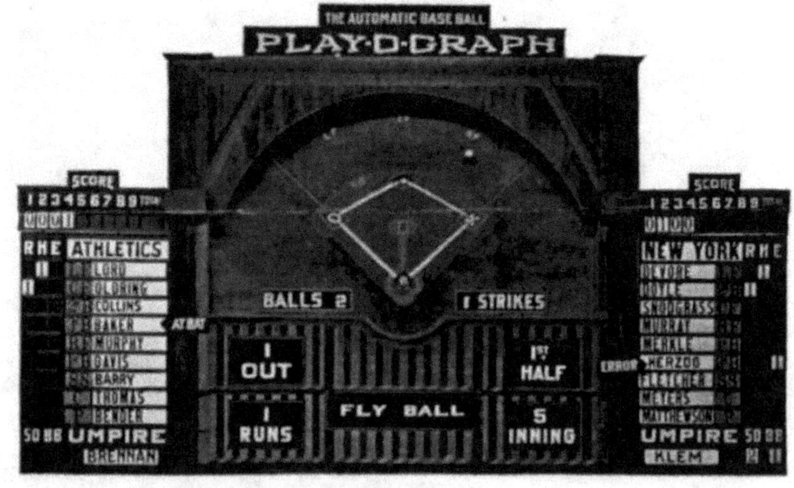

The play-o-graph was a huge billboard-sized scoreboard with a display where scores and up-to-the-minute plays were sent by telegraph during the baseball game. The play-o-graph not only posted the scores by inning, but the machine also simulated each pitch and each runner's position. The ball was moved using animatronics to show whether the ball was a bunt, curve, or fastball, and it showed where the ball was hit on the replicated baseball diamond. An "X" was displayed on the board as a runner, and an "O" was displayed if the runner was out. *The Yale Scientific Monthly* 1912-19 No. 4 (179-183)

November 1936 **Congratulations and Happy Motoring!**

"With each $20 of your Philco purchase at Sattler's you receive three entry blanks entitling you to enter the contest to win a new Plymouth car."

Asuncion Ramirez, 188 Eagle Street, was the lucky winner of the brand new 1937 Plymouth Sedan from Sattler's. (184, 185)

December 1936

Limerick Contest for Sattler's Coal and Coke Buyers

The following were the ten lucky customers of Sattler's Coal Department, each of whom won a big fat turkey. Out of the hundreds of "last lines" submitted in Sattler's limerick contest, these people were judged to have the best "last line." (Unfortunately, I don't know what their last lines were.) (186, 187)

Josephine Triller, 41 Ash Street
H. H. Poole, 148 Kings Highway, Snyder
Mrs. W. J. Sloan, 275 Huntington Avenue
Mrs. B. Davern, 72 Kirkpatrick Street
Mrs. E. Abrams, 32 Emslie Street
Mrs. F. Jeziorski, 359 Gibson Street
Royce S. Day, 18 Victory Blvd., Kenmore
Mrs. W. A. Gerlach, 727 Northumberland
Mrs. S. Butcher, 376 Main Street, Ebenezer
Mrs. W.J. Ansteth, 24 Woodlawn Ave.

1937

"Cut the Corners Squarely"

Above are Charles Hahn, John G. Sattler, Mayor George Zimmerman, Senator James Mead, and Aaron Rabow. Photograph courtesy of the Voorhees Family.

Sattler's Department Store expanded once again, starting this expansion in 1935 and finishing in 1937. This was the fourth of many expansions that Sattler's would undergo during its many years of existence.

A Sattler family motto became famous at the store: "CUT THE CORNERS SQUARELY." It was during one of the Sattler's store expansions that this family motto had been put to the test. Charles Hahn, the president of Sattler's, went to Buffalo City Hall to speak with the mayor of Buffalo about enlarging 998. It seemed the mayor at the time had quietly suggested a bribe in order to have Sattler's receive the go-ahead for the project to be approved. The mayor opened the drawer of his desk and left his office with Mr. Hahn sitting there alone. Charles Hahn realized what was going on and promptly walked out of the office. Upon the mayor's return, he discovered that no cash had been placed in the drawer. Mr. Hahn kept his money in his pocket, along with his self-respect and his dignity. After that, Mr. Hahn always reminded his children and grandchildren to "CUT THE CORNERS SQUARELY," which meant to do things correctly, rather than take the easy way out.

1937

The Scotsman Needs a Name!

Created by Robert S. Cornelius, the antics of the Scotsman were ready for any occasion. It was time for the Scotsman to have a real name, so in 1937 another Sattler's contest was announced; this time it was for giving a name to "The Scotsman." A $5.00 cash prize went to Miss Mildred Tonge of 28 School Road in Kenmore, whose winning entry was "Sandy B. Thrifty." Sandy B. Thrifty became the most recognized Sattler's mascot. Sandy changed over the years, but was always dressed for the part. (188-199)

March 1937

Circus Night

Over 400 employees and their families were guests of Sattler's store management to see the Shrine Circus at the Broadway Auditorium, located at 201 Broadway. This building is still used today by Buffalo Public Works. The groundbreaking for the building took place in 1858, with the building originally used by the U.S. Army as an arsenal, and later by the National Guard. In 1907 the building was converted to an auditorium and arena. (200, 201)

September 1937

Buy Buffalo and Boost Buffalo

The country was in the midst of a recession when John G. Sattler launched a "Buy Buffalo" and "Boost Buffalo" campaign to help the companies in Buffalo stay in business and keep their employees working. Simply stated, if you were a local manufacturer or a store that needed to buy something for your business, buy it from people in Buffalo and keep Buffalonians employed. That keeps Buffalo businesses open. This call to "Boost Buffalo" helped stimulate local business recovery, and Mr. Sattler urged businesses to continue this practice for several years. (202-206)

May 1938 **Buffalo Fire Commissioner Visits Sattler's**

From left to right, Fire Commissioner William R. Castimor; Charles Hahn, president of Sattler's; Aaron Rabow, general manager of Sattler's; Battalion Chief August W. Rath; Bob Cornelius, Sattler's promotions manager. Photograph courtesy of the Voorhees Family.

Sattler's gave a demonstration of its newly installed fire control system, which turned on if it detected a 20-degree temperature rise. When activated, the new system automatically turned on sprinklers, turned off the air-condition intakes, rang an alarm to warn people in the store and on the street of a potential fire, and sent word to the fire department of a potential fire at the department store. (207)

Properties on Beck and Gibson Streets Were Being Acquired by Sattler's by 1938

Prices for some of the properties bought by Sattler's, Inc. on Beck and Gibson Streets were as follows:

36 Beck Street $16,000, 42 Beck $13,000, 58 Beck $13,000, 64 Beck $16,000, 66 Beck $12,000, 70 Beck $12,000, 323 Gibson Street $16,000, 327 Gibson $13,000, 351 Gibson $12,000, 353 Gibson $15,000. (208)

Grantee	Grantor	Liber	Page	Date of Instrument	Date of Record	Description
Sattler's, Inc.	John G. Sattler, Inc.	2979	339	Dec. 30, 1939	Apr. 22, 1940	Beck, 300 N. Broadway
Do.	Do.	2979	348	Jan. 24, 1940	22	N.W. cor Broadway & Beck
Do.	Do.	2979	342	Dec. 30, 1939	22	Beck 330 N. Broadway
Do.	Do.	2979	351	30	22	Beck 360 N. Broadway

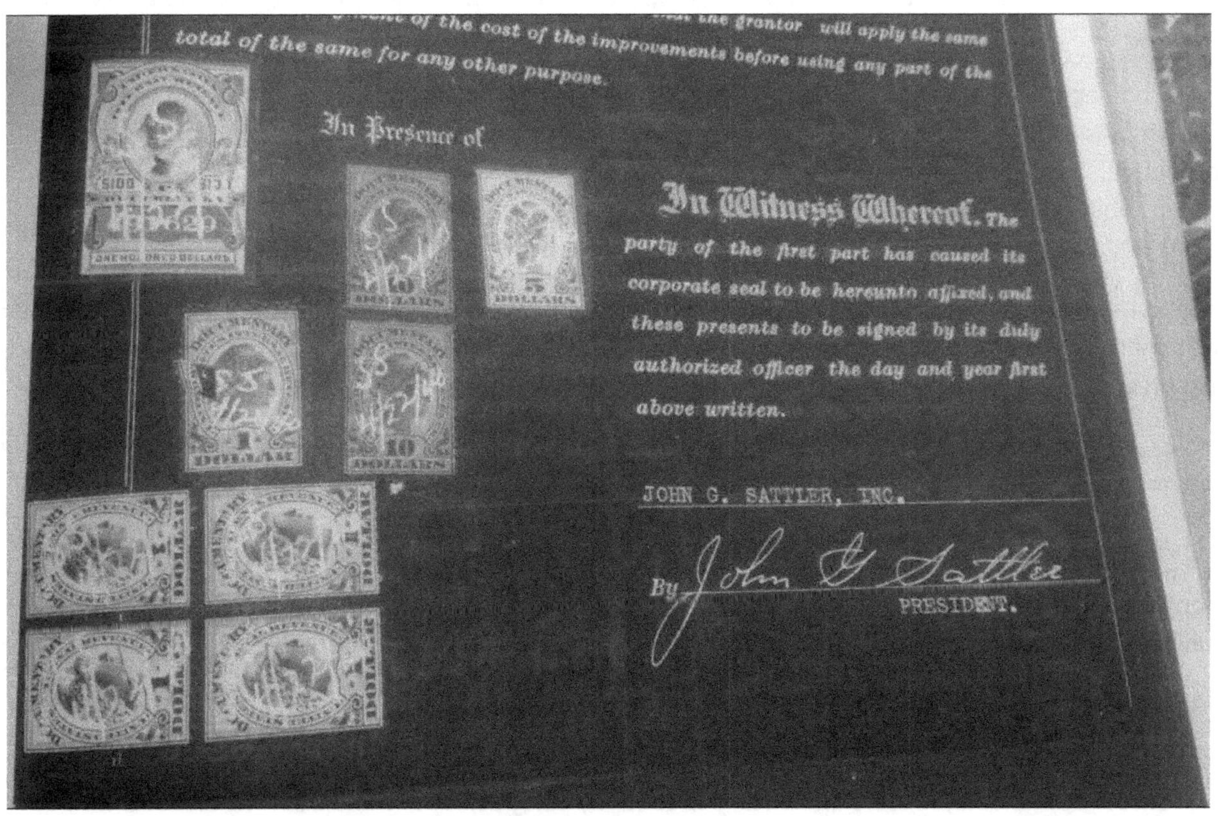

...of the cost of the improvements before using any part of the total of the same for any other purpose. ...the grantor will apply the same

In Presence of

In Witness Whereof, The party of the first part has caused its corporate seal to be hereunto affixed, and these presents to be signed by its duly authorized officer the day and year first above written.

JOHN G. SATTLER, INC.

By John G. Sattler
PRESIDENT.

Real estate information listed at Erie County Hall. Photographs courtesy of the Voorhees Family.

March 1939 Sattler's Celebrates Golden Jubilee Year

Founder Day for Mr. Sattler was September 2, 1889. The Golden Jubilee Year at Sattler's was kicked off with its "Spring Festival of Bargains." That year the front doors of Sattler's were transformed into the "Golden Gate to Thrift," as 998's entranceway welcomed customers through two large doors enhanced with golden iron grillwork and a ceiling vestibule vaulted in gold. If you looked in the windows, the displays had backgrounds of pale green with gold leaves. In the store, shimmering posts with enormous banners of gold dazzled shoppers as they experienced a "King Midas" wonderland of pageantry. (209)

An enormous helium-filled golden balloon, which bore the symbol of a spread eagle, represented Sattler's Golden Jubilee Year. The massive balloon, with a 30-foot circumference, was set afloat on March 16, 1939 and floated hundreds of feet above the department store at 998 Broadway. The balloon had colorful silk streamers that were 20 feet long, waving from its tether. This sight could be viewed from miles away and beckoned everyone to come to visit the Golden Wonder Store at 998. (209)

The formal opening of Sattler's Golden Jubilee Year of Savings was officiated by Buffalo Mayor Thomas L. Holling, Assistant District Attorney Miss Winifred Stanley and Howard L. Volgenu of the Chamber of Commerce. Congratulatory speeches were made and a golden ribbon was cut to officially open the Golden Jubilee Year. (209)

It was at that event that "Sattler's Golden Girl" was introduced: Miss Ruth Navelle, dressed in gold from head to foot. The 21-year-old beauty was chosen from among 2,000 contestants as the best-looking and most charming of the contestants. She was a representative of goodwill for the store and she received a cash prize of $25.

Music for the gala opening was performed by the drum corps of Harry E. Crosby, Post 2476, Veterans of Foreign Wars, Kenmore, NY. (209)

Telegrams and well-wishes came in from across the nation:

Thomas L. Holling, Mayor of Buffalo, wrote, "It is indeed a tribute to the integrity and policy of any individual or firm to establish such a remarkable record of continuous operation."

"Congratulations on your golden jubilee. Remember the first 50 years are the hardest. All good wishes to my Buffalo Friends." - Jack Benny

"In view of your golden jubilee, I am writing to send my congratulations and best wishes for a well-deserved celebration. "- Katherine Cornell

"Having just learned of your 50th anniversary, I take this opportunity to wish you success for your 'Golden Jubilee' celebration with it being held to commemorate the occasion. With my kind personal regards, I am yours, very sincerely, Herbert R. O'Connor, Governor of Maryland."

John G. Sattler, Charles Hahn and Buffalo Mayor Thomas L. Holling celebrate Sattler's Golden Jubilee Year in 1939. Photograph courtesy of the Archives and Special Collections Department, E. H. Butler Library SUNY Buffalo State.

"Congratulations to Sattler's ...we're early settlers ourselves." This was from Groucho and Chico Marx.

"Hardiest good wishes," wired Fibber McGee and his entire company.

"My congratulations on your success and my very best wishes to you and your employees for the continuation of that success." - Herbert H. Lehman, Governor of New York

"...an event worthy of recognition and felicitations. I want to extend my congratulations to all who have had a part in the growth and development of the great store. My best wishes for the continued success of this enterprise." - Mayor LaGuardia of New York City

"I thought we had something to brag about in June when Ida and I will celebrate 25 years in business together. But 50 years in business is something to boast of from the house tops. The fact that Sattler's has been at the same old stand for half a century is concrete evidence to me that you have served the City of Buffalo and its people well. Congratulations and all good wishes." - Eddie Cantor

"Your many years of service to the citizens of the community is concrete evidence of the success of your organization. With every good wish for the future." - Governor of Florida, Fred P. Cone

"Hearty congratulations to Sattler's as it completes 50 years of service to Buffalo and Western New York." - Governor of Kentucky, Albert N. Chandler

Other wishes of goodwill came in from Mary Livingstone, wife of Jack Benny; Governor of Maine, Lewis O. Barrows; Governor of Tennessee, William Prentice Cooper; Governor of Idaho, Barzilla W. Clark; Governor of West Virginia, Homer A. Holt; Governor of New Hampshire, Francis P. Murphy; Governor of New Mexico, John E. Miles, along with hundreds of others. (209)

This picture was taken on March 14, 1939 at the Hotel Statler. In the back row from left to right, vice-president of Sattler's, Charles Hahn, Fred J. Erion, president of Erion's, Fred C. Jahraus, president of Jahraus-Braun Co. and Aaron Rabow, general manager of Sattler's. The bottom row left to right is Samuel B. Botsford, secretary of the Buffalo Chamber of Commerce and John G. Sattler, president of Sattler's.(210, 211) Photograph courtesy of the Archives and Special Collections Department, E. H. Butler Library SUNY Buffalo State.

A banquet was given at the Georgian Room in the Hotel Statler to honor Mr. Sattler and celebrate his Golden Jubilee. The Master of Ceremony was Mr. Sattler's son-in-law, Charles Hahn. The mayor of Buffalo, Thomas L. Holling, and the Executive Vice President of the Chamber of Commerce, Samuel B. Botsford, were guest speakers. Robert Cornelius, Sattler's promotions manager, read some of the many, many telegrams and letters written by politicians, civic leaders and people from the theater and music industry, as well as from friends and fellow citizens who expressed their care, admiration and well-wishes. (210)

Mr. Sattler also spoke on this occasion. At 67 years of age, Mr. Sattler was still humble and soft-spoken as he related his recollections of the early days of Sattler's at the strategic location directly across from the Broadway Market. He spoke of his mother, Elizabeth Geise Sattler, and her involvement in the creation of the Sattler's store, which was first called The Broadway Market Shoe House. (210)

Sattler's Golden Girl
Ruth Navelle

Sattler's held a contest to choose a young woman to represent Sattler's in 1939 for Sattler's golden anniversary. The job of the Golden Girl was to be Sattler's ambassador of goodwill: to visit hospitals and charitable institutions, to deliver toys and food, and to entertain the people she visited. The Golden Girl was given a wardrobe provided by Sattler's and she won a cash prize of $25. She rode in a golden coach, drawn by a horse with golden plumes on its head, outfitted with a golden harness and golden horseshoes. Over 2,000 young women applied for the job.

The winner of the prize was a former Hengerer's Department Store tie saleswoman, Ruth Navelle. By the time she was chosen as the Golden Girl for Sattler's, she already had been discovered by a radio man from WEBR/WBEN, who came in with a friend to Hengerer's to buy a tie. After the sale was completed the radio man said that if she could sing as well as she could sell a tie, she would be in line to have a music career. Ruth informed the radio man that she could sing and was already performing at events. Soon after that encounter with the WEBR/WBEN radio men, Ruth Navelle was singing on WBEN radio as a pop soloist. At the time of her performance on the radio, the man who accompanied her on the piano for her musical numbers was the famous Buffalo Bob Smith. (212)

Ruth Navelle had her first public appearance as Sattler's Golden Girl at Sattler's Grand Opening Ceremonies to help kick off its Sattler's Golden Jubilee Year celebration. Miss Navelle was dressed in a gown of gold, accented with a gold hat and gold shoes. (213)

Photograph courtesy of Martha L. Marmion.

Photograph courtesy of Martha L. Marmion.

Ruth appeared during "Sattler's Night" at the Shrine Circus in the Broadway Auditorium. (214) She arrived and was driven around the show floor of the auditorium in her horse-drawn golden carriage, then sang for Sattler's employees and their families attending the circus show.

This picture of Ruth was taken with Ernie Watson, director of Shea's Buffalo Orchestra. Ruth was performing for a week at the Shea's Theater as Sattler's Golden Girl. (215)

Photograph courtesy of Martha L. Marmion.

September 1939

The Pope Is Not the Only Owner of a Golden Telephone

Charles Hahn, Aaron Rabow and Robert Cornelius surprised John G. Sattler in his office with the gift of a golden telephone. The Founder Day gift of the golden telephone marked the golden anniversary for Mr. Sattler. (216-218)

November 1939

Art Contest

It was so like Mr. Sattler to further the education and ambitions of the young and talented. Mr. Sattler had a history of giving scholarships to people he found to have exemplary or raw talent. We cannot always see or comprehend how our actions will affect the lives of others, or the world. An act that may seem inconsequential to us can have a profound effect on others. Such was the case of a feature event to celebrate Mr. Sattler's Golden Jubilee Year. A poster contest was held for young artists between the ages of 15 and 30 who lived in Western New York. The prizes and winners for the contest were:

First place was a year's scholarship at the Albright Art School. This was won by Victor R. Lalli of 73 Wilkes Avenue, Buffalo

Second prize was an oil painting kit with a $25.00 value, which was won by Muriel Hintermeier of Indian Church Road, Buffalo.

Third prize was an oil painting kit with a $15.00 value, which was won by Dorothy Beenau of 95 Floss Avenue.

In 1939 Victor Roger Lalli was a senior at Kensington High School. At the time that Victor accepted his award from Sattler's, it was reported that he had been interested in drawing and sculpture ever since he could remember, and his plan was to become an art teacher.

Conversations with Victor Roger Lalli's widow, Louise Lalli, were a testament to how a Sattler's contest back in 1939 helped shape the future of a great Buffalo artist and a wonderful art teacher.

Dr. Victor Roger Lalli drew comics from the newspaper at age 3, even before he could read the funny papers. In grade school and high school, his talent for art was evident to his teachers. It was during the Depression that his scholarship from Sattler's, a year's tuition at the Albright Art School, was put to good use.

Printed with permission of Louise Lalli.

In that first year at the Albright Art School, Mr. Lalli won the prestigious Isabell Ross Award for excellence in drawing with a charcoal drawing of Duke Giuliano de' Medici (at left). That was the first time a first-year student won this prestigious award.

His dream of being an art teacher came to fruition when he taught at Rosary Hill and Canisius Colleges, as well as in the Amherst Central Schools. After his retirement, he painted vivid watercolors of the architecture of Buffalo, NY. The watercolors were so precise that viewers would think they were looking at a photograph instead of a painting.

Dr. Lalli was a celebrated artist at the Albright Knox Art Gallery, showing his watercolors at a show entitled *Buffalo, My City*. Later he published a book with those watercolors entitled *The Buffalo Architectural Watercolors*.

The photographs are of watercolor prints of Our Lady of Victory Basilica in Lackawanna, NY and of Main Street in Buffalo, NY. (219-223) Printed with permission of Louise Lalli.

November, 1939

Expansion at Sattler's

On November 18, 1939, thirty homes on Gibson and Beck Street were razed for Sattler's two-acre parking lot. The parking lot was able to accommodate 500 cars. (224)

GIBSON ST.
Sept. 15, 1939

GIBSON ST.
Nov. 18, 1939

BECK ST.
Sept. 15, 1939

BECK ST.
Nov. 18, 1939

BECK ST.
Nov. 25, 1939

BECK ST.
Dec. 1, 1939

Construction of the Newest Building at 998

HEATING UNIT
APRIL 12, 1940

Sattlers Service Bldg.
Buffalo, N. Y.
Edward E. Ashley, Cons. Engr.
Louis Greenstein, Archt.
Siegfried Construction Co.
APRIL 16, 1940

MARCH 26, 1940
MARCH 26, 1940
MARCH 29, 1940
MARCH 29, 1940
APRIL 2, 1940
APRIL 2, 1940

APRIL 15 1940
APRIL 15, 1940
APRIL 16, 1940
APRIL 18, 1940
APRIL 16, 1940
APRIL 18, 1940

APRIL 19, 1940
APRIL 19, 1940
APRIL 26, 1940
APRIL 26, 1940

APRIL 17, 1940
APRIL 18, 1940
APRIL 19, 1940
APRIL 20, 1940
APRIL 23, 1940
APRIL 24, 1940

APRIL 24, 1940
APRIL 25, 1940
APRIL 26, 1940
APRIL 27, 1940
APRIL 28, 1940
APRIL 29, 1940

Sattlers Service Bldg.,
Buffalo, N.Y.
Edward E. Ashley, Cons. Engr.,
Louis Greenstein, Archt.,
Siegfried Construction Co.,
April 4, 1940.

The previous 9 pages of photographs are from a scrapbook that is courtesy of the Voorhees Family.

January 1940

Snow Party

While the new store was being built, Sattler's continued to operate out of its original 998 Broadway location. To keep up morale at the store, in January of 1940 Sattler's Social Club had a "Snow Party." Buses were provided in front of Sattler's at 6:00 PM. The Sattlerites were transported to Chestnut Ridge Park, where employees could enjoy skiing and tobogganing, with all rentals paid for by the Sattler's Social Club. At midnight, the group was treated to a midnight lunch. (225)

May 1940

Fire Prevention Achievement Award

From left to right Charles Hahn, president of Sattler's, John M. Galvin, president of Buffalo Junior Chamber of Commerce, Buffalo Fire Commissioner William R. Castimore, Battalion Chief George E. Walsh of Fire Prevention Services and Leroy H. Dehlinger, an inspector in the Fire Prevention Bureau. Photograph courtesy of the Voorhees Family.

A trophy and plaque were given by the Junior Chamber of Commerce for outstanding fire prevention services for 1939 at Sattler's Department Store. Sattler's and the Jr. Chamber of Commerce and Fire Preventative Services joined forces to display a fire prevention exhibit in Sattler's windows. (226)

Buffalo Fire Department shows off the old horse-drawn steam engine that was in service until about 1900. This steam engine can still be seen today at the Buffalo Fire Historical Society at 1850 William Street. Photograph courtesy of the Voorhees Family.

July 1940

Beach Party

Sattlerites attended a summer beach party at Bennett Beach, and the day included games, novelty events and a beauty contest. Bus rides to the event were provided by the Social Club. (227)

December 1940

"Xmas Party 1940 the Boys from Sattler's"

One of the great finds I discovered was an old 78 rpm record. The recording had a label with "Xmas party 1940 the boys from Sattler's" printed on it. It was made on December 9, 1940. It was a recording of employees from Sattler's wishing Mr. Hahn and Mr. Rabow a "Merry Christmas," and it started off with singing. **(Below is a verbatim account of the record. During the recording some of the enunciation was difficult to understand.)**

"Hail, hail the gang's all here. What the hell do we care, what the hell do we care. Hail, hail the gang's all here, what the hell do we care now." And continued with, "Yes Mr. Hahn and Mr. Rabow the gang is all here. All here to bring you a gift, our Christmas thought for you in our own voices, yours to keep through years to come. For no matter where the winds of fate or the tides of fortune may take us in our several voyages through life, you Mr. Hahn and Mr. Rabow can always, with this magical disk, turn back the hands of time, brush away the cobwebs from the silent corridors of years gone by and once again open the doors upon this night when we were all in good fellowship. This year we speak our love and friendship once as Pindar said some two thousand five hundred years ago 'whatsoever one hast well said goeth forth with a voice that never dieth, a voice the years will never drown.' This is Bob Cornelius saying, may the best be yours always. And turning it over to good old Lou Goldstein."

"'Merry Christmas' Mr. Hahn and Mr. Rabow and many, many more of them. It's a swell Christmas party and I'm proud to say through the years I've never missed one of them yet, and now here is Charlie Greenberg."

"Thank you for a swell party fellows. It looks like we are certainly beating last year's figures tonight. I'd like to take lots more time to say all the nice things that I am thinking, but here is Jack Reznick pushing me away."

"Thank you Charlie; hello Mr. Hahn and Mr. Rabow. I'd like to stick my hand out of this loudspeaker and shake yours and wish you a 'Merry Christmas and a Happy New Year.' Now here is that nationally famous regular eight fifty to ten fifty value Harry Herman."

"I've heard they have big parties in the west, but they can't be any bigger or better than those Christmas Eve shindigs here at Sattler's. Now let me introduce that intermittent rubber goods collector, Harold Gus Fink."

"'Season's Greetings' bosses. Mighty swell for you to give us this swell party every year; in fact it's a swell party. Really I'm having a wonderful time; now here comes someone who looks like he wants to talk, Mike Stark."

"Say Bob, get out of my way. Well ah, here we are again; another Christmas party is nearly over. It was a peach too; best of luck Mr. Hahn and Mr. Rabow, and here's Benny Battell."

"You're all wool and the odd wire for my money, fellows. It's a pleasure and a privilege to work with and for two such fine men, but look who is here-White Meat Willy Pudding himself."

"Well I tried to cook up something to say good enough to express my feelings, but the record isn't big enough to say all the things I'd like to say, so to keep things from getting into a stew, I'll turn it over; dish it out Al Zolar."

"Greetings gents in sizes 1 to 6X main floor rear. It's the best party ever. Best of luck to you for a new year, and here is that zinfmeta zimfamen from the South, Al Okin."

"Hello everybody, plenty yule this country never seen like this before. Yawl sure know how to mix business with pleasure, and it's a mighty nice party alright; here come Mush."

"Howdy chiefs, yes sir it's another home run. I'll lay you two to one that there's not another store in the country where the bosses and the fellows got what we got here tonight. More power to you and everything you do. Now Johnny Homer has a long one for you."

"Yes, but tonight I'm going to cut it short just a 'Merry Christmas and a Happy New Year'; take it away Joe Kay."

"It's fun to paint the town this way. If everybody has as good a time as I do, this is a party none of us will forget for a long, long time. How 'bout it Otto Kasin?"

"Right you are Joe, this is my second Christmas party at Sattler's, and I'm mighty happy to say that nobody has taken any picture of me yet tonight. But if they do, I'm going to use Johnny Hellmer as a stand in. Here's a real sport Art Pfeiffer."

Side 2 of the record.

Mr. Cornelius says, "Thank you Goldie, now here's Art."

"Say Mr. Hahn, have you got any more of those clay pigeons? The boys want to do a little shooting Sunday, no foolin', everything is swell and I'm mighty happy to be here tonight. Here's old bloody Bill Brighten, the pork chop king."

"Hello bosses, it's mighty nice to be here with you tonight. And that's no bologna; take it from me it's a ducky party, everybody veals fine, nobody's getting porky and there's certainly nothing to beef about, is there Mr. Dooley?"

"Not by a jug full Bill. Now don't any of you men at the party put glasses down on this combination radio. If you do, Joe Block will sure raise hell. Now Martin Lablock."

"'Peace on Earth', peace on everybody. It's a skiffle, it's a real 23-point hand-tailored party all right. Isn't it Mr. Hinel?"

"I'll say it is. If I can just stay this happy till Thursday morning I'll be happy. Just a moment, you say there's a light on in the main floor; where is Gordon?"

"Right here Mr. Hinel. It's a jam-up party gentlemen; I'm having the time of my young life. Now here is Morad with a big smile?"

"Why shouldn't I smile; this is the best party I've been to, ah Mr. Hahn?"

"Ah Mon, it's a bonnie party it is (this gentleman had a very heavy Scottish accent and was difficult to understand). I dinna ken when I had such a good time. I can surely say it's a braw bricht moonlicht nicht tonicht. How about it Bill Storm?"

"What a party. It's great gentlemen. I can assure that we're all having the time of our lives. What about it Jerry Schriber?"

"You bet your boots Bill. Just want to say 'Merry Christmas' Mr. Hahn and Mr. Rabow; now here is Ferdinand the Bull Smith."

"This is wonderful and that's no bull! Well, I finally made it. And to tell the truth it's the best party that I've ever been to in my life. The best of everything to you gentlemen; here's Lou Cooper who keeps the pet shop ship shape."

"A scout is honest so I must say that this is the swellest surprise I've ever experienced. Thanks for a wonderful time. What do you say Bill Cranston?"

"I say I'm glad to be a Sattlerite on a night like this. 'Merry Christmas' Mr. Hahn and Mr. Rabow. Take it away Norm Marion."

"Well as far as business goes, Christmas is all over, but in my memory this Christmas will always be fresh. It's a humdinger!"

"You said a shovel-full Norm. I think the bosses deserve 33 and 1/3 cheers just for being so nice. Don't scratch your furniture on the way out Paul Line?"

"I've got to admit though, was a sure load of groceries when it comes to throwing a swell party. All I can say is that I'm mighty happy to be here and having a wonderful time. What so you say Lee Smith?"

"I'm sure happy to be here at my first Sattler's Christmas party. Now I know why everyone was so excited. Hey brother it sure is wonderful. And now here is Lorie Henny."

"Hello and a 'Happy Holiday' to you both. Now, but not least, Bernie Hersher."

"Well Hersher my mouth, but I'll be doggonned if this isn't even better than last year's party, if that's possible! Yes Sir Mr. Hahn and Mr. Rabow. I think I speak for all the fellows when I say you are tip tops when it comes to real 22 karat men. You are what we all call good friends as well as good bosses. God bless you both."

"Thank you Bernie. And now good old Eddie Branson had got a space saved for him on the end of this disc and we are just waiting for him to get back from New York. Meanwhile we all join Mr. Hersher in saying God bless you both."

January 1941

Can You Estimate How Far Sandy Rides In 38 Days?

This promotion for Sattler's started in November of 1940 and concluded in January of 1941, so it must have been a cold and snowy ride for Sattler's mascot, Sandy B. Thrifty, for those 38 days! The ad that was in the newspaper stated: "First, see the giant mechanized figure of Sandy B. Thrifty on Bailey Avenue at Manhart. Imagine he is pedaling along a straight highway. Then guess how far he would travel in 38 days. The prizes are worth trying for!

All the information you need will be found on an entry blank. You can receive an entry blank with each purchase of boys' or girls' items at Sattler's. Be sure to ask for yours. Age limit, 8 to 18 years." (228)

The Final Estimate Showed Sandy B. Thrifty Traveled 24,108,000 Feet.

The prize winners were as follows:

FIRST PRIZE - $25 in cash won by Charles Gabryel, age 17, of 213 Playter Street.

SECOND PRIZE – A bicycle, won by Robert Upper, age 18, of 403 Olympic Avenue.

THIRD PRIZE – A bicycle, won by Donald Kelly, age 15, of 21 Spiess Street.

FOURTH PRIZE – A bicycle, won by Esther Sadkin, age 12, of 344 East Ferry Street.

FIFTH PRIZE – A bicycle, won by Paul Soloman, age 18, of 1949 Union Road, Gardenville, NY. (229)

I spoke on the phone with one of the winners of this contest, Esther Sadkin Kaufman. She has been living in Pittsburgh as an artist for the last 50 years. Esther was a joy to speak to and reminisce about Sattler's. She said that her cousin, Rose Cooper who worked at 998, put an entry form into the contest collection box for her at 998. She was a bit disappointed with the bike because she had won a boys' bike. That was a problem because of the high top crossbar on the bike. On the street where she lived, she could only ride on the sidewalk, and because of the unevenness of the sidewalk she did not ride it often. Nevertheless, it was a thrill for her to be a winner. (230)

Sandy's Enormous Bike

One of Sattler's typical promotions was Sandy B. Thrifty riding his bike for 38 days. What was not typical was the amount of work it took to have such a promotion. Sattler's had a 14' x 20' billboard constructed to promote Sandy's bike riding contest. Attached to the billboard was an enormous metal mechanical bicycle with one huge front wheel and a smaller back wheel that Sandy B. Thrifty would ride. The bike extended over the top of the billboard. It was made by Bernhard Spielberger, who was a mechanic for the Wolf Machine Company, 1200 Clinton Street. The bicycle was constructed so that the pedals were kept in motion for 38 days. A huge replica of Sandy B. Thrifty sat on the bike, and Sandy's feet were attached to the bike pedals. (231)

January 1941

Going to Skateland

300 employees of Sattler's enjoyed a skating party at the new Skateland on Main Street. The evening was sponsored by Aaron Rabow, Sattler's vice-president. (232)

February 1941

Dance, Dance, Dance

A Sattler's year of service lapel pin is given in recognition of an employee's years of work for Sattler's.

The 11th annual dinner dance took place at the main ballroom of the Hotel Statler, where over 500 employees enjoyed the evening of food and dancing. A total of 42 service pins were given out to employees. (233)

Diamond Pins for fourteen years, six months and over: Mildred Banacha and John Wojcinski.

Gold pins for nine year and six months to fourteen years and five months: Louis Bystrak, Margaret Geist, Pauline Goldstein, Harry Herman, Mabel Klinck and Sophie Michaels.

Silver pins for four years and six months to nine years and five months: Walter Barry, Raymond Huenniger, Joseph Knasiak, Alice Koeppel, Virginia Kraska, Virginia Manion, George Pappas, Anita Piernik, Morris Schaffron, Hattie Skulicz, William Britton, Ann Miller, Emil Young and Goldie Levinson.

Bronze pins for two years and six months to four years and five months: Genevieve Doherty, Marguerite Hanse, Bernard Herscher, Edwin Kresinsaki, Thomas Kennedy, Loretta McGuire, Evelyn Nassau, Viola Riesen, John Ruhland, Paul Ryan, Kathryn Schuster, Frank Stelmach, Theresa Strnelec, Celia Sulkowski, Henry Sypniewski, Marian Tyran, Catherine Wald and Sophie Winiecki

April 1941

Doris Grace Sattler Marries

Doris lived with her father (John G. Sattler) until she married John Rooney on April 12, 1941 at the age of 31. She was married on a warm Saturday afternoon in the Presbyterian Church of LeRoy, the Rev. Evan M. Jones officiating. Mr. and Mrs. Rooney made their home at 800 West Ferry in Buffalo. (234, 235)

Doris Sattler Rooney

John Rooney

Photographs courtesy of Marilyn Clement.

April 1941

"Fun–A-Plenty"

Photograph courtesy of Michael Stark's Family.

Sattler's Social Club put on a charity variety show called "Fun-A-Plenty" to a crowd of 2,200 at the Buffalo Masonic Consistory auditorium located at 1180 Delaware Avenue. (Today the building is used as classrooms for Canisius High School and is known as Berchmans' Hall.) (236-238)

The 60-member cast was made up of Sattler's employees. The opening skit was a half-hour staged dispute over the front row seats in the audience. That was followed by impersonations, comedy routines, drama skits, dance, song, a colorful red white and blue "Spirit of 76"patriotic skit, a parade of flags of the British Commonwealth and a musical bullfight number. The final skit incorporated that front row dispute in the audience once again. (236, 237)

The show was written and directed by David Rothenberg, a Sattler's employee. This raucous show brought the house down with riotous laughter and numerous curtain calls. A dance in the Consistory ballroom followed this event. (236)

The show was a charity event to raise money for "Bundles for Britain," a project started in 1940 by a New York City woman, Mrs. Natalie Wales Latham. The project started as a group of Mrs. Latham's friends who formed a knitting circle to make socks, hats and gloves to aid the British people as war relief during World War II. By 1941, "Bundles for Britain" was sending medical relief, such as operating tables, ambulances, medicine, medical supplies, cots and bedding. (236, 239-241)

Some Extras for Sattlerites To Enjoy in 1941

"On the right you see Sattlerites enjoying the delightful roof garden provided for them, atop the store. There they revel in sunbathing, horseshoe pitching, miniature golf and flower gardening." (242)

"Sattler's free lending library, for the exclusive use of employees, is one of the most popular spots in the store. There Sattlerites may read good books or enjoy cards, checkers, mahjongg and other games. Books may also be taken home by employees." (242)

July 1941

Sattler's Knows How To Keep Their Employees Happy

Every Wednesday in July and August, each permanent Sattler's employee received an extra day of rest and recreation (with pay). The picture and poem below are from a July 1941 Sattler's ad that was in *The Buffalo Evening News*. The ad was to remind the Sattler shopper not to come to 998 Broadway on Wednesdays during the summer because Sattler's was closed. (242)

OH, WE'RE four happy water sprites;
Ready for waves or water fights,

Or any other kind of fun
That folks enjoy beneath the sun!

You see, we sprites are Sattlerites
With Wednesdays off, to see the sights,

Or simply lie around and rest—
Or do whatever we like best.

And that's why miles of happy smiles
Beam on you, down Sattler's aisles!

July 1941

Bennett Beach Outing

On a warm day in July of 1941, you could see those Sattler's employees and their families at Bennett Beach for a summer outing. This time employees were digging for buried treasure in the sand where the Sattler's Social Club had buried eight pounds of coins for a buried treasure event. The day also included a softball game and the crowning of a new Miss Sattler for 1941. (243)

Photograph courtesy of Michael Stark's Family.

August 1941

Death of John G. Sattler

Sattler's Department Store
Is Closed Today, Tuesday,
Due To The Death Of

JOHN G. SATTLER
Founder and President

The store will also remain closed all day tomorrow, in accordance with our custom of closing Wednesdays in July and August. However, the store will reopen Thursday, when, as usual, the hours will be 9:30 A. M. to 5:30 P. M. and 7 to 9:30 P. M.

SATTLER'S
998 BROADWAY

Photograph courtesy of the Voorhees Family.

John G. Sattler lived his life well. He truly loved and cared about Buffalo and its people. He was a quiet, gentle man whom I have the honor of writing about. His family has recordings of John as he sings in German while his daughter, Marion, plays the piano. There are the touching letters to his cousin, who was ill, as he wrote inquiring about her health. Also there is correspondence with his only grandson, Jack, written while "Grandpa" was out of town. And he was a man who would no longer eat chicken because he had a few chickens of his own running around in his barn in Eggertsville.

In addition to his business at Sattler's, John was a leading home builder who helped shape the Kensington and Kenilworth areas. He also developed much of the Clover Bank and Highland area on the Lake Erie shore, as well as parks in Tonawanda. In order to provide a summer camp for children in need, he lent out his summer property in Chippewa, Ontario. During the Depression years, he started a "Buy Buffalo" campaign to help keep Buffalonians and manufacturers working. John believed in fellowship and was quick to encourage education. For example, he provided his building at 703 Main Street, rent-free, for WPA adult education classes. His store was a happy place for people to work, where a family atmosphere was the only way he would let the store be run.

John's funeral service was conducted in his home on LeBrun Road in Eggertsville by Rev. Lester L. Ross of the Central Presbyterian Church. Read at his service were: the 23rd psalm, "The Eternal Goodness" by John Greenleaf Whittier and "Crossing of the Bar" by Alfred Lord Tennyson.

He was laid to rest with his bride Alma and his daughter Katherine in the Sattler mausoleum at Forest Lawn Cemetery in Buffalo, NY. (244-246)

September 1941

Cake Auction

Sattler's Social Club held a cake auction. The cakes were decorated in patriotic colors and auctioned for the benefit of former Sattler's employees who were serving in the military. The money raised bought gifts to be sent out to "the boys." (247)

September 1941

Sattler's Fishing Contest

Sattler's had yearly contests to draw sportsmen into the store. This year's winners of Sattler's fishing contest were: Bob Mahoney of 25 Rapin Pl., who won $10 for catching the heaviest bass (5 lbs. 7 oz.) and L. Spislak of 11 Moreland Street, who won $10 for catching the heaviest yellow pike (10 lbs. 12oz.). Congratulations gentlemen! (248)

November 1941

Winner, Winner Pheasant Dinner!

Sattler's not only catered to fishermen, but to all types of sportsmen. The $10 winner in Sattler's largest pheasant contest was Ed Luderman of 4602 Broadway, Depew. He brought in a pheasant that weighed 4 lbs. 2 oz. (249)

November 1941

Hoot Gibson Draws a Packed Crowd of Spectators

Hoot Gibson was a movie cowboy and rodeo star who was performing in the Western New York area with a championship rodeo troop. He drew a huge crowd at Sattler's when he appeared at 998 on a Tuesday in mid-November. That day, 3 shoplifters were caught in the store and one of Sattler's store detectives was quoted in City Court as saying "There were so many people that some of them thought it was a good time to help themselves." 2 female shoplifters were fined $25 for having lifted $3.79 and $8.00 in merchandise respectively. One man who shoplifted an .88 pair of rubbers received a fine of $10.00. (588, 589)

December 1941

"This Day Will Go Down In Infamy"

On December 7, the United States Naval Base at Pearl Harbor was bombed by Japanese air assault. More than 2,300 American lives were lost. The battleship U.S.S. Arizona was destroyed, and the U.S.S. Oklahoma capsized. The attack destroyed 12 ships, which were either sunk or beached, and damaged 9 others. 160 aircraft were destroyed and 150 aircraft were damaged. The next day the United States Congress declared war on the Empire of Japan, and President Roosevelt's famous speech in which he declared that "this day will go down in infamy" was broadcast. (250)

December 1941

Defense Bonds

That year the Christmas bonuses for Sattler employees were war bonds. Bond value was based on the length of service to the department store, and all employees received war bonds ranging in value from $3.00 to $100. In addition to war bonds, Sattler's full-time and part-time employees were given a paid winter vacation of 3 days, plus a 3-day weekend for Christmas. (251)

December 1941

Sattlerite Reminder

From *The Sattlerite*, Sattler's employee paper: "Incidentally, if you would like to write to our men in service, personnel has most of the boys' names and addresses on file. We're sure they'd like to hear from you, because if there's anything a serviceman really appreciates, it's a letter from the old gang back home."(252)

December 1941

Bonuses for "The Boys"

Aaron Rabow, vice president of Sattler's, sent out a letter to all former Sattler's employees who were called into military service. The body of the letter was as follows:

"You will receive the increased Christmas Bonuses just as though you had been working in the store. This is one of the store's ways of showing you how proud we are to number so many of our boys among those who are doing their part and giving their time in training for national defense. Let me take this opportunity to assure you that employment is waiting for you at the store and that we shall all be happy to welcome you as a Sattlerite when you return from Military Service." (253)

January 1942

Please Donate

In January of 1942, Sattler's set the record for the largest number of blood donors for the Red Cross in the Buffalo area. 500 Sattler's employees pledged to donate a pint of blood to the Red Cross. This number of donors was overwhelming, and the Red Cross mobile unit had to revisit Sattler's several times to collect all the blood that was pledged. (254)

March 1942

Beatrice Kay

March 1942 Sattler's had a visit from singer, television and movie star, Beatrice Kay. She came to Sattler's to promote her Gay '90's records. During the first two weeks of March 1942, she sang at the Glen Park Winter Gardens. (255-258)

April 1942

Company Paid Pension and Life Insurance

President Charles Hahn put into operation a life insurance and pension plan for Sattler's employees. Employees who had been with the store continuously for 8 years and were between the ages of 21 to 55 were eligible to receive monthly pension benefits which began on December 20th of the year the employee reached his or her 65th birthday. If you were an employee with less than 8 years of service, you became eligible for these employee benefits once you reached your 8 years of service.

"Should an employee die before retirement age, his beneficiary will receive at least 100 times the monthly pension amount, or the cash value, whichever is greater. In no case will the insurance be less than $1,000. If the employee dies after retirement, his beneficiary will receive the balance of the sum he would have received if he had lived for ten years after retirement." All costs for these benefits were paid for by the management of Sattler's. This plan was underwritten by Massachusetts Mutual Life Insurance Company and the Northwestern Mutual Life Insurance Company. (259)

May 1942

Elsie the Cow

Sattler's had another big star visit 998! For five days, Sattler's hosted Borden's famous Elsie the Cow, who participated in a War Bond Tour. This beautiful bovine came to aid in the sale of war bonds and stamps. She traveled via a specially outfitted DC-3 airplane with her two companions, Edith and Ann Perrine. The Perrine sisters, who were brought up on a dairy farm, became Elsie's caregivers, attendants and travel companions.

Elsie, as glamorous as ever, wore her signature necklace of daisies at Sattler's. She was given a luxury bedroom in Sattler's basement. On the curtains that hung around the maple four-post bed that Elsie stayed in, a sign read "Elsie Says Buy War Bonds Now." In Elsie's room there were pictures of Elsie with her husband Elmer and her daughter Beulah. Elsie's Red Cross knitting bag could be seen on a wheelbarrow-shaped chair. Peeking out of the bag was what appeared to be the beginning of a red afghan. The attendants explained that Elsie knits to help the Red Cross with the war effort.

Elsie, the Jersey cow from Elm Hill Farm in Brookfield, Massachusetts, became famous first for her appearance in the movie *Little Men,* where she played the part of Buttercup. But it was her contribution to the war effort during World War II that was critical to raising money by promoting war stamps and war bonds. By February of 1942, Elsie had helped to raise over $1,420,500 for the aid of war sufferers in Britain. By the end of WWII, she had helped raise over $10,000,000 in war bonds in the United States. (260-263)

June 1942

Scrap Rubber Drive

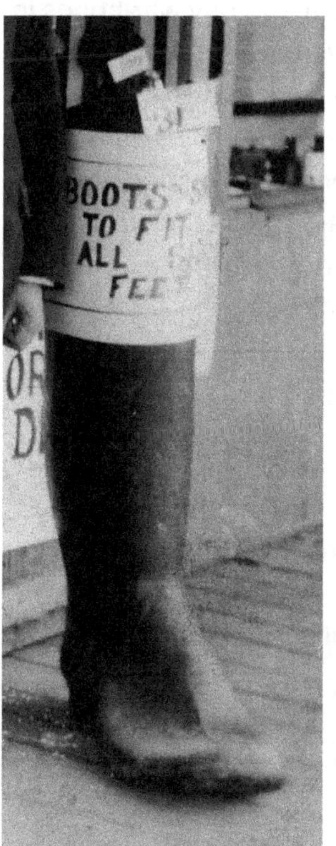

Japan invaded Malaya on midnight of December 8, 1942 and the British troops were driven out of Malaya. As a result, Japan held Malaya's resources, which included 38% of the world's rubber production and 58% of the world's tin production. Earlier in the war, Japan also invaded the Dutch East Indies on January 10, 1942, and by March 8, 1942 the Dutch surrendered the Dutch East Indies, where 35% of the world's rubber was produced.

Rubber was a critical need for the USA military. Rationing of tires and gas was initiated to encourage people to use alternative transportation during WWII so that rubber could be saved for military uses. Scrap drives of all kinds became necessary, so during June of 1942 Sattler's had a scrap rubber drive to aid the nationwide shortage of rubber.

Sattler's gave up one of its oldest display items to help support the war effort. A size 40 rubber overshoe, filled with 77 pounds of rubber from overshoes and boot heels, was Sattler's contribution to the nation's scrap rubber drive.

Governor Lehman of New York stated, "It is the patriotic duty of every citizen to join the scrap rubber drive. I call upon them to do so." (264-268)

Photograph courtesy of the Voorhees Family.

July 1942

Whiteout for Victory

A war stamp and bond drive took place during the month of July, as the National Retailers for Victory Drive set a goal of $1,000,000,000. The Victory Campaign quota set by the Erie County Retailers for Victory was $7,512,000. During this campaign, the local retailers observed a 15-minute Whiteout for Victory Stamp and Bond Sale. The Whiteout began at noon, during which nothing other than war stamps and bonds were sold for 15 minutes.

Some of the local stores had soldiers, sailors and Marines selling bonds. There were Hollywood celebrities setting up booths in Lafayette Square to sell bonds during the Whiteout Campaign. Near the Hollywood stars' booth, both firemen and Boy Scout bands played patriotic music to encourage people to buy bonds. Some of the retailers had likenesses of the Axis Bullies depicted on their floors that one could stomp on; others had effigies that one could give a slap to when buying war stamps or bonds. When stores weren't running the Whiteout promotion and somebody bought merchandise, change was available in war stamps. (269-279)

July 1942

American Heroes Day

After the first Whiteout Sale, Sattler's sold an additional $30,000 in stamps and bonds. The Retailers for Victory designated July 17, 1942 as American Heroes Day. This publicity encouraged people to get out and buy war bonds in honor of family members and neighbors who were in the military. Sattler's bond sales boomed on American Heroes Day, sending their bond sales total to $100,000. That was $3,000 over Sattler's pledged quota. (280)

"Shop where your money goes farther, so that you will have extra money to buy War Stamps and help your country. You'll save on needs for home and family at Sattler's." (281)

United States Defense Savings Bonds

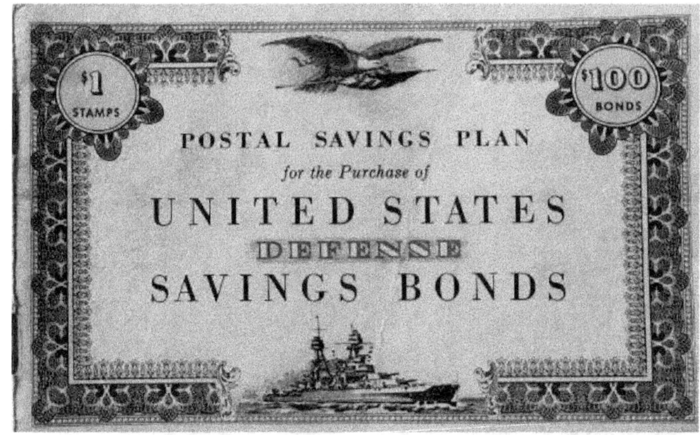

"By the end of the war, 85 million Americans (out of a population of 131 million) had purchased $185.7 billion dollars of bonds - over $2,000 per person, at a time when the average income was $2,000 per year. The patriotism and personal sacrifice of the average citizen played a significant part in the Allied war effort. "(641)

DEFENSE SAVINGS BONDS

When you fill this album with $1.00 stamps, it will have a total value of $75 and it will buy a Defense Savings Bond worth, in 10 years, $100. Your postmaster will give you, or you may secure from the Treasury Department at Washington, details of the Regular Purchase Plan, which has been adopted by many thousands of investors who are buying Savings Bonds each month and at other intervals of their choice. Under this plan you can buy as often as you please and, without penalty, stop buying at any time. But if you buy a $100 (maturity value) bond each month for 10 years and hold all your bonds, you will then own $12,000 (maturity value) of Defense Savings Bonds. These would be redeemable by your Government at the rate of $100 per bond each month for the following 10 years.

THE UNITED STATES POSTAL SAVINGS SYSTEM

All items shown on this page are courtesy of Alberta Daugherty.

August 1942 **Lettuce Auction To Benefit Prisoners of Bataan**

A Lettuce Auction took place at the Niagara Food Terminals at Clinton and Bailey. Pictured holding the case of lettuce are Sattler's employees Harry and Louis Benatovich. Above from left to right are Charles Hahn, Sattler's president; Auctioneer Harold E. Koch, president of the Buffalo Wholesale Grocers, Inc.; and Warren B. Wilkes who recorded auction bids. Photograph courtesy of the Voorhees Family.

The Benatovich brothers managed Sattler's produce department, which was located in Sattler's basement. The brothers were originally produce hucksters via horse and buggy, and they had their business in the Humboldt Park area where they lived. They later opened a stand in the Broadway Market and eventually moved to Sattler's, where they ran the produce area for the store. (282)

In August of 1942, an auction was held for the benefit of the prisoners of Bataan. A Red Cross Mercy Ship with food, medicine and other supplies left San Francisco on August 14, 1942 in the Aid to Bataan Campaign. The items were purchased from the proceeds of the nationwide Lettuce Auction. The lettuce was donated by the Salinas Valley Produce Exchange of California. Cities across the nation shared in the effort to support this worthy cause. The Pittsburgh Lettuce Auction totaled over $15,000, Chicago $12,450 and New York City $4,200. Buffalo's efforts exceeded $13,000. Sattler's was the top bidder for a crate of lettuce in Buffalo, with a winning bid of $1,100. The usual price for a crate of lettuce ran $3.75-$5.00. (283-285)

December 1942

Sattler's Will Buy War Bonds

"WITH EVERY DOLLAR YOU SPEND IN THE STORE ON MONDAY"

"Sattler's entire gross receipts for Monday ("Remember Pearl Harbor Day") will be invested by the store in War Savings Bonds. That means every dollar you spend at Sattler's tomorrow, goes to work immediately to help win the war!" (286)

April 1943

Double Pay for Easter Week

Sattler's gave an Easter bonus to over 1,000 employees who had worked for the store since February 16, 1943. Employees who had one year or more of service received an extra full week's pay, while those employees who had worked for less than a year received a half-week of extra pay. The announcement was made over the store's public address system by Sattler's Vice-President and General Manager Aaron Rabow: "This is just another way the store takes to express its appreciation for the fact that you are doing your jobs as soldiers on the home front, in a manner befitting true Sattlerites. Remember, ours is the task of keeping the wheels of distribution turning so that all Buffalo can continue to work with full efficiency in doing its great wartime job." (287)

July 1943

Fishing Anyone?

Sattler's Department Store and Buffalo Parks Commissioner John A. Ulinski teamed up for a fishing contest. One dozen calico bass were given a numbered tag on their tails and set free in South Park Lake and Delaware Park Lake. Anyone catching a tagged bass who brought the fish into Sattler's received a $25 war bond and was able to keep the fish too! This contest helped encourage fishing in these two city park lakes. (288, 289)

November 1943

Sandy Jr.

Did you know that there was a Sandy B. Thrifty, Jr.? I didn't! The only information I could find out about him was that the public wanted him back. Back from where? This is the only reference I found about Sandy's son.

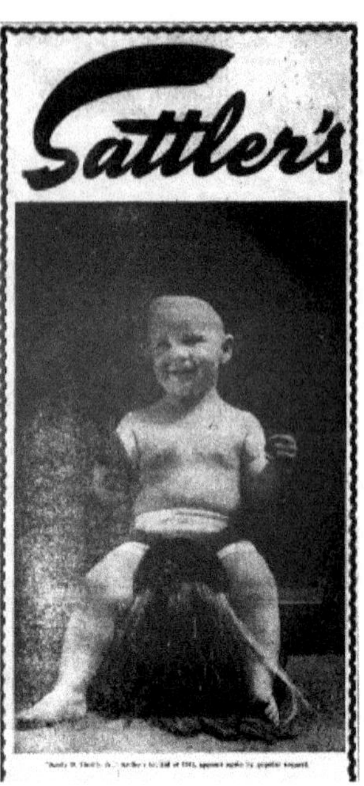

"'Sandy B. Thrifty Jr., Sattler's hit kid of 1941, appears again by popular request." (290)

November 1944

Flocks of Pheasants Are Disappearing

Sattler's addressed a serious problem with the growing fox population in Western New York by offering a $2 bounty for each dead fox brought into the store. This Sattler's advertisement appeared in the local newspaper, and within 24 hours the first fox was brought in for a bounty by a 14-year old boy who shot it near Como Park. It was only a few minutes later that another man brought in his fox carcass to Sattler's sporting goods department. That fox was shot near Belvedere Road in South Buffalo.

"Rudy Karnath, agent for the Society for the Prevention of Cruelty to Animals, has said foxes had been coming within the city limits for the last year. He reports there must be a considerable number in South Buffalo, for he has answered several calls from the section along Cazenovia Creek. Foxes have also been seen for the last few months in the stockyards."

Local residents and hunters have noticed a significant reduction in the flocks of pheasants. Newspaper interviews with locals report seeing foxes attacking pheasants and pigeons in the city of Buffalo.

More than 60 hunters have already participated in the fox bounty program that has been in effect at Sattler's for one week. One hunter from Attica has already turned in 19 fox carcasses. Al Obrochta of Orchard Park, NY brought in the largest fox. From the fox's nose to the tip of its tail measured 47 inches. (291-295)

January 1945

Buffalo Blizzard

EVEN STORE EXECUTIVES HELP CLEAR AWAY SNOW FOLLOWING BUFFALO BLIZZARD

Photograph courtesy of the Voorhees Family.

In January and February of 1945, Buffalo was the lucky winner of several weeks of blizzard-like weather. Buffalo Mayor Joseph J. Kelly sent out official announcements of a continuing snow emergency, and Sattler's was closed. On Monday, February 5, 1945, as the city of Buffalo was trying to recover from the huge snowfall, Gordon Holman, Sattler's building superintendent, needed a little help of his own. So Aaron Rabow, who was Sattler's vice-president and general manager, gave marching orders to 45 department managers and their assistants that they were on snow shovel duty. The group volunteered their time and cleared away the snow for 75 feet on Broadway and 125 feet on Beck Street. With shovels in hand and the loan of construction trucks from the Iroquois Gas Company, cleanup began.

It was reported by Robert S. Cornelius, advertising manager, "We handled about 50 tons of snow... We took it off the street, as well as from the sidewalk, and we opened up the storm sewer receivers just in case." (296-298)

March 1945

Double Pay

Aaron Rabow announced that all Sattler's employees would receive double pay for the week before Easter because of their hard work and dedication while working one of the busiest Easter seasons ever. (299, 300)

April 1945

Sattler's Service Awards

The annual Social Club dinner dance brought out 600 people at the Hotel Statler. Included in those employees were Major Charles Hahn, president of Sattler's, Sgt. Norbert Jedrzejewski, Joseph Prusak and Henry Intrator, all of whom were home on furlough. (301)

Sattler's Social Club elections were held during the dinner dance, and 119 Sattler's service pins were handed out by Major Charles Hahn. A bronze service pin was given to Marion Sattler Hahn, wife of Major Charles Hahn. Mrs. Hahn served as executive vice-president of Sattler's during her husband's absence due to military service. In addition, a bronze pin was given to the father of Major Charles Hahn, Charles L. Hahn, who then served as assistant treasurer. There were 88 other bronze service pins awarded for 3 years of service, 19 silver pins for five years of service and 12 gold pins for 10 years of service.

May 1945

"Symphony No. 998"

Guy Lombardo and his Royal Canadians, Danny Kaye, Ben Wain, and singer Barry Wood came to Kleinhans Music Hall for a War Bond Rally. (302) This was a huge event, as it was going to be broadcast on the radio coast-to-coast. The rally was a thank-you to volunteers at a recent war bond drive for all their hard work.

It just so happened that Robert Cornelius, advertising executive at Sattler's, gave tickets for the rally to his son, Bob, who was honored to go to this event. Bob remembers that when Guy Lombardo and his Royal Canadians were playing one of their musical numbers, the music suddenly became very familiar for all of the Buffalonians there. Guy Lombardo had his Canadians play the Sattler's music theme song. It was unexpected and exhilarating for Mr. Cornelius to have Sattler's recognized in the musical program. (303)

The piece that was played at the War Bond Rally was called Symphony No. 998. The Sattler's theme song was written by Robert Cornelius, but the music played that night was arranged by Ivan R. Beatty. Beatty was a prominent musical arranger and musician living on Harding Road in South Buffalo. He was the special arranger for Shea's Buffalo Symphony Orchestra and arranged all the music for their stage presentations. He played saxophone, clarinet and violin for Shea's Buffalo, The Alley Peacock Orchestra, The Yankee Six and the Buffalodians. His musical arrangements played on radio stations in New York and Pennsylvania. His popularity enabled radio stations to use him as a draw to their stations, by advertising in newspapers in New York City, Philadelphia and Buffalo. Ivan Beatty's Symphony No. 998 was advertised to be played by the Buffalo Philharmonic in musical programs until 1953. (304-313)

Photograph of Ivan R. Beatty, courtesy of Shirley M. Kessler.

Above photo is of the Buffalodians (Ivan R. Beatty is in the back row fifth from the right) during a 1926 Revue at Monte Carlo on Broadway in New York City. Photograph courtesy of Shirley M. Kessler.

July 1945

War Veterans Come Back to Sattler's

In July of 1945, Sattler's announced that 90 veterans who were former Sattler's employees would be reinstated to their former jobs at Sattler's with no loss of their benefits while they were in military service. These Veterans were given their pay increases, vacation, bonuses and insurance plans as if they had continued with their working careers at Sattler's. **Photograph courtesy of the Voorhees Family.**

This also included handicapped Veterans and part-time employees who wanted to continue their education. (314)

During World War II, Sattler's netted an increase of 75,000 square feet of space from recent additions to its building. Due to more selling space, "We shall be able to absorb our service men and women without disturbing our present personnel setup," said Mr. Rabow. (314)

December 1945

$25 Victory Bond

A $25 victory bond was the prize for the hunter who brought in the most foxes that had been either shot or trapped in Western New York by December 1945. Each fox submitted to Sattler's sporting goods department received a $2 bounty. The offer "is being made in an effort to help cut down the wholesale slaughter of small game by these predators," said Art Pfeiffer, manager of Sattler's sports department. Leo Obrochta won the $25 bond by bringing in 17 foxes.

(315-317)

June 1946

Monkey Business from Sattler's

In 1937, the Buffalo Zoological Gardens was the worksite of WPA projects that employed 500 laborers, carpenters and masons. In the northwest corner of the zoo was constructed Monkey Island, whose rectangular area had a 16-foot limestone hill and was surrounded by a shallow water-filled moat.

The antics of the monkeys were one of the biggest draws for the zoo. Over the years, the enclosure for the monkeys held a playground of items for the enjoyment of the simians. There were rubber tire swings, a jungle gymnasium and a spinning wagon wheel mounted so that it could be used like a merry-go-round. In addition, there were several unbreakable chromium-plated mirrors installed.

The famous Buffalo Zoo curator turned movie star, Marlin Perkins, once was quoted as saying, "This may sound strange to you, but those monkeys actually hold swimming races. I've seen a lot of them disporting themselves in the water. But a visitor informed me last week that several of them leaped into the moat and started racing. Each time one would get ahead, another would pull him back. That went on until they had an argument and the event was postponed until tempers had cooled."

Over the years, the monkeys escaped the confines of their home on Monkey Island and enjoyed the surroundings of Delaware Park, including visiting the properties at neighboring homes where they were enjoying treats given to them by local residents.

In June of 1946, Sattler's donated 50 rhesus monkeys to the Buffalo Zoo for their Monkey Island exhibit. It was one of many years of such donations to the zoo. That year 6,000 zoo-goers were on hand for the reopening of Monkey Island at the Buffalo Zoo. (318-338)

June, July and August 1946

Sattler's Expansion Was Completed

During World War II, Sattler's President Charles Hahn had a job working for the War Department in the U.S. Army Air Forces in New York City. Charles Hahn was asked by the War Department to work for the military because of his expertise in managing Sattler's. (339) He was promoted to the rank of Major.

While Major Hahn was away serving his country, his wife Marion Sattler Hahn ran Sattler's. It was actually Marion who instituted Sattler's latest expansion. (340) Under Marion's leadership, the store thrived and her husband came back from his job in the military to a Sattler's store that was intensely profitable.

Photographs courtesy of the Voorhees Family.

July 1946

Sattler's Summer Frolic

Employees never had to worry about transportation to and from Sattler's sponsored events. Buses were always waiting at the store to take one to the event and back to 998. **Photographs courtesy of the Voorhees Family.**

SATTLER'S SOCIAL CLUB

Summer Frolic

AUTOMOBILE CLUB, CLARENCE, N. Y.

TUESDAY, JULY 9TH, 1946

Admit Mr. Ball

(MEMBER)

Free Buses Leave Store at 5:30 P. M.

October 1946

Skeet Shoot for Employees

Sattler's held its annual skeet shoot at the Hamburg Rod and Gun Club. Thaddeus Wozniak took first place, breaking 25 clay pigeons in a row, followed by Michael Stark in second place with 24 and Albert Kurek breaking 23. (341, 342)

Pictured on the top row from left to right: Michael Stark, Unknown, Unknown, Unknown, Aaron Rabow, Unknown and Charles Hahn. Bottom row: Unknown, Unknown, Unknown, Bob Cornelius, Unknown. I am hoping that we will someday have names for the unknown faces. Can you help? Please leave information on *The Sattler's Diary* Facebook page. Photograph courtesy of Michael Stark's Family.

October 1946

Time Capsule Placed behind Cornerstone

Left to right: Aaron Rabow, Sattler's vice president; Mayor Bernard J. Dowd; Charles Hahn, president of Sattler's. The trowel on the right was used in the laying of the Cornerstone. Photographs courtesy of the Voorhees Family.

A time capsule, consisting of a filled copper box, was buried behind the cornerstone at 998 Broadway on October 17, 1946. Forty-one years and one day later, it was opened on October 18, 1987. (343) The Sattler's time capsule was revealed at the Sattler's Reunion that took place at Hearthstone Manor in Depew. It was attended by Sattlerites and guests. Inside the time capsule were: the recording of a speech by President Franklin D. Roosevelt, a recording of Sattler's jingles and a book entitled *The Egg and I,* written by Betty MacDonald.

January 1947 Additional Board of Directors at Sattler's

Sattler's was expanding. The recent 106,000 square foot addition to the store with new elevators, escalators, modernized lighting and larger store departments led to the need for a larger board of directors. This was put in motion with the appointment of four additional new board members: Aaron Rabow, vice president of Sattler's; Robert S. Cornelius, Sattler's director of publicity; John T. Madden, Sattler's secretary-treasurer; and president of the board Lewis G. Harriman of Manufactures Traders and Trust Company.

President Charles Hahn expressed his gratitude to the new board members and stated that, "We expect the experience and counsel of Mr. Harriman will prove extremely valuable to us in our growth program for the coming years." (344)

January 1947 20 Years of Service

From left to right, Unknown, Robert S. Cornelius, Charles Hahn, Marion Sattler Hahn, Aaron Rabow, Unknown, Jack Hahn. Photograph courtesy of the Voorhees Family.

Aaron Rabow receives a watch at the annual Sattler's Social Club gathering, which 750 people attended at the Hotel Statler. (345)

July 1947

Sattler's Teen Town

On Sattler's second floor in the rear of the store was ***TEEN TOWN!*** Open on Saturdays, it was hosted by teens from local high schools and was a hangout for teenage girls. Every Saturday, Teen Town had weekly guessing contests. How many buttons in a bobby sock? How many seeds in the giant pumpkin displayed at the club? My favorite is: how many movie stars do you know, revised to how many movie stars can you name? There were 10 winners each week. Names of the winners of the previous week's contest were posted at Teen Town on Saturdays. Prizes were dandy sweatshirts with your high school's name. If the store didn't carry your school's sweatshirt, you won a pair of nylon stockings!

"Besides groovy date-bait glad rags, Sattler's Teen Town offers some swell free features for the enjoyment of the high-school crowd. One is our dandy free-wheeling juke box: and the others you'll see when you come in." (346-350)

PLAY JUKE BOX FREE

HEAR ALL THE RECORDINGS YOU WANT! NO NICKLES NEEDED— JUST PUSH THE BUTTON FOR YOUR FAVORITES!

Sattler's Teen Town, second floor, rear, will be the gathering place for smart teenagers, all day tomorrow. So come out to 998 for a free juke session!

Here Are Tomorrow's High School Hostesses!

Miss Joanne Oldstrom

Miss Oldstrom will represent Bennett High and be your juke box hostess for the day.

Miss Betty Tyler

Miss Tyler will represent Amherst Central High, and model latest fashions.

Teen Town was the precursor to the extremely popular Teen Scene at Sattler's during the mid-1960's

The following was from an advertisement: "SHAKE those bones, RATTLE those timbers, ROCK and ROLL to the boppesting jam session that a teen's ever seen or heard! Do you hear me talking teens? Be sure to make the scene! It's the first THEATER PARTY of Sattler's TEEN SCENE CLUB and it's free, every living bit! You'll see such swing favorites as Fats Domino, Joe Turner and Tough Corners in a great movie with 10 'Golden Goodies' – SHAKE, RATTLE & ROCK…

"You can converse with your leader DANNY NEAVERETH of KB. You can see the great NEIL DARROW in person and hear him sing his new hit 'ONE MORE MOUNTAIN'. You can see the BEATLES themselves…Ringo, Paul, John and George…on film! And you may win FREE DOOR P R I Z E S including record albums and merchandise…

"TEEN SCENE members may pick up their FREE TICKETS in Sattler's. If you're not a member, now is the time to join." (351-355) Photographs on this page courtesy of the Voorhees Family.

September 1947

Sandy B. Thrifty Presents

Sattler's Jingles

"A memento of the Grand Opening of the Newer, Greater Sattler's September 3rd, 1947"

Recordings of all the Sattler's Jingles

When little Jimmy yells "They're Playing Our Song," he means it! Whether you sing it, hum it or whistle it . . . it's the song of savings that's become the theme of smart shoppers throughout Western New York! The wee ones love the catchy tune and the happy beat of Sattler's jingle. The parents (and grand-parents, too) instantly associate it with bargains and saving money.

Though we change the words from time to time and vary the tempo from waltz to cha-cha . . . the meaning always remains the same. "Shop and save at Sattler's 9-9-8 Broadway, in Buffalo . . . 9-9-8 Broadway . . . go there today!" Its Buffalo's Happiest Shopping Habit . . . and practically everyone's got it!

Brad Fisher, a retired Ford Motor Co. worker, sparked my interest when he told me that he owned a QRS piano roll with a hand-typed label with the words "Sattler's Jingle." The piano roll is in the original QRS box, and Mr. Fisher, a piano roll collector, did his research and found that QRS did not have records of making the "Sattler's Jingle" piano roll in quantity. This may be the first Sattler's jingle. And it may have been made just for Mr. Sattler's store.

We may never know for sure who wrote the melody for that first Sattler's jingle. However, "Sattler's Jingle no. 2" was recorded in 1941. The words and melody are accredited to Lanny Grey. There are other Sattler's jingles, and I understand that they were written by Bob Cornelius, Sattler's advertising genius. Bob Cornelius was a multitalented guy. He was not just an artist who could draw, but he and his advertising department also created several more famous Sattler's jingles. And boy, did those jingles do their job! During Sattler's heydays in the 1940's, I would dare to say that 998 Broadway was the most recognized address to Buffalonians, perhaps even better known than the address of 1800 Pennsylvania Avenue!

Bob Cornelius certainly did not skimp when it came to getting the best talent possible to record those commercial jingles. No studio musicians for Sattler's! Only tiptop professionals with national reputations. The Air Lane Trio: Tony Mattola, the famous jazz guitarist, with Slam Stewart on bass and Don Elliot on trumpet. The singers on the jingles were none other than those singing sweethearts of radio commercial jingles, Lanny and Ginger Grey. This married couple was jingle-singing royalty in Buffalo. Whenever Sattler's tried to change the well-known jingle, hundreds of complaints were received.

Sattler's jingles are the first and oldest retail singing commercials in the nation. When I heard them from the record shown on the previous page, I imagined them playing on the radio. Do you remember any of these famous Sattler's jingles?

Shop and save at Sattler's,
998 Broadway, in Buffalo
998 Broadway
Go there today.

Perhaps this jingle from 1944, with the first three lines that imitate an old police call, will spark your memory:

998, calling Buffalo,
998, calling Buffalo,
Come in Buffalo,
Oh we're coming into Sattler's
Right on the bargain beam.
For that one-stop shopping center
Is a bargain lover's dream.
We shop this whole town over
So believe us when we say,
You'll make a lucky landing
At 998 Broadway.

Here is another jingle sung by Lanny and Ginger Grey in 1945:

There's variety at Sattler's to make you dust your eyes.
They have jeans and beans and magazines and ties and pumpkin pies. Oh boy!
They've stakes and rakes and layer cakes and shirts and skirts. OK!
She means they sell just everything at 998 Broadway.
Shop and save at Sattler's
998 Broadway in Buffalo, 998 Broadway.

This 1946 jingle had musical accompaniment by The Air Lane Trio:

Say those builders work like beavers, there at 998 Broadway,
Yes that big new home for Sattler's is growin' every day.
But if you're after bargains, you don't have to wait.
Just keep on with your shopping at good old 998.
(356-358)

October 1947

Coloring Contest

Sattler's never forgot the kids when it came to contests! The children received a picture of a rooster from the Weatherbird Shoes logo and had to color it for Sattler's coloring contest. It was time for the kids to go back to school, and they would be needing those new school shoes made by Weatherbird!

Sattler's advertised June Neuner as one of the winners of a coloring contest, and she won a G. E. Radio. She recalls that Sattler's put a picture in the newspaper to be colored. She and her sister, Jean, sent their artwork in to Sattler's. While June recalls receiving a letter from Sattler's complimenting her coloring, she does not recall winning a radio. However, she pointed out that it might just be that she does not remember the radio in her childhood home.

Winners for the contest were announced in October 1947:

Bicycles: Raymond H. Stage, 571 South Park Ave., Stephen Dembinski, Jr., 18 Keystone St., Betty Koselanski, 28 Theodore St., Mary Amy Wells, 120 57th St., Niagara Falls

G. E. Radios: Audrey Dryja, 94 Strauss, Jean and June Neuner, 138 Oakmont, Mary Helen Donovan, 83 Lakeview

Dandy Train Set: Ronald Nosal, 59 Lombard, Thomas Kolasa, 51 Rommel, Donald Alessi, 642 Plymouth

Hutchinson Basketballs: Ted Ostrowski Jr., 38 Townsend, Otto Plinzek, 56 Feugeron, Robert Raczka, 26 Lombard

Daisy Air Rifle: Billy Nauman Jr., 1541 Eggert

Chicago Roller Skates: Edwin Kwandrans, 8 Brownell, Elaine Pochylska, 80 Mohr, Joan Dankowski, 122 Haller

Ping Pong Set: Alice Hyziak, 72 Rother, Bernard Komlsarek, 137 Sobieski

Knife and Axe: Jackie Pascall, 79 Buffum, John Dudkowski, 39 Strauss, John Colling, 235 Herman

Baseball Gloves: Richard Milligan Jr., 634 S. Tierundra, Billy Snyder, 104 Landon, Michael Rick, 14 French

Doll Carriage: Delphine Szaframski, 79 Courtland, Lorraine Franc, 297 So. Ogden, Jeanne C. Bell, 150 Mulberry

Tennis Rackets: Marion Nytz, Irving, N.Y., Elaine Stefaniak, 104 Guilford, Lucille Petrino, 365 14th St.

Shoe Ice Skates: Eleanore Martin, 68 Lathrop, Frances Szymanski, 253 Peckham, Stephen Graczyk, 64 Goembel

O. K. Footballs: Johnny Wilber, Freedom, N.Y., Ferris Klink, 349 Gold St., Richard Kraska, 403 Gibson

Street Roller Skates: Bernice Flakiewlez, 139 Gilbert, Barbara Depowski, 75 St. Florian, Donna Gardner, 37 Parkview (359)

Mme. Alexander Dolls: Lorraine Krawczyk, 134 Goodyear, Dorothy Kubicka, 142 Townsend, Delphine Smania, 382 Gibson, Maryann Wisniewski, 94 Weaver

Badminton Set: Donna Geary, 97 Peabody

Binoculars: Anthony Molisse, 359 Eagle St., Michael Geryak, 54 Benzinger, Grace Chojnacki, 93 Woodell, Jean Thomas, 127 Baits

Fishing Kits: Leonard Wrona, 567 Fulton, Eugene Osika, 825 Eagle, Robert Roberts, 58 Strauss (359)

November 1947

Virginia Mayo

November 1947 brought Virginia Mayo to town. The actress not only visited Sattler's for Drene Shampoo, but also starred in the movies *White Heat* and *Along the Great Divide.* Rumor has it that when Virginia Mayo came to Sattler's, Robert Cornelius, Sattler's publicity and advertising department manager, altered his wife's picture in his office by adding horns to her. Just a little fun that stayed up on his office wall in Sattler's for many years! (409, 410)

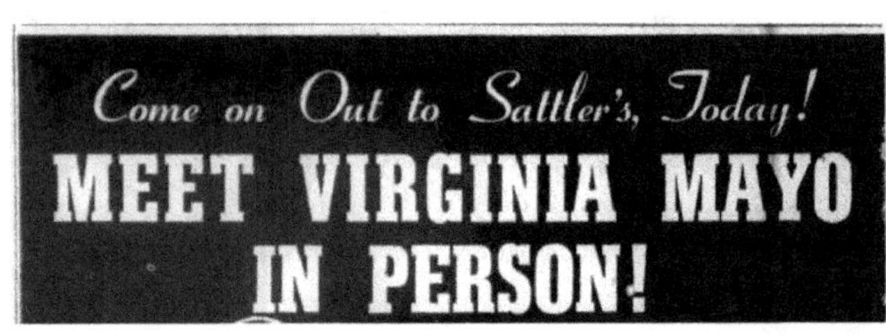

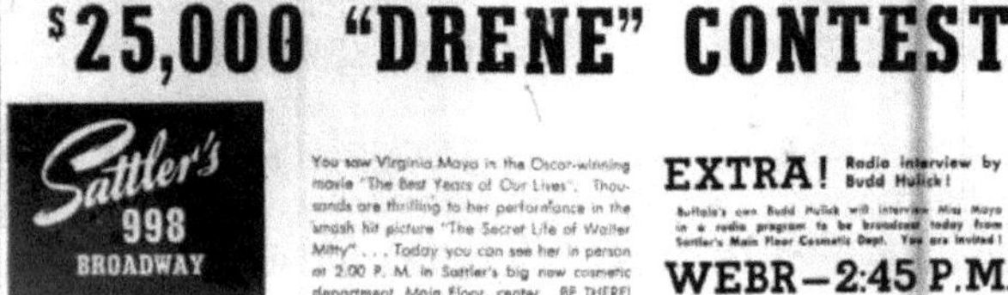

The small print in the ad reads:

"You saw Virginia Mayo in the Oscar- winning movie *The Best Years of Our Lives*. Thousands are thrilling to her performance in the hit picture *The Secret Life of Walter Mitty*...Today you can see her in person at 2:00 P.M. in Sattler's big new cosmetic department, Main Floor, Center. BE THERE!

EXTRA! Radio Interview by Budd Hulick! Buffalo's own Budd Hulick will interview Miss Mayo in a radio program to be broadcast today from Sattler's Main Floor Cosmetic Dept. You are invited! WEBR-2:45 P.M."

November 1947

Name the Stars

Name the movie stars at Sattler's Teen Town contest on the second floor at 998! Sattler's is giving away 10 pairs of Ice Capade tickets and 10 school sweaters to the winners of the contest. (362)

September 1948

Sattler's Giant Food Fair

Photograph courtesy of Michael Stark's Family.

The Food Fair had a carnival-like atmosphere with music, prize giveaways, demonstrations and free samples - all the fanfare you expect from a Sattler's event. Over one half million people were projected to visit the store at 998 Broadway over the 8-day event. Many food packers, producers and distributors had exhibits, plus there were cooking demonstrations by nationally-known home economist Martha Logan. Menu planning and serving suggestions were featured, and customers received a multitude of free samples, recipe booklets, novelty items and product information during the Food Fair.

One of the huge attractions was a 3,000-pound tub of butter. The tub in which the butter was encased cost $400 to manufacture and it took 85 dairy workers to fill it with butter. There was also a giant cake, 8 feet in diameter.

It was Robert Cornelius, Sattler's promotions manager, who encouraged shoppers to "come equipped with bushel baskets to tote the load of free gifts and merchandise." (366)

Prizes given away included: a refrigerator, two cocker spaniel puppies, toys, key rings, dog leashes, goggles, paint books and kitchen items. Over $5,000 in prizes were distributed to those who visited the store. (363-365)

A 14-foot long, 10-inch diameter Armour Thuringer sausage was featured at Sattler's Food Fair. It took 14 men to bring in the sausage and secure it in place over the meat counter! Customers were given chances to guess the weight of the sausage. The customer who guessed the closest weight won a year's supply of Armour Thuringer sausage. Who would believe that during the Food Fair you could sell three and a half tons of sausage in one day? Only at Sattler's! (363, 366, 367)

Shown in the picture with the Armour Thuringer sausage are Aaron Rabow, vice president and Charles Hahn, president of Sattler's. Photograph is courtesy of the Archives & Special Collections Department, E. H. Butler Library, SUNY Buffalo State.

This pair of cute pups, held by Aaron Rabow on the left and Charles Hahn, were given away during Sattler's Food Fair. All you had to do was provide the winning name! Photograph is courtesy of the Archives & Special Collections Department, E.H. Butler Library, SUNY Buffalo State.

October 1948

Coronet Magazine

"Yes, you're in it…all Buffalo is in it, for all Buffalo has helped to make Sattler's the Hellzapoppin' Store about which the whole nation is reading.

"You'll remember it all, if you've watched Sattler's grow up thru the years…Elephants in the store, weddings in the window, the clowns, the trained seals, the live bears and the whole parade of zany stunts that have kept you laughing with folks at 998 Broadway since you were a child.

"But whether you've grown up in Buffalo with Sattler's or just moved to town last week, you're sure to get a real kick out of the article that begins on page 77 of the October *Coronet* Magazine, now on sale at all newsstands! Read it!" (368)

October, 1948

Eddie Polo Visits Sattler's

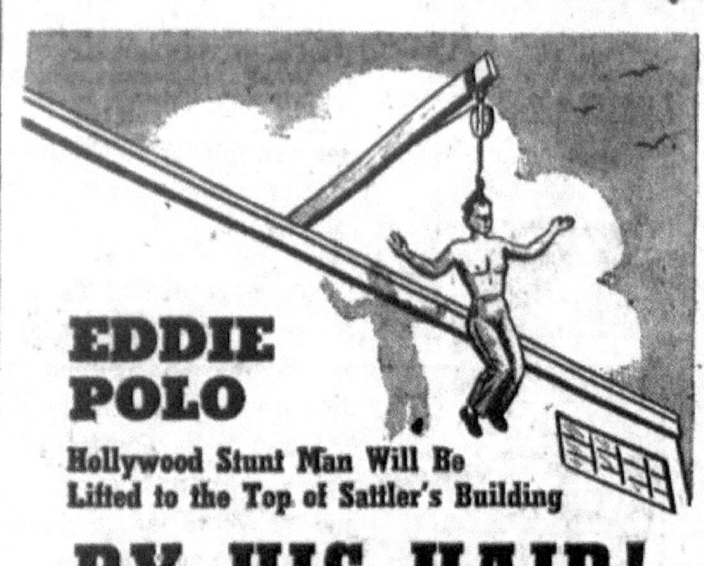

Eddie Polo's nickname was "Hercules of the Screen," and he was a stunt man, a circus acrobat and a popular film star in the early days of Hollywood. Eddie Polo appeared in the films: *The Broken Coin, Graft, The Adventures of Peg o' the Ring, Liberty, The Gray Ghost, Bull's Eye, Lure of the Circus, King of the Circus, The Plow Woman, The Vanishing Dagger, Do or Die, The Secret Four, The Daredevil Reporter, Witness Wanted, Of Life and Death and All is at Stake*. (369-371)

January 1949

Another Sattlerite Hit Show

A variety show and buffet dinner for 1,100 Sattler's employees was held at the Elks Lodge auditorium. During the evening, Miss Julia M. Gosztyla was chosen as Miss Sattlerite 1949. Four taxi cabs were filled with gifts and sent to her Titus Street home. The gifts, from the different departments at Sattler's, included: a mattress, dresses, a gallon of pickles, boots, loafers, 5 pounds of chocolate, a radio, a rug, shoes, record albums, a canned ham, 2 pounds of cookies, a watch bracelet, layer cake, a corsage, a full size jukebox, an electric blanket, a set of silver, assorted lingerie, a china lamp, nail clippers, cleaning and glazing for a fur coat, a brunch coat, a photograph and aprons. (372, 373)

March 1949

Mrs. Homer Stanton

I was told the story of a customer, Mrs. Homer Stanton of Mill River, Massachusetts. She was the wife of a farmer and mother of three young girls. Mrs. Stanton read about Sattler's in the October 1948 edition of a national magazine called *Coronet.* She decided to send 50 cents with her letter and asked the store to send her a "bargain." (374, 375)

WHAT Mrs. STANTON WROTE...

Her letter dated February 14, 1949 is as follows: (376, 377)

Dear "998",

I have just read all about the One-Stop Wonder Store in last October's *Coronet* magazine and I am not going to let the fact that I live "way down East" keep me from getting a Sattler's bargain. So I am sending you 50 cents in stamps just to see what kind of bargain I'll get. You pick it out and I'll accept it.

Sincerely yours,

Thelma R. Stanton

And indeed Sattler's did give Mrs. Stanton a bargain! Mrs. Homer Stanton and her husband received the red-carpet treatment by the City of Good Neighbors, as Sattler's provided a 4-day holiday for the couple with their 50-cent bargain request. (374, 375)

First, a car dealership in the area where Mrs. Stanton lived drove her and her husband from Mill River to the Albany, NY airport, with a parade of motor cars following them. Sattler's flew Mr. and Mrs. Stanton to Buffalo on a round trip, first class ticket, via American Airlines' Convair flagship. The Stantons were met at the airport by a welcoming committee of executives, headed by Aaron Rabow, vice president of Sattler's. The couple was taken by limousine to the Hotel Statler, where they stayed in the honeymoon suite. The suite at the Statler had gifts waiting for Mr. and Mrs. Stanton and gifts for their daughters who were still back home in Mill River, Mass. (376)

On the day of the Stantons' arrival, Sattler's ran eight pages of sale ads in Mrs. Stanton's honor and proclaimed the sales were for "Mrs. Stanton Day." She was in Buffalo to launch the start of a Great Bargain-Lover's Dream Sale. (376, 378) **Photograph courtesy of the Voorhees Family.**

The following morning, before Sattler's opened to the public, Mrs. Stanton was taken from the Hotel Statler by her chauffeur-driven Packard limousine to 998. An orchid corsage and 1,200 employees waited for her to lead a store parade. A special throne on wheels was her chariot, as she was taken from one department at Sattler's to the next.

In each department, the manager gave her an item of merchandise. She received electric blankets, a 3-piece bedroom set with a mattress, 4 lamps, 5 rugs, an Admiral radio, 2 pairs of shoes, a purse, an iron, 3 record albums, a sweater, 3 dresses, a hat, a scarf, a spring suit, smoker's supplies for her husband, inlaid kitchen linoleum, 24 packages of Jiffy starch, a case of dog food, 24 pounds of coffee, perfume, electronic appliances, material to make dresses for her three girls, foundation garments, groceries and a fur coat. By the end of her stay in Buffalo, the Stanton Family received over $3,500 worth of merchandise and gifts. (376).

Mr. and Mrs. Stanton were also the guests of the city of Buffalo as they received a key to the city, a miniature policeman's badge and a courtesy card from Mayor Bernard J. Dowd. A trip to Niagara Falls and different points of interest was on the agenda for the 4-day stay. They continued to enjoy that chauffeur-driven Packard limousine throughout their stay. The Stanton's were at Laube's Old Spain for breakfast, and in the evening they danced, wined and dined at the Town Casino and Chez Ami.

On stage from left to right: Mrs. Homer Stanton and Billy Keaton (who is wearing a 998 tie) from WEBR Radio. Photo courtesy of the Voorhees Family.

Mrs. Stanton also had personal appearances at nightclubs and was interviewed on WEBR radio. She had a total of 6 radio interviews.

The four-day whirlwind trip ended with a limousine ride back to the airport. As the Stantons were about to board the plane, they were bid farewell by Mr. Rabow and left with a parting gift of 11 cents, change left over from the 50-cent bargain shopping trip. (376, 379, 380)

May 1949

Truth or Consequences

Ralph Edwards was the host of *Truth of Consequences*, a radio quiz show that aired on NBC-WBEN in 1949. The show had guest participants who were allowed two seconds to answer an outlandish question. If the contestant was unable to answer the question, that contestant was given a zany, wacky, or embarrassing task to perform.

Such was the case for Joe Grebb, who tried to get a hen to lay an egg on his head in a specific amount of time. Unfortunately for Grebb, he was unable to benefit financially from this ridiculous stunt, as the hen did not cooperate and lay an egg. Joe Grebb could have won $1,000 on the NBC Radio show, and the host thought that a second chance could take place. Edwards agreed that if 10 people in 10 cities could perform the same stunt, each contestant had the opportunity to win $100. At the same time they could redeem Joe Grebb, and perhaps Joe could still win some cash.

Ralph Edwards had chosen Buffalo as one of the cities for the gag, and the stunt would take place at the Sattler's window at 998 Broadway. The first step was to find a contestant willing to take on the challenge! A 48-year-old Marine Trust Mortgage employee, Robert C. Grimmer of West Hazeltine Avenue, Kenmore, NY, volunteered to undergo this egg-straordinary opportunity for his chance to win $100 while enjoying some notoriety and fun.

Grimmer received plenty of attention for being the volunteer egghead, including interviews during *Breakfast at Laube's Old Spain*, a morning program on WBEN radio, and on the *WBEN Luncheon Club* the next day. There were also several repeat broadcasts of the egg-targeting event itself.

A white leghorn hen named Grim was placed in a chicken coop that was suspended above Grimmer's head as he sat in Sattler's window. A chute that led from the bottom of the chicken coop was positioned over Mr. Grimmer's head so that if the hen laid an egg it would land eggs-actly on top of the contestant's bald noggin. 11:00 A.M. to 1:00 P.M. was the time Mr. Grimmer was allowed to entice, coerce and maybe even plead with this hen to lay an egg. The window also had a play-by-play announcer, Clint Buehlman, with his microphone. A cherry cream pie, which sat near Buehlman, would be the booby prize if a successful day in the hen house wasn't accomplished. Time clucked by.....the crowd was packed in front of Sattler's to watch this spegg-tacular event! No egg was laid. No $100 prize awarded. But yes, a consolation prize of a pie in the face was awarded to a good sport, Robert Grimmer.

The good humor of Grimmer was apparent as he left the window at Sattler's and was consoled by his wife and four children, only to remark "I'll get even, we're going to have fried chicken for dinner tonight." (381-389)

May 1949

Operation Thrift – the Mighty Bargain Airlift Sale

Sattler's buyers pose for the Bargain Airlift Sale. Photograph courtesy of the Voorhees Family.

Sattler's Airlift Sale ran for a span of 9 days in May of 1949, and it was one of the biggest promotions that Sattler's had undertaken. It took place at the same time that the Berlin Airlift was at its most dramatic height. The trio of Hahn, Rabow and Cornelius had their game hats on for the Bargain Airlift Sale, which they called Operation Thrift. Operation Thrift was so successful that it was the National Retail Dry Goods Association's winner of the year for the best-coordinated campaign.

What better way to receive free publicity than to invite Buffalo Mayor Bernard J. Dowd and other government officials, who were trying to bring Buffalo to the forefront by becoming a "top-flight aviation city." Sattler's brought in aviation experts from Capitol Airlines, Pan American World Airlines, American Airlines, Robinson Airlines, British Overseas Airline Corporation, the Airport Advisory Board of the Buffalo Airport, Mastercraft Aviation Services and the Jr. Chamber of Commerce Aviation Committee. But most importantly, it brought in all that free advertising by inviting newspapermen and radio executives.

The Sattler's executives and buyers were invited to dinner with these men at the Buffalo Club, where the dinner was as delicious and as fresh as possible. Lobster was flown in from Gloucester, MA, shrimp from Louisiana, green beans from North Carolina, canapes from Europe, and the cocktails had ice (hewn from the 7,000,000-year-old Mendenhall Glacier) that was flown in from Juneau, Alaska.

The following pictures of the buyers for this event are enhanced versions of the above photograph. Do you recognize anyone in these photos? If so, please go to *The Sattler's Diary* Facebook page and let everyone know whom you recognize! (390)

Photograph courtesy of the Voorhees Family.

Memories from Jack Hahn about his father, Charles Hahn, president of Sattler's and Operation Thrift:

"We went to the Pentagon with this brainstormed thing that people told us was ridiculous and came back with an all-day show, with three jet teams, two of them from the Navy and one from the Air Force.

"The Canadian Government heard about our air show and said 'Can we put in a jet team?' I told them yes, if you will send down thirteen bombers to escort them, and they did. We had an air show that lasted from nine o'clock in the morning until six o'clock at night. Everyone in Buffalo had a sunburned face that day, May 8, 1949, when we had over $60,000,000 worth of aviation equipment flying for a Buffalo department store.

"Our brainstorming airlift wound up with such things as: every airline in the entire area rerouting its planes to fly over Sattler's. We had floodlights going up into the sky. Three airlines banded together and flew a seven-million-year-old cake of ice from Juneau, Alaska, to cool the cocktails at the press luncheon."

"Although this was such a crazy idea that nobody had ever dreamed of–let alone seen - it is believed to be the first of what we now call "air shows."

This invitation was printed on the bottom of the ad shown on the left: "Come early and stay late for the first great day of America's first Bargain Airlift – tomorrow, at Sattler's. Tomorrow is the grand and glorious opening day of Sattler's mighty Bargain Airlift – Operation Thrift. Be sure to be on hand at 9:30 A.M. when Mayor Dowd and a score of other dignitaries will conduct the colorful sendoff ceremonies. Thrill to the sight of a thousand gas-filled balloons floating in the sky when Operation Thrift officially begins. Read all eight bargain-crammed, full-page Sattler's ads in today's paper and see how your One-Stop Wonder Store has made good on its promise to make Sattler's Bargain Airlift the year's most thrilling sale. Fill every need of home and family now and take months to pay! Remember, a small deposit reserves any purchase in 'Layaway.'" (391)

TOMORROW, SUNDAY, MAY 8th
FROM 9:30 A. M. TO 5:30 P. M.

(Buffalo Municipal Airport)

This free Air Show, the greatest in Buffalo's history, is a public service feature of Sattler's mighty Bargain Airlift. It is presented in co-operation with the Buffalo Junior Chamber of Commerce Aviation Committee who share with Sattler's the aim to advance Buffalo as a great aviation center.

Airlines Sightseeing Flights

Beginning at 9:30 A. M., American Airlines, Capital Airlines, and Robinson Airlines will fly sightseeing trips over the Buffalo area, using standard airlines transport planes. These nominally-priced flights will enable new thousands to experience the thrill of modern air travel.

Thrills by the Hundred!

Co-ordinated by Mr. John Olmstead of Mastercraft Aviation Service, the Airlift Air Show will bring to Buffalo one of the most complete and exciting aviation spectacles ever presented in this part of the country!

Beginning at 12:00 noon, you'll see the world's fastest planes, United States and Canadian jet-propelled miracles of speed, as they streak through the sky in precision formations! You'll see Buffalo's own Bell Helicopters in a spectacular "sky dance!" You'll see awe-inspiring mass flights of both regular and reserve Airforce and Navy planes. You'll see thrilling formation flights of Air National Guard planes!

You'll see a flying exhibition of the newest in personal aircraft by America's leading manufacturers. You'll see the Shawnee Airport glider team pick up and tow a motorless sailplane. You'll see a thrilling "sea rescue" executed by Frontier Helicopter Service. You'll see the Civil Air Patrol in an inspiring flag ceremony! You'll see spine-tingling aerobatic stunts! You'll see all this and many more never-to-be-forgotten sights at the Airlift Air Show, tomorrow!

(392, 393)

SAVINGS UNLIMITED

in this, the world's first bargain airlift!

FIRST department store in the world to use air transportation on this huge scale, Sattler's is proud to bring you the freshest foods, the newest fashions—Yes, and the newest home furnishings, at bargain-low planeload prices. Don't forget to bring the children; they'll get the thrill of a lifetime.

FIRST to rally the nation's civil airpower behind a great merchandise event. Sattler's entire store will be a thrilling sight to see . . . with searchlights raking the clouds, windsocks on the roof, colorful displays throughout the store, contests, prizes, and many other big attractions.

Civic and Aviation Leaders Congratulate "998"

MAYOR BERNARD J. DOWD: "The Airlift which you plan to hold will be, I am sure, another of those novel and successful promotions for which Sattler's is famous, and will reflect great credit not only on '998 Broadway' but on the city of Buffalo as well."

CAPT. WM. MARQUARDT, AMERICAN OVERSEAS AIRLINES PILOT: "Hello, Sattler's, and congratulations on your big 'Bargain Airlift.' Like the Berlin Airlift, in which the American Overseas Airforce flies every day, your 'Operation Thrift' is a dramatic demonstration of the power of modern aviation to serve the citizens of the world. Buffalo can be proud of this pioneer move in the progress of air transportation."

JAMES H. CARMICHAEL, PRESIDENT, CAPITAL AIRLINES: "Congratulations, Sattler's, on your thrilling idea. Capital Airlines will be proud to take part in America's first Bargain Airlift."

BILL ODUM, WORLD-FAMOUS FLYER: "Congratulations to Buffalo on being the scene of America's first commercial airlift. Sattler's great airborne bargain event is sure to make news from coast to coast and deservedly so for this is one of the biggest boosts ever given to American commercial aviation."

WALTER H. JOHNSON, VICE PRES., AMERICAN AIRLINES: "It is going to be a real pleasure to work with you in making this the most successful merchandising promotion that Sattler's has ever developed."

MAJOR ALFRED E. ANSCOMBE, PUBLIC INFORMATION OFFICER, CIVIL AIR PATROL: "I know you can depend on every civilian flyer in Western New York to help make this the greatest tie-up between progressive aviation and progressive retailing that America has ever seen."

COLONEL BOB SCOTT, AUTHOR OF "GOD IS MY CO-PILOT": "I want to congratulate Buffalo on being the scene of America's first commercial airlift. I think both the city and Sattler's can be proud of the big boost this unusual event is doing to give American commercial aviation."

W. H. HUFF, MGR. EASTERN DEPT., AIR EXPRESS: "Air Express salutes Sattler's on the occasion of its thrilling Bargain Airlift. We are proud to cooperate in this event for we believe it is a vital demonstration to the world that American Commercial Aviation and American Retailers can join hands to serve the public in new and important ways."

SATTLER'S

998

n Airlines

AMERICAN AIRLINES

SATTLER'S

998 BROADWAY

BROADWAY

(394)

"Don't fail to see the big Navy fighter plane in Sattler's parking lot! Visit the unified services aviation recruiting booth on our main floor! See the many and exciting educational aviation displays in our windows and throughout our store! Watch for the huge searchlight beams that will sweep the skies above Sattler's every night!" (394, 395)

100,000 people came to the Buffalo Airport for the airshow that was sponsored by Sattler's and the Buffalo Junior Chamber of Commerce Aviation Committee. The day was fair with abundant sunshine, perfect for a day of flying. A flag-raising ceremony was presented by the Civil Air Patrol Cadets at 11:30 in the morning. Then there was an hour to let people have a closer view of the planes, both military and private aircraft, before the start of the airshow.

Bob Cornelius, Aaron Rabow, Ralph Hubble, Charles Hahn with Secret Service-type guys. Photograph courtesy of the Voorhees Family.

June 1949

MORE MONKEY SHINES FROM SATTLER'S

Sattler's

PRESENTS AN EXHIBIT OF

50 MONKEYS

For a Summer-Long Stay

On MONKEY ISLAND

This was the fourth summer that Sattler's presented 50 monkeys to the Buffalo Zoo for a summer-long stay on Monkey Island. (396)

August 1949

That's No Bull!

Sattler's bought an 870-pound Black Angus steer at the 4-H Baby Beef Sale held at the Erie County Fair auction for .65 per pound or $565.50 . This grand champion steer was raised by Philip Taylor, a 16-year-old 4-H enthusiast from the hamlet of Lawtons, NY. (397) Philip Taylor became the "owner/operator of the Dancote Farms of Lawtons, NY, specializing in Aberdeen Black Angus cattle, at one time the largest herd of this breed in the US." (587)

This is a photograph of 16-year-old Philip Taylor with one of the Black Angus steer from Dancote Farm in Lawtons, NY. Photograph courtesy of Sylvi Taylor.

September 1949

Dr. I.Q. In Person

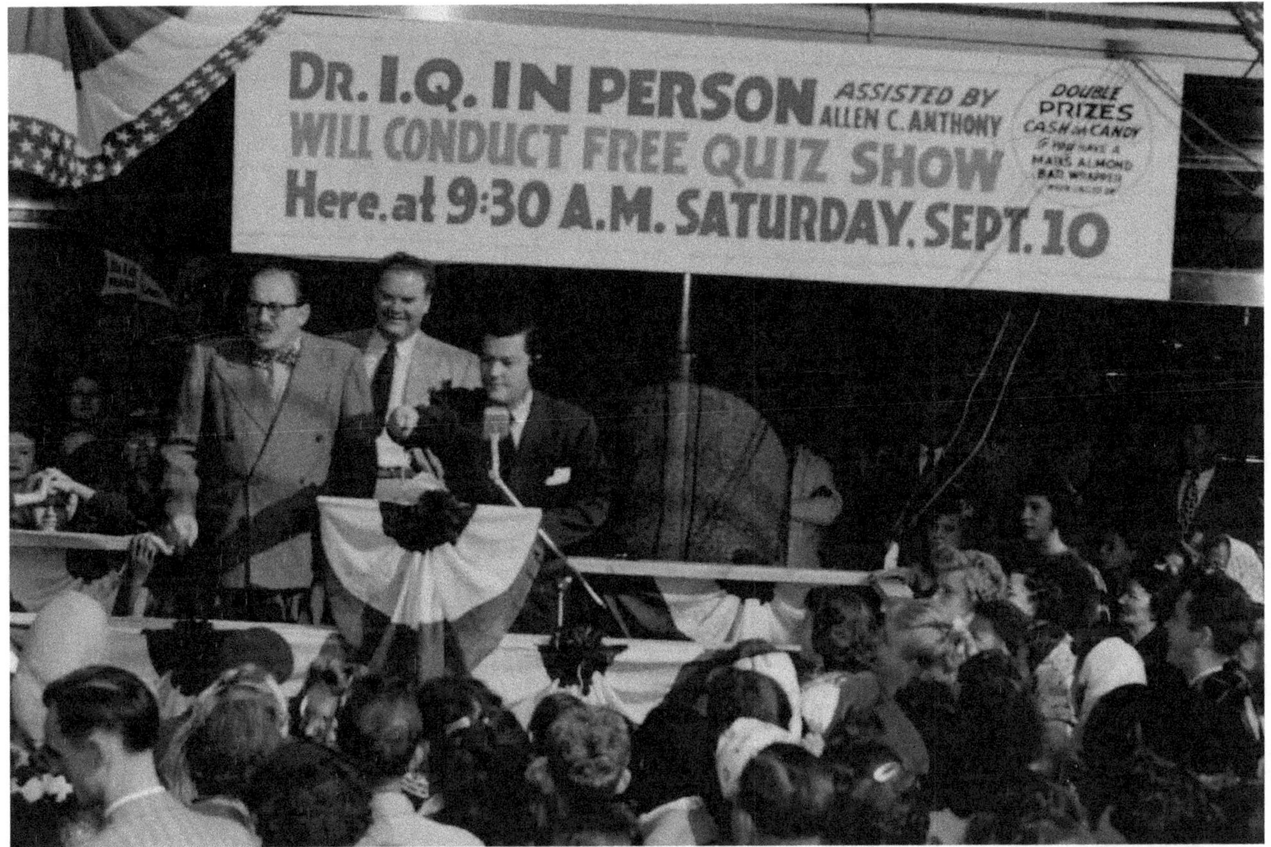

Standing on the stage in the photograph from left to right are Aaron Rabow, Robert Cornelius and Dr. I.Q., Lew Valentine. Photograph courtesy of the Voorhees Family.

In 1939, the Mars Company manufactured a candy bar called the Dr. I.Q. Candy Bar. It was a bar made of nougat, caramel and roasted peanuts, covered in milk chocolate. (398) The Mars Company used the *Dr. I.Q. Quiz Show* as an advertising enticement. It was a fast-paced radio and television quiz show that started in 1939 to promote the Dr. I.Q. candy bar.

Lew Valentine was "the genial master of wit and information" from the *Dr. I.Q. Quiz Show*. He conducted a free quiz show at Sattler's while announcer Allen C. Anthony, from the show, assisted the Quiz Master. If you were a contestant with a Mars Toasted Almond wrapper, you would receive double the prize. If you had the correct answer the prize was a silver dollar, and if you had the wrong answer the prize was a box of Mars candy bars. (399-401)

DR. I. Q., IN PERSON,

Conducts A FREE QUIZ SHOW at Sattler's!

At 9:30 A. M., Saturday, September 10th (note: that's more than a week from now, not this coming Saturday), Lew Valentine, the genial master of wit and information, assisted by Allen C. Anthony, will conduct a special Free Quiz Show at 998 Broadway. Remember, if you have a Mars Chocolate Covered Almond Bar wrapper in your possession you'll win double the regular prize in case you are called up to participate in the quiz. There'll be big cash prizes for the right answers and boxes of Mars candy for those who miss their questions.

Mars Chocolate-Covered

ALMOND BARS 3 FOR 24c

(5 BARS FOR 39c)

Main Floor and Basement Candy Depts.

When Dr. I.Q. was in Buffalo and not in front of Sattler's, his show played at the Shea's Buffalo Theater in 1942, 1943, 1949 and 1950. The show was broadcast locally over WBEN radio.

October 1949

Drawing for Two Studebakers

Drawing for 2 Studebakers

to Be Held at 9:40 A. M. Tomorrow!

Be on hand when Mr. David West, president, and Mr. Dal Lewis, manager, of the Automobile Club of Buffalo, and Mr. Wade Stevenson officiate at the drawing for the two new Studebaker automobiles Sattler's is giving away. (Tickets were distributed during our recent Fair.) Winners will each receive over $200 in extra prizes if present at the drawing, 9:40 A. M. tomorrow, in front of Sattler's

(402-404)

Sattler's gave away two 1959 Studebaker Champion Regal De-Luxe 4-door sedans. Unfortunately I don't know who the winners were. If you know who won the cars, please let everyone know through *The Sattler's Diary* Facebook page. We would love to see some photographs if you have them!

Sattler's was never slow to take advantage of an opportunity to draw more customers into its store. During the drawing for the Studebaker Champion Regal De-Luxe, another contest entry form was available at Sattler's for Miss Flame of 1949. The ad read: "Who will be Miss Flame of 1949? You may be the redhead that wins this honor! Miss Flame will win a stunning outfit of apparel and a full ten-week course in Fashion Modeling at the Continental Models Guild, 92 Main St. Besides this, she will take part in the Junior Chamber of Commerce Fire-Prevention Week activities throughout the city. Sattler's photo studio will supply your contest-entry photo absolutely free! (Second floor, rear.) Hurry!" (403)

November 1949

Sattler's Famous Bargain Train Pulls into Buffalo

During my research, I came upon a speech that was written and delivered by Jack Hahn, son of Sattler's president Charles Hahn, to members of the Saturn Club. "Now, Sattler's has throughout the years brainstormed many things and come up with such ideas as our Bargain Train, where we dramatize the idea that 'Sattler's buys by carloads so you can buy for less,' " said Jack Hahn.

"'Fast Freight to 998'! That is our well-known store address in Buffalo. We say 'From the Eastern Shore to the Wonder Store, from the Golden Gate to 998, the Bargain Train is rattling across the country to bring you the best buys; best because Sattler's buys in carload lots.'"(405) **Voorhees Family photo.**

In days gone by, the Central Terminal Train Station was a constant beehive of activity. It was there that the boxcars with Sattler's banners were placed for all to see. (406) Sattler's department store sought permission from the Buffalo Common Council to erect signs at various railroad viaducts in the city of Buffalo to advertise their Bargain Train from November 10th to the 19th in 1949. (407)

"SEE THE BARGAIN TRAIN! Huge sections of Sattler's famous Bargain Train may be seen on the New York Central's Memorial Drive siding, near the terminal; on the Lackawanna's Team Track, South Park Avenue near Lower Main Street; and on the Erie and Nickel Plate siding, Bailey Avenue near Clinton." (408)

The fine print on the above ad reads "On the same track where the Freedom Train stood, see this thrilling reminder of Sattler's and leading Buffalo railroads' constant effort to free you from the high cost of living." (409)

February 1950

Hollywood Star

★ SATTLER'S OPEN TILL 5 P. M. WEDNESDAY!

FRANCIS *The Talking Mule Will Give a FREE SHOW At Sattler's Wednesday, 9:30 A. M. to 10 A. M.*

NOTHING TO BUY! Just Be At Sattler's Main Entrance Wednesday at 9:30 A. M. and You'll See Francis in An Amazing Half-Hour Show **FRANCIS** Universal - International's Biggest Comedy Hit in Five Years, NOW SHOWING AT BASIL'S LAFAYETTE

Who could forget that comic kick from Francis the Talking Mule? In the 1950's, Francis starred in seven movies: *Francis, Francis Goes to the Races, Francis Goes to West Point, Francis Covers the Big Town, Francis Joins the WACS, Francis in the Navy and Francis in the Haunted House*. Again, Sattler's spared no kicks to get people to come to their store! (410, 411)

April 1950

Circus at Sattler's

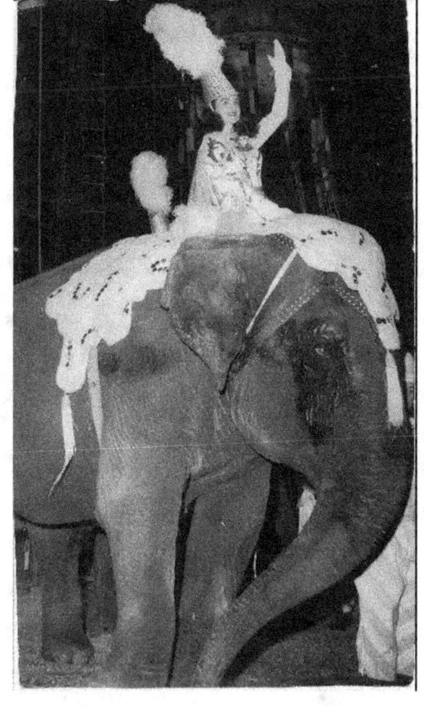

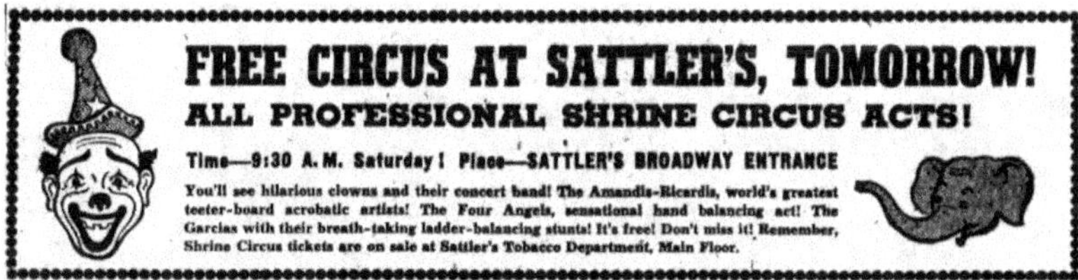

The parking lot at Sattler's was the place to be one Saturday morning during April 1950. That crazy Sattler's store was at it again, with barkers shouting outside the store trying to coax you to a circus spectacle, all for free!

"You'll see hilarious clowns and their concert band! The Amandis-Ricardis, world's greatest teeter-board acrobatic artists! The Four Angels, sensational hand balancing act! The Garcias with their breath-taking ladder-balancing stunts! It's free!"(412)

Pictured is Helen Amandis, of the famous circus act of Amandis-Ricardis. Photograph is courtesy of Laura Amandis.

May 1950

Sattler's All-American Roundup

Sattler's All-American Roundup took place in 1950. The best products from all 48 United States (Alaska and Hawaii became states in 1959) were shipped to Sattler's for their store. It took Sattler's buyers five months and 342,000 miles of travel to bring this sale to 998. American Airlines flew 48 state flags to the Buffalo Municipal Airport, where the plane was met by Sattler's executives and 48 U.S. Army soldiers who were driving Army Jeeps. Passengers in the Jeeps included D'Youville College students dressed in caps and gowns, while each Jeep flew one of the state flags as the parade of military vehicles headed to Buffalo City Hall. In an outdoor ceremony, Aaron Rabow, vice president of Sattler's, gave Buffalo Mayor Joseph Mruk a bronze nameplate from the retired American Airlines' flagship *Buffalo*. Mr. Rabow also extended greetings from the governors and members of the Heads of the Chamber of Commerce of the 48 states. (413)

"I think Buffalo should be proud to be the scene of this nationally important event. I accept with great pleasure the greetings of the governors of the 48 states, as well as the well-wishes of heads of Chambers of Commerce all over the nation for this roundup," said Mayor Mruk. (414-416)

June 1950

Monte Carlo Nite

These Sattlerites were off to another great Social Club outing - a Wiener Roast and Monte Carlo Nite held at the AAA Club! **Photographs on this page courtesy of Michael Stark's Family.**

August 1950

Howdy Doody Day

HEY KIDS! Monday is HOWDY DOODY DAY at 998 Broadway!

COME MEET "BUFFALO BOB" SMITH IN PERSON!

C'mon and let's give Buffalo's Own World-Famous Television Star a Rambunctious, Rousing Welcome!

BIG FREE SHOW at 9:15 A. M.!

SEE "Buffalo Bob" and Clarabell, his faithful clown, as they conduct a riotous 45-minute variety show on a specially constructed stage in front of Sattler's, tomorrow morning!

SEE the thrilling wire walker! He juggles fire! SEE the trained dogs! SEE the educated monkey! Join in as "Buffalo Bob" leads the community sing!

FUN for everyone as Clarabell, the clown, releases 2,000 gas-filled balloons to fill the sky with color. It's really going to be sensational, so be there!

"Movies of tomorrow's big party soon to be shown on television, Coast to Coast! Yes sir, we are going to take movies of all you folks who come to our show at Sattler's tomorrow morning, and when I get back to New York I'm going to put these pictures on my television show! So be on hand tomorrow and then look for your face on the television screen in a week or two!" **-BUFFALO BOB SMITH**

"**SEE** 'Buffalo Bob' and Clarabell, his faithful clown, as they conduct a riotous 45-minute variety show on a specially constructed stage in front of Sattler's, tomorrow morning!

SEE the thrilling wire walker! He juggles fire! SEE the trained dogs! SEE the educated monkey! Join in as "Buffalo Bob" leads the community sing!

FUN for everyone as Clarabell, the clown, releases 2,000 gas-filled balloons to fill the sky with color. It's really going to be sensational, so be there!**"** (417)

September 1950

Pooch Parade

Sattler's S.P.C.A Pooch Parade took take place on a Sunday afternoon in Humboldt Park. The parade was for "unpedigreed pups." Competing were 750 pets with their handlers, and the parade line was so long that it circled twice around the dry wading pool. Additionally, over 10,000 people were in attendance to cheer on their favorites.

Jack Hahn, assistant treasurer of Sattler's, was chairman of the Pooch Parade, which also served as a reminder that National Dog Week was coming up. The S.P.C.A. had dozens of volunteers to register people as members of its organization. Membership fees were .25 to $1.00.

Photo courtesy of the Voorhees Family.

The parade was led by Blackie, the goat who was owned by S.P.C.A. Chairman Allen Spaulding. Blackie was followed by a four-year-old drum majorette, Bonnie Lou Burns of Springbrook, NY, then by dogs of all varieties, including some in costumes. There were dogs dressed in hats and skirts, a dachshund sandwiched between two rolls to be the official hotdog at the parade, and a dog feeding on a baby bottle while being wheeled in a baby carriage.

There were twelve contest classifications: largest, smallest, fattest, skinniest, longest hair, shortest natural hair, longest tail, shortest natural tail, longest ears, shortest natural ears, most originally dressed and best trick dog. Prizes varied by contest category, but all contestants and their owners were eligible to compete for the grand prize, which was a Shetland pony, complete with saddle and bridle. (418-426)

Winners were:

Largest dog: 1 Katherine Koeppl, 2 Alan Terryberry, 3 A. Pickery
Smallest dog: 1 Carol Garrowski, 2 Diana Dorst, 3 Sharon Armentrout
Fattest dog: 1 Carol Schreiber, 2 Ronald Strom, 3 Carol Wattlief
Skinniest dog: 1 Patricia Nowak, 2 Patty Ann Firta, 3 Michael Krzystak
Shortest Natural Hair: 1 Pamela Rieth, 2 Gayle Towart, 3 Michael Mize
Longest Tail: 1 Kathleen Macey, 2 Gerald Brown, 3 Ronald Rudnicki
Shortest Ears: 1 Patricia Szymanski, 2 Alice Czaja, 3 Franklyn Lambers
Longest Ears: 1 Christian Day, 2 Barbara Weick, 3 Richard Hooper
Shortest Natural Tail: 1 William Mango, 2 Raymond Jedd, 3 Donald Howard
Trick Dog: 1 Donald Getrin, 2 Geraldine Harris, 3 Barbara Wieck
Most Original Dressed Dog: 1 Vincent Coigno, 2 Janice Bujnicki, 3 Richard Brooks
The grand prize, the Shetland pony, bridle and saddle, was won by 13-year old Bess Mae Greenberger of 83 Blaine Avenue.

Unfortunately, Bess Mae, Sattler's grand prize winner, passed away several years ago. I did speak with her son, Alan, who was unaware of the pony his mother had won and was delighted to hear the story of the Pooch Parade. Alan did mention that his mother was an only child with strict parents. She lived in the city of Buffalo and he was rather certain that his mother would not have been able to keep the pony. However, Alan did say that in her later life his mother worked as a secretary at an equestrian school for the handicapped in Florida. (427)

September 1950

Sign the Freedom Scroll

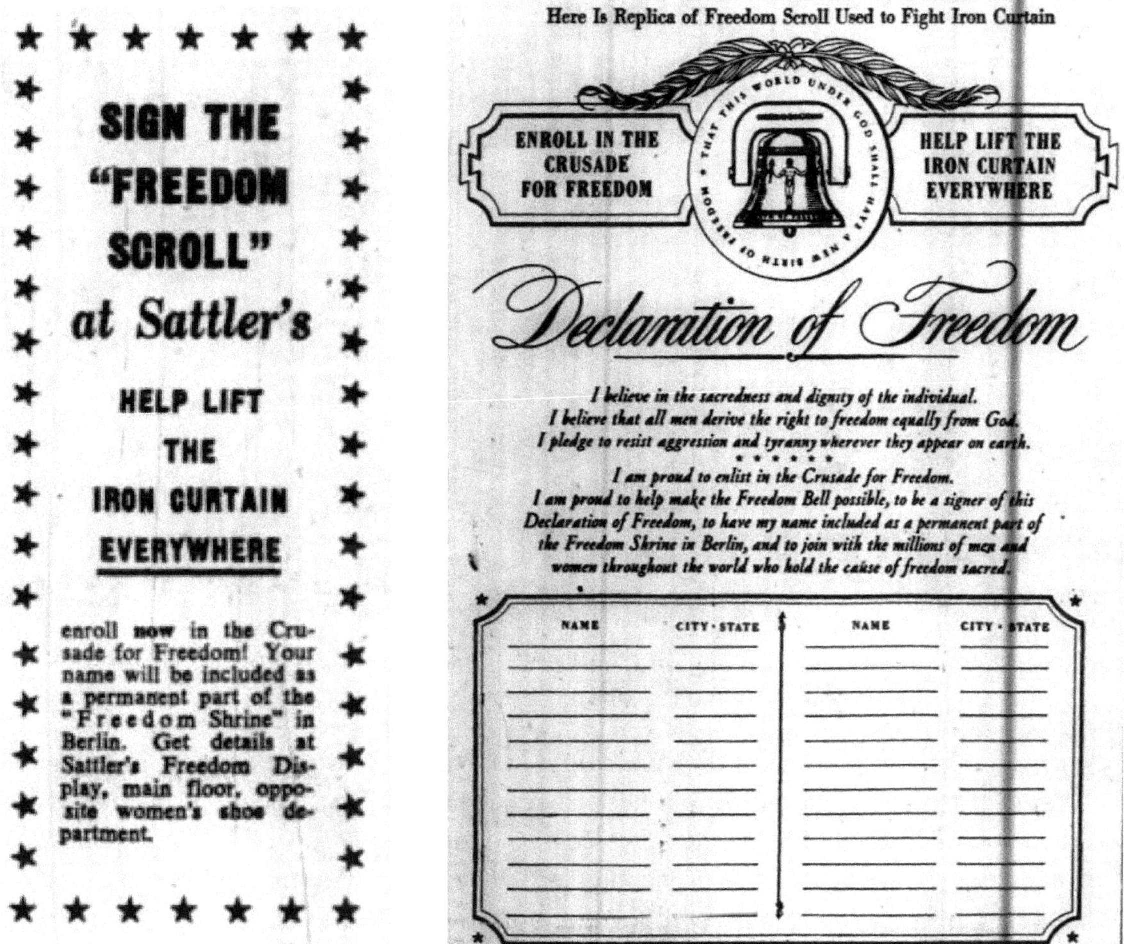

SIGN THE "FREEDOM SCROLL" at Sattler's

HELP LIFT THE IRON CURTAIN EVERYWHERE

enroll now in the Crusade for Freedom! Your name will be included as a permanent part of the "Freedom Shrine" in Berlin. Get details at Sattler's Freedom Display, main floor, opposite women's shoe department.

Here Is Replica of Freedom Scroll Used to Fight Iron Curtain

ENROLL IN THE CRUSADE FOR FREEDOM

THAT THIS WORLD UNDER GOD SHALL HAVE A NEW BIRTH OF FREEDOM

HELP LIFT THE IRON CURTAIN EVERYWHERE

Declaration of Freedom

I believe in the sacredness and dignity of the individual.
I believe that all men derive the right to freedom equally from God.
I pledge to resist aggression and tyranny wherever they appear on earth.

* * * * * *

I am proud to enlist in the Crusade for Freedom.
I am proud to help make the Freedom Bell possible, to be a signer of this Declaration of Freedom, to have my name included as a permanent part of the Freedom Shrine in Berlin, and to join with the millions of men and women throughout the world who hold the cause of freedom sacred.

NAME	CITY · STATE	NAME	CITY · STATE

On Labor Day in 1950, General Dwight D. Eisenhower initiated the *Crusade for Freedom*, which was an attempt to raise funds and awareness for Radio Free Europe. In the early part of the Cold War, a replica of the Freedom Bell that was modeled after the Liberty Bell, but not cracked, toured across the United States. Along the tour, people were asked to sign the *Declaration of Freedom*, which eventually was signed by more than 15,000,000 people and was given by the American people to the people of West Berlin. The Freedom Bell was hung in the Rathaus Schoneber in West Berlin. The bell was rung in the presence of 400,000 Berliners on October 24th, 1950 on United Nations Day. In addition, churches, schools and government buildings rang bells in unison with the Freedom Bell on that day. A simultaneous broadcast of the Freedom Bell's chime could be heard around the world, as its sound was broadcast by news organizations and by Radio Free Europe. After that, the bell was rung every day at noon.

Contributions collected during the tour of the Freedom Bell totaled $1,288,000 and were donated to Radio Free Europe, which broadcast to radio stations in Iron Curtain Countries by a short-wave transmitter. (428-435)

October 1950

Eddie Cantor and Hildegarde at Sattler's Fire Prevention Show

Pictured with the feathered hat is Hildegarde, and sitting next to her is Eddie Cantor. Photograph courtesy of the Voorhees Family.

A *Fire Prevention Show* and ceremony took place outside of Sattler's during National Fire Prevention Week. The special guests at the show were performer Eddie Cantor and singer Hildegarde. Participants also included fire officials, the U.S. Marine Corps Color Guard and local school children. There was a demonstration of high ladder and rope firefighting techniques. 30,000 school children in the city of Buffalo signed a Fire Prevention Pledge which was presented by the stage star, Eddie Cantor, to President Harry Truman in Washington. (436, 437)

November 1950

You Never Know Whom You'll See at Sattler's

In November of 1950, Sattler's Social Club had another successful Masquerade Party. (438) **Photograph courtesy of Michael Stark's Family.**

Do You Remember Sattler-Scrip?

The first Sattler-Scrip reference I found was dated November of 1950. Sattler-Scrip was used just like money at Sattler's and was often given away as a prize since it could be redeemed in the same way as cash at the store.

A story was told to me by Julian Rabow about his dad's appearance on a local television sports show. (His father was president of Sattler's at that time.) After the show, his dad received a call from a local Sattler's shopper. It seemed that the shopper had seen Mr. Rabow on the sports show and had a large collection of military memorabilia from World War II that he had acquired during his military service. He really didn't want the collection anymore and was wondering if there was a chance that Mr. Rabow would want to buy it from him. It seems that a deal was struck, and $500 dollars in Sattler-Scrip was exchanged for the memorabilia. Both parties were ecstatic with the deal!

November 1950

Mrs. Casey Jones Visits Sattler's

Left to right, Aaron Rabow, Mrs. Casey Jones, Charles Hahn. Photograph courtesy of Fredrick L. Avery.

The 80-year-old widow of American railroad engineer Casey Jones started the Bargain Train Sale at Sattler's by pulling the cord of a diesel engine whistle.

What the newspapers wrote about the story of Mrs. Casey Jones coming to Buffalo could never convey the heartwarming truth about two wonderful southerners who met and became friends.

This story was told to me by Bob Cornelius, who is the son of Robert Cornelius. Bob Cornelius became joyfully animated when he spoke so lovingly of his father and Mrs. Casey Jones. Bob began by telling me about himself as a boy and his intense love for trains.

Bob and I were seated together on a sofa in his living room. Bob turned to show me a beautifully painted picture, on the wall behind us, of a locomotive engine.

He spoke of how he, like so many young boys, loved trains. Bob owned a biography of Casey Jones the famous engineer, and he began to recount Casey's story for me:

Having earned the reputation of being a punctual engineer, Casey Jones prided himself on getting the train he was driving to the station on time. Such was the case on the fateful day that Casey and his fireman, Sim Webb, replaced the regularly scheduled engineer on a train that was running late. Legend is told that Casey ran the late train as hard as she could go, as he was trying to make up lost time and get back on schedule. Suddenly Casey saw the back of a train which was occupying the same track. Unable to stop his train, a crash was unavoidable. Casey told Webb to jump off the train and Webb jumped to save his life. Casey Jones, however stayed on the train and applied the brakes. He pulled the cord and made the train's whistle scream as loud as it could to warn anyone of the rapidly approaching train and the upcoming collision. There was a terrible crash which ended Casey's life, and the story of Casey Jones and that fateful train ride has been retold in songs, books and movies.

Bob then continued his story about how Casey Jones's wife ended up at Sattler's:

As it happened, it was Bob's copy of the book, *Casey Jones,* that Bob's father, Robert Cornelius, saw lying about their house one day back in 1950. The book gave Bob's father the idea of bringing Mrs. Casey Jones to Buffalo! After all, what is the good of working as the vice-president of promotions at Sattler's if you can't have a little fun with the job while impressing your son at the same time? So Robert

Cornelius set out to find Mrs. Casey Jones, the wife of the legendary train engineer and American folk hero. He found her at home in Jackson, Tennessee. She agreed to come to Buffalo and help promote the 1950's version of Sattler's Bargain Train Sale by promoting the Mrs. Casey Jones Sale.

"Wife Of The Greatest Railroad Hero Of All Time!"

"From her home in Jackson, Tennessee, Mrs. Casey Jones has come to take the position of honor when prominent railroad officials and community leaders gather at Sattler's tomorrow morning for the opening of Sattler's nationally famous sales event, the Bargain Train! Come and help us give Mrs. Casey Jones a rousing welcome to the City of Good Neighbors." (439)

SHE'S HERE! IN PERSON!

to Blow the Whistle That Will Signal the Start of Sattler's Historic Bargain Train Event

Mrs. Casey Jones

WIFE OF THE GREATEST RAILROAD HERO OF ALL TIME!

From her home in Jackson, Tennessee, Mrs. Casey Jones has come to take the position of honor when prominent railroad officials and community leaders gather at Sattler's tomorrow morning for the opening of Sattler's nationally famous sales event, the Bargain Train! Come and help us give Mrs. Casey Jones a rousing welcome to the City of Good Neighbors.

Ceremonies Begin 9:45 A. M. Thursday

Be on Hand for an Event You'll Never Forget

AMERICA'S LEADING RAILROADS HAVE CO-OPERATED WITH US TO BRING YOU A DAZZLING ARRAY OF ENTERTAINING AND EDUCATIONAL FEATURES

Sattler's prepared the public for the upcoming event as its store mascot, Sandy B. Thrifty, was decked out in railroad attire and appeared in full-page newspaper ads that enticed the public to come to meet Mrs. Casey Jones and see the wonderful store displays, while picking up a bargain or two.

Mrs. Jones arrived by train in Buffalo. During her three-day visit, Mrs. Jones stayed in the bridal suite at the Hotel Statler. She appeared on nine separate radio and television shows, including *Meet the Millers*. Each interview was an opportunity to retell the story of her husband, the great railroad hero, Casey Jones. She also mentioned that she was being hosted by Sattler's to open Sattler's Bargain Train promotion for the year of 1950.

On the big day of the store's Mrs. Casey Jones Sale, November 8, 1950, at two minutes before 10:00 A.M., train whistles throughout the city were sounded in honor of Mrs. Jones' visit to Buffalo. (440) At 10:00 A.M. on that day, the opening ceremonies of the sale promotion at 998 started as Mrs. Casey

Jones pulled the cord on a diesel train whistle to signal the beginning of the sale at Sattler's. The ceremonies continued with The Melody Men Quartet singing "The Ballad of Casey Jones."

Sattler's had the store decorated to impress any railroad buff. On the third floor of Sattler's, there was a full-size replica of a Chesapeake and Ohio locomotive cab complete with throttle, bell and whistle.

The front windows of Sattler's held the B&O Railroad's historical display, which included scale models of famous trains, as well as oil paintings and etchings.
(441)

In typical Sattler's fashion, Mrs. Casey Jones was given a wad of Sattler-Scrip, which gave her the opportunity to spend the scrip in Sattler's for whatever she wanted.

There were lunches and hospital visits for Mrs. Jones to attend, but that still left plenty of time for her and Robert Cornelius to share stories about their families. At one of these meetings, Robert Cornelius brought his son Bob's book, *Casey Jones,* to Mrs. Jones. Mrs. Jones was gracious enough to autograph the book with a note of personal wishes to young Bob Cornelius.

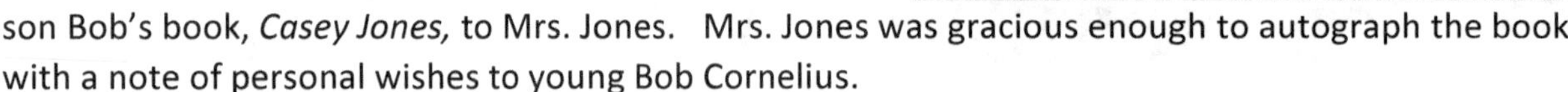

Sometime later, Mrs. Casey Jones sent Robert Cornelius a package by mail. Inside was a hand-crocheted antimacassar she had made for the Cornelius family. Two weeks after sending her package, she wrote Bob the personal letter below:

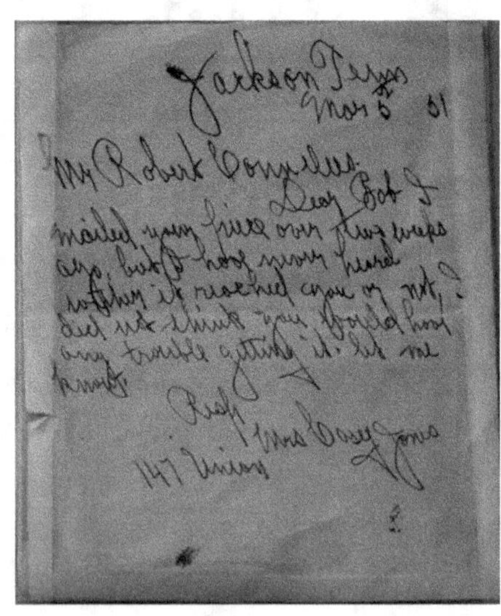

Jackson Tenn.
March 5, 51

Mr. Robert Cornelius

Dear Bob I mailed your piece over two weeks ago, but I have never heard whether it reached you or not? I did not think you would have any trouble getting it. Let me know.

Resp.
Mrs. Casey Jones
147 Union

January 1951

20 Years of Sattlerite Fun

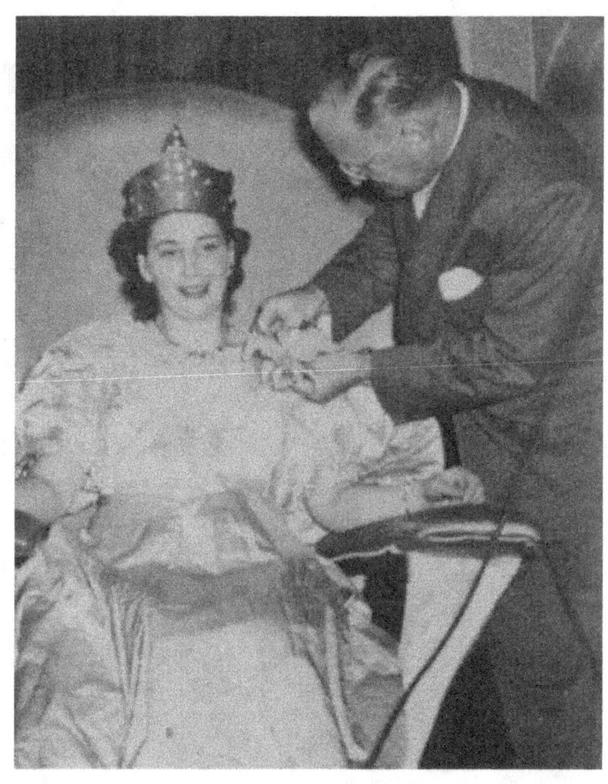

Candidates for Offices in Sattler's Social Club **Aaron Rabow pins a corsage on Miss Sattlerite**

Pictures above are from *The Sattlerite,* souvenir edition, Vol. 20, No. 1, January 23, 1951. Photographs courtesy of Michael Stark's Family.

For President: BILL WILSON or JOHN WOOD

For Vice President: PAT RYAN or JOEY WARE

For Secretary: JEAN COUGHRAN or BETTY PETEIT

For Treasurer: VICKY PLEGIER or GRACE HARRISON

The Sattlerite was a newsletter publication that told what was going on with the employees working at the store. In 1949, there were 1,175 members in Sattler's Social Club.

The following is what was written by an anonymous member of *The Sattlerite* staff on the 20th anniversary of the Sattler Social Club:

"It's the Social Club's twentieth birthday, so let's look backward for a moment. Twenty years ...that's quite a chunk of time, no matter how you look at it. And as we reminisce over the Club's past 20 years, each of us thinks of many things. Some of us remember the grand old get-togethers during the Thirties...the Forty-Niners' Party at Eagles Hall... the big family outings at Bennett Beach...the "Big Apple" shindig at the Knights of Columbus Auditorium (remember when the dance was 'the thing'?)... the nights of fun at Scott's Roller Rink...Others of us remember the wonderful times we had during the Forties. One of the most outstanding was the Social Club's laugh riot "Fun-A-Plenty." Staged at the Consistory in April 1941, this production featured over 60 Sattler stars, with all proceeds going to Bundles for Britain. After the war, in the later Forties, many bright memories were created... there was a continuous 'round-the-calendar series of exciting indoor and outdoor events, all of which added genuine pleasure to our lives.

Fresh in our minds, of course, are memories of the past year...highlighted... our gay summer outings and the very successful Masquerade in November. Yes, from back through the years we can recall scores of picnics, plays, dances...a whole string of Social Club parties that were real honest-to-goodness fun for all of us. But, when we think a little more seriously, we realize that the Club has meant more to us than just those parties...enjoyable though they were.

To all of us, the Social Club has had a deeper meaning. During the past twenty years, it has broadened and enriched our lives...by fostering good will, cooperation, teamwork and, above all...friendship.

May the Social Club go on for the next twenty years and beyond...continuing to inspire the same fine spirit of good fun and good fellowship its members have enjoyed for two memorable decades." (442)

Photograph courtesy of Julian Rabow.

Memories from Julian Rabow about His Dad, Aaron Rabow

Social Club Party 1951

"This picture was taken 65 years ago at a Sattler's Social Club party. My father is the one dressed like a child (it brought the house down when he walked out on the stage, as no one had ever seen him in anything but a conservative suit!). I am the one providing the lap. I was 25 years old and at that time working at Sattler's. We were doing a song act based on Al Jolson's song 'Sonny Boy'. I wrote the script.

I typed the words for each of us and attached them to the back of the lollipop. It was talked about in the store for weeks!"

Julian Rabow worked in the record department and was 998's public address announcer. Julian's father, Aaron Rabow, was vice president of Sattler's. (443, 444)

February 1951

Bonzo Visits

BONZO *Hollywood's Newest Star Will Give a FREE SHOW in Sattler's Broadway Window, Thur., 9:40-10 A.M.*

BRING THE FAMILY TO SEE BONZO, THE 5-YEAR-OLD CHIMPANZEE, WITH HIS TRAINER, HENRY CRAIG, and JESSE WHITE, THE HOLLYWOOD MOVIE ACTOR!

SEE Universal-International's "Bedtime for Bonzo," the Howling Comedy Success Starring Bonzo, Ronald Reagan and Diana Lynn, Starting Tomorrow at the Lafayette Theatre!

Coming to visit Sattler's was Bonzo, the famous chimpanzee that starred in the 1951 movie comedy *Bedtime for Bonzo* with future U.S. President Ronald Reagan and Diana Lynn. Jesse White, a Buffalo-born actor who played Babcock in the movie, joined Bonzo for a 20-minute free show at Sattler's.

White, an actor in dozens of films and television shows, was best known as the Maytag repairman. He appeared in commercials as the Maytag repairman from 1967-1988. (445)

April 1951

Joseph Dunninger

Joseph Dunninger, world-renowned mentalist and escape artist, is known for the quote: "For those who believe, no explanation is necessary; for those who do not believe, no explanation will suffice." He performed outside of Sattler's in April 1951. Dunninger was joined by three well-known and respected Buffalo citizens who were given the task of assisting him in his performance. They were the first Polish mayor of Buffalo, Mayor Joseph Mruk; the Erie County Budget Director Edward A. Rath; and Aaron Rabow, vice president of Sattler's.

The task of these three assistants was to put three ordinary objects into a steel box four days before Dunninger's stage performance, a job which these 3 men took to heart. As they gathered in the mayor's office with the shades drawn, the men put the 3 items into a steel box and then sealed it with a padlock. Mayor Mruk held the only key to open the box. The box was then placed in a plastic bag that was stapled shut and then placed in another plastic bag that was stapled shut. The doubly sealed metal box was frozen in a 300-pound block of ice and was stored in the brine tanks at City Ice & Fuel Division, City Products Corporation. At 9:00 A.M. the day of the performance, the block of ice was delivered to Sattler's and placed on the performance stage.

Eight hundred onlookers attended the performance at 998's storefront. Both Aaron Rabow, executive vice president of Sattler's, and Budget Director Edward A. Rath were on the stage with mentalist Dunninger. Mayor Mruk was at a funeral that morning and was unable to attend the performance.

Dunninger correctly guessed the 3 items in the sealed box, which were: a key to the city, a police parking ticket tag numbered C68770 and a police badge numbered 222. One slight error in Dunninger's telepathic talents was his contention that the police badge was numbered 220. (446-449)

May 1951

The Big Cheese

In 1951, Sattler's displayed a mountain of cheese!

"Another first—at Sattler's…this mammoth cheese stands five feet high, is four and one-half feet wide, required 31,479 pounds of milk to manufacture. Product of Kraft Food Company's Lowville, New York plant, made in June 1950 and fully cured for more than a year…patiently aged to satisfy the most discriminating taste." (450)

May 1951 **Sattler's Salute to American Communications**

Sattler's small print reads as follows: "We sent 522 Telegrams and Made 612 Long Distance Calls to Round Up the Huge Array of Super Savings!

Although the public never sees Sattler's buyers in operation, this phase of our business is so immensely important that we could never bring you the kind of bargains that have made our store famous, unless our buyers kept in constant daily touch with the great wholesale markets of the nation.

How Long-Distance Communications Help!

Not only do Sattler's buyers burn the wires in an endless search for outstanding bargains, but leading suppliers, the country over, telegraph or phone us every day with news of outstanding merchandise offerings. In this way, no opportunity is missed to save you extra dollars!

Come, yourself, and bring the children, to see the wonderland of telephone and telegraph miracles provided for your pleasure by America's two great pioneers in long-distance communication, the Bell Telephone System and Western Union.

You'll see a magically controlled animated window show which graphically demonstrates how the fabulous dial system actually works. Just place your hand on the magic spot on the show-window glass to set this wonderful demonstration in motion!

See the interesting and educational historical displays combining the oldest and newest in telephone and telegraph developments. School teachers are invited to bring their entire classes. See Western Union's amazing Desk-Fax demonstration! See New York Telephone Co.'s mystery switchboard, over which lucky customers will make telephone calls, free!

Send Mother's Day telegrams from Western Union's model office, at Sattler's! See the baseball scores projected on "Trans-Lux" as they come in over Western Union wire." (451-454)

August 1951

Baseball Game at the Corn Roast

Photograph courtesy of Michael Stark's Family.

Photograph courtesy of Michael Stark's Family.

Sattler's employees knew that the Sattler's Social Club was the place to be. Baseball, beer and best friends; that's what summer memories are made of! The bartender pouring the beer in the above photograph is Jack Hahn. Do you recognize anyone in these photographs? If so, please go to ***The Sattler's Diary*** Facebook page to let us know.

September 1951

'Winter in Western New York'

SEE SATTLER'S SHOW of "PORTERFIELD" MASTERPIECES

'Winter in Western New York'

We proudly present a preview of the coming season in 75 superb scenes by Wilbur H. Porterfield, Courier-Express pictorialist and dean of Buffalo photographers. Mr. Porterfield's work has won him international acclaim. See his great winter-scene exhibit tomorrow, on our main floor, center.

A premier photographic artist of his time, Wilbur H. Porterfield was a gem who lived and worked in Buffalo. Known for his pictorial art, some called him "the man who made Buffalo beautiful." Porterfield worked for the rotogravure printing staff of the *Buffalo Courier* and the *Courier-Express*. His work could be seen in the Sunday inserts that were featured under the title of "As Porterfield Sees It." After his death in November 1958, the *Buffalo Courier* changed the name of the Sunday insert he was featured in to "As Porterfield Saw It." This section ran for an additional 10 years after Porterfield's death.

Porterfield won over 150 local, national and international photographic prizes. He was featured at the Albright Art Gallery in exhibitions during 1921 and 1941, and the Burchfield Penney Art Center had exhibitions of Porterfield's work from October 1999 to February 2001.

Sattler's was always trying to support local talent. The show of 75 scenes by Porterfield was entitled *Winter in Western New York*, and the artwork was displayed in the center of the main floor at 998. (455-458, 593)

Photograph is courtesy of the Archives and Special Collections Department, E. H. Butler Library, SUNY Buffalo State.

November 22, 1951

Thanksgiving Day Parade on Broadway

Photograph courtesy of the Voorhees Family.

Over 150,000 people showed up for the 1951 Thanksgiving Day Parade in the Broadway Fillmore District of Buffalo. Master James M. Cole, the world's youngest elephant trainer, guided a family of three elephants in the parade. Master James M. Cole and his troop of three elephants were sponsored by Sattler's. (459)

Photograph is of Master James M. Cole.
Photograph courtesy of Yates County History Center.

the SATTLERite

VOL. 21 JANUARY, 1952 No. 1

Our All Star Revue for '52!

For whom will be the victory? . . . that we all must wait and see.

Proudly we hail these worthy sons and daughters of our social fraternity, loyal . . . enthusiastic . . . hard-working all.

To each and every club member who, each in his own way, has contributed to this past year's success, we say . . . "thank you!"

Since 1951 is through . . . let's RAISE OUR SIGHTS ON '52.

Clockwise from left to right: VICKI FLEGIER — MARY KLUCZYNSKI — OLIVE WETZEL — DOROTHY FALLON — JOHN WOOD JOE WARE — JEAN COUGHRAN — CEIL BURZINSKI

Another memory of bygone days from the staff at Sattler's in 1952. (460)

March 1952

Tuesday, 10:45 AM

A suspect was arrested in connection with the armed robbery of Sattler's, 998 Broadway, in March of 1952. Cashier Patricia R. Kacprowica, a 17-year-old resident of Sobieski Street, was held up by 30-year-old Arthur Stanley Noworyta, of 172 Metcalfe Street. Noworyta wielded a gun at the young employee and demanded "the money."

Noworyta took $2,500 and fled to the rear of the store, where he crashed through a glass door and injured his hand, which later required 10 stitches. Several of the store employees chased the bandit, and Noworyta was finally overtaken by former Marine Dale W. Zenner of 336 Hinds Street, Tonawanda, NY. Zenner was an employee at Gordon Vacuum Store on Broadway, and he decided to join the pursuit when he saw the robber run by the Vacuum Store while being chased by Sattler's employees.

Zenner told police, "He had both arms tucked against his chest and he held a gun in one hand. He ran into an alleyway and I figured he would come out on Sears Street, so I planned to head him off. I was right, but he got back to Broadway before I reached him. He tried to stop a motorist by flashing his gun, but the auto kept going. He was having trouble hanging onto a bundle of money he was holding against his chest. I took one smash at him and he went down. I got my knee against his wrist and took the gun away from him. I kept my foot on it until the police arrived."

The $2,500 was recovered within 15 minutes of the armed robbery. Police Commissioner Michael C. Noeppel stated, "The Police Department is grateful to these citizens for such fine cooperation... The fact Buffalo has such a brave and alert public should be a warning to would-be lawbreakers not to try anything here." The suspect was charged with first-degree robbery and illegal possession of a dangerous weapon. Noworyta pled guilty to first-degree armed robbery and he was sent to Attica State Prison to serve his sentence of 15 to 30 years. (461-465)

Upper left "Police Lieut. Nelson Canteline of the 8th Precinct is shown with the .32-caliber Belgian automatic and ammunition taken from Arthur S. Noworyta." The upper right is "Charles E. Clarey, Sattler's store parking lot attendant as he stands beside a door shattered by the gunman in his escape attempt."

At the lower left is "Gale W. Zenner, former Marine, who knocked down, disarmed and pinned Noworyta to the pavement." On the lower right is "Patricia R. Kacprowicz, Sattler's cashier at whom the holdup man pointed a gun and demanded 'the money.'" (462, 463)

Photographs are courtesy of the Archives & Special Collections Department, E.H. Butler Library, SUNY Buffalo State.

July 1952

Buffalo Bob Smith Visits Buffalo

**The crowd outside Sattler's when Buffalo Bob Smith came to town.
Photograph taken by Gerard C. Myers, courtesy of Myers Studio, Inc.**

It's Howdy Doody Time at Sattler's in 1952! Sattler's ran ads stating that, "It's going to be a gay and glorious party when thousands of boys and girls welcome Buffalo Bob Smith and his motorcade tomorrow, in front of Sattler's store. Buffalo Bob, creator of television's *Howdy Doody Show,* has always been one of Buffalo's most enthusiastic boosters. Now it's our turn to show Buffalo Bob how much his hometown folks love him and appreciate his work!

"Get your free balloon in front of Sattler's 998 Broadway, when you come to welcome Buffalo Bob Smith tomorrow. You'll get the thrill of your life when you see Sattler's breathtaking balloon release to be staged in honor of Buffalo Bob and his motorcade. **CLARABELL IS COMING, TOO!"** (466)

Pictured is a 20-car motorcade of Buffalo Bob Smith and Clarabell the Clown coming from 186 Roehrer St., where Bob Smith's mother lived. (467)

Two of Buffalo Bob Smith's "officially scheduled" visits to Sattler's were in 1950 and 1958. (468) Bob Smith also had another connection with Sattler's, as Bob's sister was the manager of the drapery department at 998. He came often to visit his sister at the store and he was known to bring Howdy Doody with him on many surprise visits. Those surprise visits were an unexpected pleasure for the patrons and staff at Sattler's. (469)

August 1952

Sattler's Annual Corn Roast

Photograph courtesy of Michael Stark's Family.

It was another sunny 80-degree Tuesday, with no rain in sight, when hundreds hopped a ride on the buses waiting outside of Sattler's after work for an evening of festivities at the Buffalo Automobile Club in Clarence, featuring games, music, food and fellowship. On Wednesdays, Sattler's was closed during the summer months so that a late night bonfire and roasting corn with friends never got in the way of work the next day.

June 1953

Time for the Family To Sell Sattler's

Charles Hahn, with all of his marketing wizardry, could not stop the arrival of the suburban malls and the population shift of the Polish and German immigrants and their families, who left Buffalo's East Side homes to move to the suburbs. This well-oiled and profitable machine's president and principal stockholder saw the suburban malls drawing shoppers, who now had cars, to new and exciting malls. One might wonder why such a successful store as Sattler's would be worried about malls? The store was doing a whopping $27,000,000 in annual sales. With a shifting population and increased competition in the malls, Mr. Hahn recognized that change was coming. Being the president of Sattler's and the majority stockholder, he sold all of his shares in the store. With Mr. Hahn's 80% of the company shares sold, other family members sold their remaining 20%. All of the store's shares were bought by Associated Investor, Inc. (470, 471)

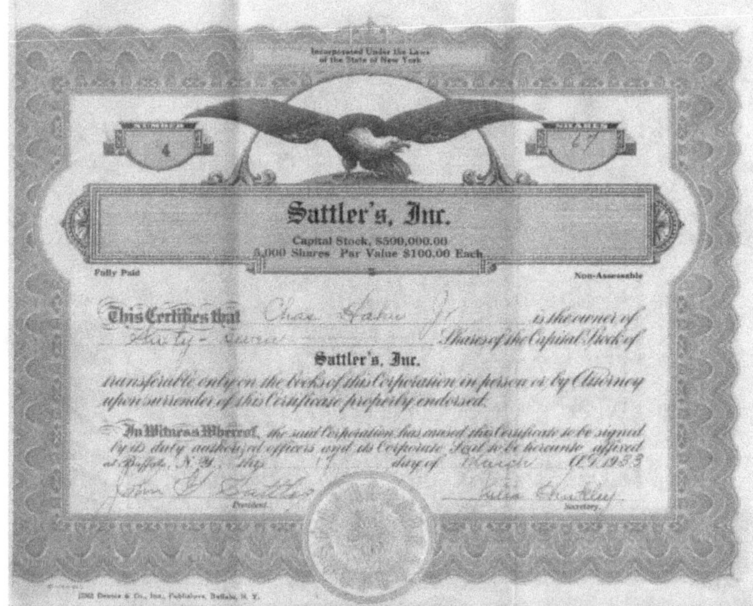

Incorporated Under the Laws of the State of New York

Sattler's, Inc.

Capital Stock, $500,000.00
5,000 Shares Par Value $100.00 Each

Fully Paid — Non-Assessable

This Certifies that Chas Hahn Jr is the owner of ... Shares of the Capital Stock of

Sattler's, Inc.

transferable only on the books of this Corporation in person or by Attorney upon surrender of this Certificate properly endorsed.

In Witness Whereof, the said Corporation has caused this Certificate to be signed by its duly authorized officers and its Corporate Seal to be hereunto affixed at Buffalo, N.Y., this 17 day of March A.D. 1953

President — Secretary

Sattler's, Inc.

CERTIFICATE

CAPITAL STOCK

ISSUED TO

DATED

The Hahn-Rabow-Cornelius alliance was broken. Aaron Rabow became Sattler's president, and Robert Cornelius became executive vice president. A new owner now had control of the "Hellzapoppin" store.

The front and back of Sattler's stock certificates.

June 1953

Sattlerama

What better way to reassure the people of Buffalo that Sattler's hadn't changed with new owners than to start a new Sattler's tradition and to add a new word to Buffalonians' vocabulary…. ***SATTLERAMA!*** (472, 473)

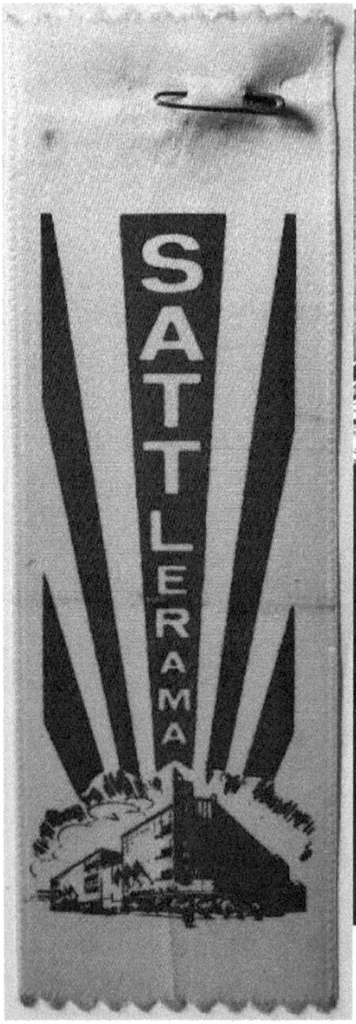

SATTLERAMA

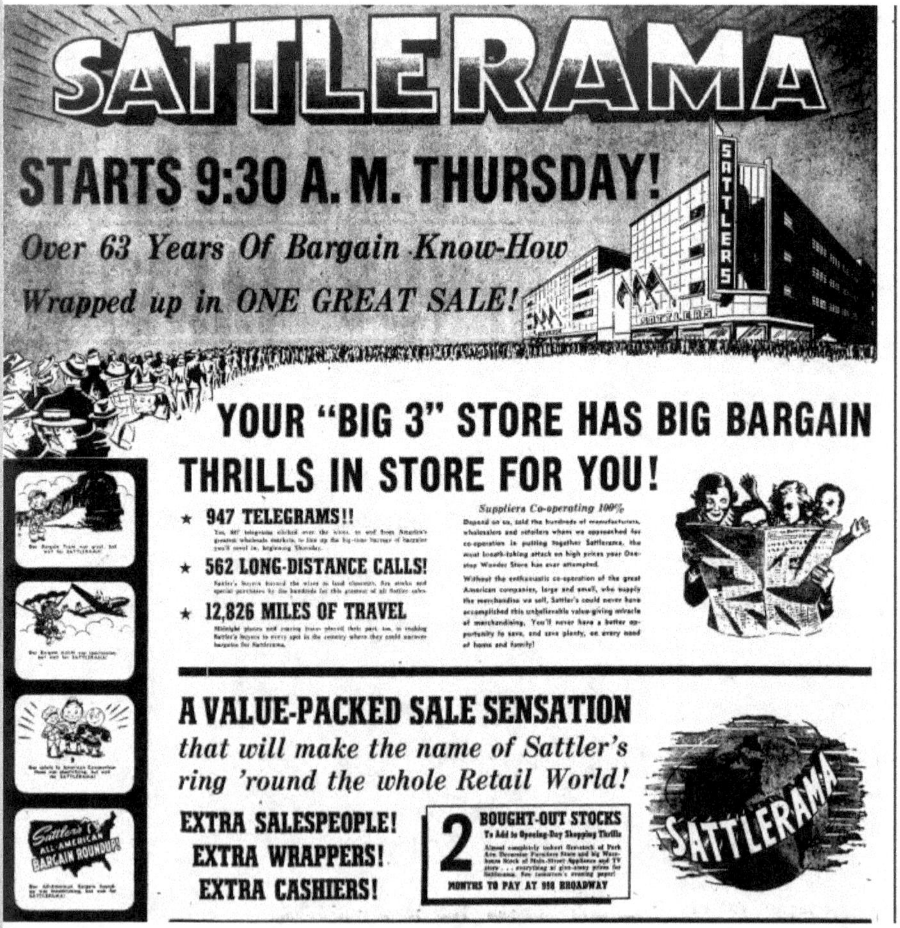

SATTLERAMA

STARTS 9:30 A. M. THURSDAY!

Over 63 Years Of Bargain Know-How Wrapped up in ONE GREAT SALE!

YOUR "BIG 3" STORE HAS BIG BARGAIN THRILLS IN STORE FOR YOU!

★ 947 TELEGRAMS!!

★ 562 LONG-DISTANCE CALLS!

★ 12,826 MILES OF TRAVEL

Suppliers Co-operating 100%

A VALUE-PACKED SALE SENSATION

that will make the name of Sattler's ring 'round the whole Retail World!

EXTRA SALESPEOPLE!
EXTRA WRAPPERS!
EXTRA CASHIERS!

2 BOUGHT-OUT STOCKS

MONTHS TO PAY AT 998 BROADWAY

Sattler's ALL-AMERICAN BARGAIN ROUNDUP!

SATTLERAMA

September 1953

Space Patrol Rocket at Sattler's

Photograph is courtesy of the Daily Sentinel, Rome, NY

Do you remember the 1950's TV series called *Space Patrol*? This is a replica of the spaceship *Tara V* from that sci-fi show about a family on a space adventure. One of the major sponsors for the show was the Ralston Company, who was the maker of Chex cereal at the time. This mobile replica was called the *Ralston Rocket*. It was a 35-foot long exhibit that you could walk through. This was one of two traveling models built by the Coach Company of Los Angeles, California. Admission to the *Ralston Rocket* was one Ralston Wheat or Rice Chex cereal box top, or the box from those Chex cereals. Chex just happened to be on sale at Sattler's that week for 19 cents a box! That admission pass would let a person onto the rocket where you could, "See how ships of the future are made...fire the rockets...and operate the controls!" (474,475)

July 1954

Picnic Time

The Annual Sattler's Social Club Picnic was at Genesee Park. A sign-up for Red Cross blood donations brought in 200 pledges from the almost 1,700 employees and their families at the picnic. Thus, the mobile blood unit from the Red Cross would be visiting Sattler's store in the near future. The day also featured games, contests and prizes, as well as a special treat for picnic goers: a demonstration by the Sheriff's Mounted Division. (476)

August 1954

" Shop and Save at Sattler's"

Another crazy contest at Sattler's was "Can You Teach Your Parakeet to Say 'Shop and Save at Sattler's' ? If You Can, He May Win a Big Cash Prize!" $200 would be awarded to the owner of the first parakeet who could repeat Sattler's slogan, $100 to the second and $50 to the third. This contest started on Sept 2nd and entry blanks were given out until September 11th. The deadline for the contest was December 31st. (477)

September 1954

Giant Treasure Cake

Sattler's 7th Annual Food Fair promised a chance at prizes. A slice of tasty cake was given to each customer who came to the store, as long as quantities lasted. This enormous cake was full of capsules containing certificates for wonderful prizes. The prizes included: 15 sixteen-place setting starter china sets, 12 swing-arm can and bottle openers, 4 General Electric irons, 4 ten-piece kitchen cutlery sets, 3 electric hair dryers, 2 General Electric table radios, 50 bags of groceries, as well as one $29.95 American Character Doll (32 inches tall). (478)

September 1954

Elephant Show at Sattler's

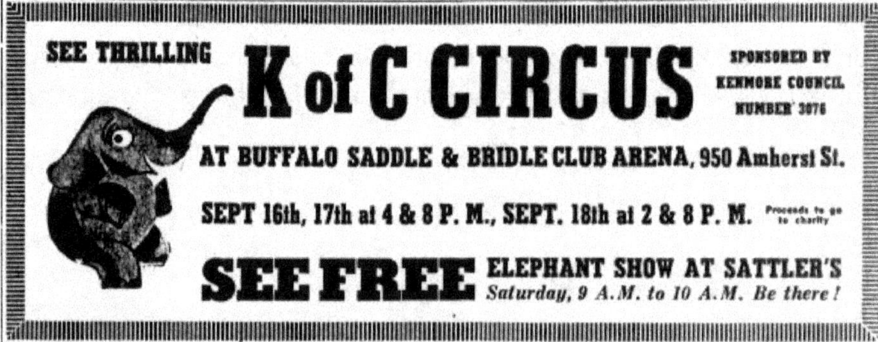

Elephants in Sattler's parking lot! The circus was in town, so why not enjoy a Saturday morning visit with the Knights of Columbus-sponsored Pachyderm Circus? The Knights were thrilled to have the extra publicity, as the proceeds from their circus would purchase air conditioning units at Children's Hospital and help St. Rita's Home for Children in Williamsville, NY. (479-482)

June 1955

Erie County Day

Satter's made a promotional spash that was heard all over Buffalo and Western New York State when it teamed up its annual Erie County Day promotion with National Swim for Health Week. Highlights of the spectacular storewide event were: bathing beauties performing in a swimming pool in front of the store, a full-hour on-the-spot broadcast featuring prominent officials in a *Salute to Erie County* program, a realistic rescue demonstration by the Buffalo Fire Department and a smashing swimsuit sale playing up the Go Caribbean With Catalina Contest. (483, 484)

Photograph courtesy of the Voorhees Family.

June 1955 **25th Anniversary of the Sattler's Social Club**

At the American Automobile Association (AAA) in Clarence, NY, the 25th anniversary of Sattler's Social Club's Summer Picnic event was held with 1,300 employees and their families in attendance. (485)

You may be asking yourself the same question I was wondering. AAA Club? Where is there such a facility owned by AAA? This facility was (and actually still is) located in Clarence, NY, just 17 miles from downtown Buffalo. It is presently owned by the town of Clarence, who bought the clubhouse and the surrounding property in 1957. (486)

The Buffalo Automobile Club in Clarence, NY joined the American Automobile Association in 1903 and owned a large 2-story clubhouse with acres of gardens, woods and fields surrounding the property. The Club also had tennis courts, traps for shooting, an outdoor facility for cookouts and other events, as well as a small lake. (486)

September 1955

Big Quiz Show

$100 in PRIZES!

"Billy Keaton to conduct the show near Sattler's Broadway entrance.

"All contestants will be chosen from the audience; correct answers will win one to twenty-five silver dollars each. Free Peter Paul's Mounds even if you don't know the answer when called on. Double prizes for contestants who have a 'Mounds' wrapper in their possession and are called on in the quiz." (487)

Photograph courtesy of Michael Stark's Family.

October 1955

Operation Good Times

Take a ride on the "998"! Over 1,000 Sattler's employees and 150 guests did just that when the 16-car railroad special pulled out of the Central Terminal to take their passengers on Operation Good Times to Dunkirk. The ride was to kick off Sattler's 8th annual salute to the 13 railroad companies that served the Western New York area.

This was no ordinary train ride for the employees and their guests! The train was decorated with buntings and banners, and Sattler's executives played the roles of engineer, brakeman and conductor. They roamed the railcars in their railroad attire, entertaining and encouraging singing as the cars chugged along.

During this four-hour ride, prizes were awarded every mile. Some of the prizes included hams, turkeys and clothing. When the passengers arrived at the Dunkirk Station, they were greeted with a release of 1,000 helium-filled balloons. Those balloons signaled the beginning of lunch, as southern fried chicken was brought onto the train. Then Wade Stevenson, Buffalo Chamber of Commerce president, boarded the train to talk about the Buffalo Bisons Baseball team and to give away some prizes. Those prizes were blocks of stock for the Buffalo Bisons. (488, 489)

January 1956

Sattlerite Dinner Dance

From left to right: John Woods, Irving Lerick, Aaron Rabow, Grace Harrison, Judge Joseph Sedita and unknown woman. Photograph courtesy of the Voorhees Family.

Sattler's Social Club Dinner Dance took place at the Hotel Statler and was attended by more than 1,000 employees. The large group had to be split into two rooms, but due to the kindness of WBEN-TV, the event was watched on a closed-circuit television so that the entire group was able to enjoy the awards ceremony. Guest speaker was Judge Frank Sedita, who spoke about the work of Small Claims Court, which began proceedings in September of 1955. (490, 491)

August 1956

Outing in Island Park, Cheektowaga

The annual Sattler's Social Club Summer Picnic was held at Island Park in Cheektowaga and was attended by more than 1,000 of the 1,200 Sattler employees. Games were the call of the day with a plethora of prizes, merchandise gift certificates and Buffalo Bisons game tickets. (492)

1957

"Our Hooch Is Pure Hooch"

The sign above the stage reads:

"SATTLER'S SPEAKEASY
.OUR HOOCH IS PURE HOOCH
.NO CHILDREN OR DOGS
.DRINK AT YOUR OWN RISK"

The sign on the right part of the stage reads: *"The Helen Morgan Story." The Helen Morgan Story,* a movie about a sassy jazz singer, starred Ann Blyth and Paul Newman and was big at the box office in 1957. This Sattler's Social Club event had the Jerry Lee Orchestra accompanying an unknown singer. Any information on the singer or the event would be appreciated, and you can let everyone know through *The Sattler's Diary* Facebook page. (493)

Photograph courtesy of the Voorhees Family.

August 1958

Redwood Roadshow

"See the Rings of History"

An 891-year-old redwood log was hauled across the country from the Redwood Forests of California to Sattler's. The redwood log on display was cut down in 1957 and came from a tree that began its life in the year 1066. The first growth ring of 1066 is marked with the Battle of Hastings. Other significant historic dates are also marked on the growth rings throughout the tree. A history of the logging process, from the forest to the sawmill to the finished planks, was on view at the Redwood Roadshow. (494-500)

Ad used with the permission of Georgia-Pacific

September 15 1958 **Robert S. Cornelius Leaves Sattler's**

Robert Cornelius resigned from Sattler's after being Sattler's top promotional and public relations man for over 25 years. He began working at Sattler's in 1932, became the director of marketing and promotional manager of Sattler's in 1946, and by 1953 was Sattler's executive vice president.

Mr. Cornelius left Sattler's to take a job as President of Bahama Sales Planning, Ltd. in Nassau. He was sorely missed by the employees at Sattler's, but continued to see his many friends from the store until his death. (501) When Mr. Cornelius resigned from Sattler's, Aaron Rabow was the only one of the "Three Fine Fellows" remaining at Sattler's.

Governor Nelson Rockefeller (left) with Robert Cornelius.
Photograph courtesy of the Cornelius Family.

September 1958

Christmas Drawing Contest

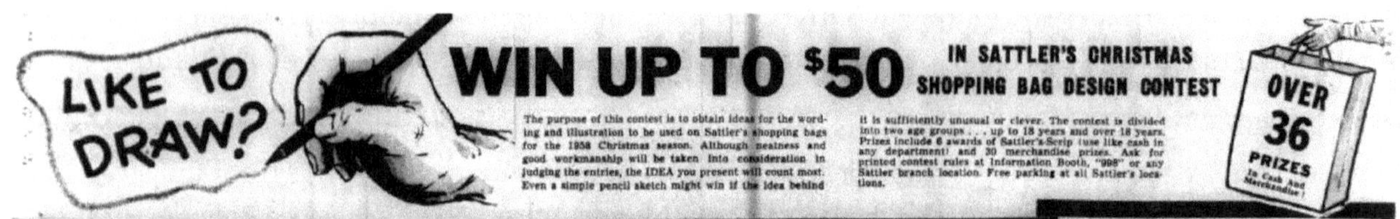

"The purpose of this contest is to obtain ideas for the wording and illustration to be used on Sattler's shopping bags for the 1958 Christmas season. Although neatness and good workmanship will be taken into consideration in judging the entries, the IDEAS you present will count most. Even a simple pencil sketch might win if the idea behind it is sufficiently unusual or clever. The contest is divided into two age groups...up to 18 years and over 18 years. Prizes include 6 awards of Sattler's Scrip (use like cash in any department) and 30 merchandise prizes. Ask for printed contest rules at Information Booth "998" or any Sattler branch location. Free parking at all Sattler's locations." (502, 503)

Sattler's Christmas shopping bag design contest winners:

Group 1: 1st Prize, Patricia Xander, Hamburg, NY
2nd Prize, Emilie Woltz, 755 Best Street, Buffalo 11, NY
3rd Prize, Ruth P. Roberts, 189 Ganson Street, Buffalo 3, NY

Group 2: 1st Prize, Charles Merrifield, 27 Hewitt Avenue, Buffalo, NY
2nd Prize, Pamela Snell, 18 Grandview Avenue, Buffalo 23, NY
3rd Prize, Eileen Connors, 421 Abbott Road, Buffalo 20, NY

November 1958

Dave Irwin, Arctic Explorer

Featuring the Exciting Exhibit of
ESKIMO LAND
With DAVE IRWIN, Arctic Explorer
IN PERSON ON OUR 3rd Floor
SEE! ESKIMO PUPPIES
And Interesting Arctic Souvenirs of Eskimo Land!
FREE! ESKIMO PUPPY

Dave Irwin was an explorer who traveled by dog sled for 3,600 miles across the Arctic. He wrote the book *Alone Across the Top of the World*. He visited Sattler's with an exciting exhibit called *Eskimo Land*, which included his team of huskies, live bear cubs and arctic souvenirs. This exhibit also offered a "simulated dog sled ride across the top of the world." (504-506)

January 1959

Autograph Party at 998

The movie *Perfect Furlough* - starring Tony Curtis and Janet Leigh, and co-starring Brazilian actress Linda Cristal - opened at the Lafayette Theater. Sattler's sponsored the Perfect Furlough Contest and an Autograph Party in the juniors' department at 998, where actress Linda Cristal announced the contest winner.

During the contest you could nominate your favorite service person by entering a written statement, using 50 words or less, expressing why you thought the person you nominated deserved the Perfect Furlough. If your entry was chosen, that service person won an all-expenses-paid weekend in New York City - including round ticket airfare for two, a stay at the famous Hotel Delmonico, tickets to a Broadway show, night club entertainment and tours of New York City. (507-510)

Feb 1959

A Valentine in the Window

The windows at 998 were decked out with antique valentines from the Norcross Greeting Card Museum. At the time, the museum held the most extensive collection of antique valentines in the country, with the collection's earliest valentine dating from 1710. Among the displayed valentines were lacy cards featuring cupids, turtledoves and love-knots, all popular subjects in the 1840's. Included were portraits framed in gold decorations that were all the rage from 1849 to the time of the Civil War. (511, 512)

Photograph courtesy of the Voorhees Family.

March and April 1959

Bannister Baby Display

Constance Bannister, a famous photographer of babies, visited Sattler's photo department in March 1959. In April of 1959, a collection of her baby photographs was displayed in Sattler's windows in connection with Baby Week. It was reported that there were large crowds of spectators who viewed the display.

Bannister was world-renowned for her photograph work featuring children and babies. Her photographs had appeared on magazine covers for *Woman's Day, McCalls, LOOK, Country Gentlemen, Everywoman's, Collier's* and many more. She is also known for her photo calendars and the books: *Bannister Babies, We Were Spies Behind The Iron Curtain and Senator, I'm Glad You Asked Me That!* (513-515)

October 1959

70 Years Young

Sattler's celebrated 70 years in business with fashions from 1889 decked out in its windows. The clothing was on loan from the Buffalo Historical Society. Additionally, the 1889 front pages of both *The Buffalo Evening News* and the *Courier-Express* were enlarged and displayed in the windows at 998.

A bonus during the 70th Anniversary Sale was Sattler's Lucky License Plate Number Game. You had to listen for the public address announcement while shoppping at 998, and the cars that were parked in the lot at Sattler's were randomly chosen. If the owner of that car heard his or her license plate number, $10 in Sattler-Scrip was the prize. (516-518)

October 1959

"If I Were President of Sattler's" Contest

On the 16th of this month, *The Buffalo Evening News* published the following Sattler's ad: "The winner of Sattler's recent 'If I Were President of Sattler's' contest, 14-year-old Michael Mize of 242 Gold Street, Buffalo, will preside as 'President for a Day' at Sattler's tomorrow. Michael will report to work at 10 A.M. and will tour the store with President Aaron Rabow until 11 A.M. He will preside at an advertising meeting, and at noon he will lunch with store executives in the Employees' Cafeteria. From 1 to 4 P. M. he will tour the Broadway & Downtown Home-Stores, the University Plaza, Hamburg & Thruway Plaza Branches, returning in time to close the '998' store at 5:30 P.M. In addition to presiding as President of Sattler's , Michael has won a trip to Washington, D.C. via Capitol Airlines. He will be accompanied by his mother. A freshman at Emerson Vocational High School, Michael is studying commercial food courses. He is a member of the Boy Scout Trinity Troop 87 and is a Junior Aide at the Cradle Beach Crippled Children's Camp School. Congratulations, Michael! Tomorrow is Your Day at Sattler's!" (519, 520)

November 1959

Miss America

Come Meet LEE MERIWETHER
(Formerly Miss America and Featured on Dave Garroway's "Today" Show)
AT SATTLER'S—THURSDAY AT 5 P.M.
Miss Meriwether, Now Starring in "The 4-D Man," Will Be in Our American Girl Shoe Dept., Street Floor, to Meet the Public and Autograph Pictures.
500 AUTOGRAPHED PICTURES FREE.
"The 4-D Man" Opens Nov. 13 at Basil's Pictures.

Lee Meriwether, who is known for being a model and actress, was originally thrust into the public eye when she was crowned Miss America in 1955. Her acting roles included playing Catwoman in the 1966 *Batman* movie and two appearances in the 1967 *Batman* series. She also appeared in episodes of *Star Trek, The Fugitive, Time Tunnel, Mission Impossible, Perry Mason, Barnaby Jones* and many other TV series and movies. (521, 522)

December 1959

Employees Wear Christmas Buttons

"Sattler's Has That 'Home-Town' Touch!

"Can't you just feel that homey atmosphere the minute you step inside the door at '9-9-8'? There's something electric and exciting about the atmosphere at Sattler's, and despite the crowds that are natural during the Holiday Season, you still get that friendly greeting and cheerful attention from every member of the Sattler Store Family.

"Approach anyone wearing the big plastic Christmas button with your problem or question and you will get a prompt, courteous and helpful response.

"Because, you see, Sattler's is just like home and we always take time to greet our friends and neighbors. So do your Christmas shopping at Sattler's and enjoy your gift buying more." (523)

"This will give you a lift if Christmas shopping is getting you down...

"Last week we installed (thanks to the N.Y. Telephone Co.) a series of red telephones in our children's division on the second floor at '9-9-8'. When the youngster picks up the phone which has a sign saying 'Listen to Santa on our special Christmas Phone' he hears a jolly 45-second recorded message from ol' Kris Kringle himself.

"Well, you should see the looks on the faces of the kids while they're listening on the phone! They glow like a sunbeam and their eyes light up like a sky full of stars. It warms your heart to see such rapture. Merry Christmas Shopping at Sattler's!" (524)

March 1960

Sandra Dee

Sandra Dee was scheduled to make a personal appearance at an Autograph Party on March 28th. Dee was touring and making personal appearances promoting the full-length feature cartoon *The Snow Queen,* which was being shown at local theaters. Days before Dee's scheduled appearance at Sattler's, she was mobbed in a department store in Syracuse, NY by 4,000 fans. "My dress was torn and they took my gloves," she said. "I was really delighted." Dee ended up cancelling her appearance at Sattler's because of illness, and she was replaced by 14-year-old Patty McCormack, whose voice was also featured in the motion picture *The Snow Queen*. Dee was a motion picture star who appeared in movies such as *Gidget* and *Tammy*. (525-531)

May 1960

Tanks in the Parking Lot

"See the 'Power of Peace' in the Armed Forces Display in Sattler's '998' Parking Lot"

Another crowded parking lot event at Sattler's! In the past, Sattler's parking lot had elephants, clowns, a Navy fighter plane, a 35-foot spaceship, dancing dogs and trick ponies. But on this Armed Forces Day, a "Nike" 2-piece mobile unit, 155-MM self-propelled Howitzer and an M-48 Patton Tank were on display. There was Army personnel in constant attendance to answer questions, courtesy of 27th Armored Div. NY National Guard. You never knew what you would see when you visited Sattler's! (532, 533)

June 1960

Andy Williams Visits Sattler's

In June of 1960, Andy Williams made a personal appearance at Sattler's. He was in town for a show that evening at the Glen Casino. (534) Unfortunately, that is all the information I have about this event. If you remember it or have any details, please go to *The Sattler's Diary* Facebook page and share your story.

I remember my parents' playing their Andy Williams albums back in the 1960's. "Moon River," "The Hawaiian Wedding Song," "The Shadow of Your Smile" and "Born Free" were just a few of the hits back then, most of which were not recorded until after his appearance at Sattler's. Andy Williams' songs "It's the Most Wonderful Time of the Year" and "Happy Holidays" are still being played on the radio every Christmas season as holiday favorites.

June 1960

Imogene Coca and King Donovan at Sattler's

More movie stars visited Sattler's in the summer of 1960! Both Imogene Coca and King Donovan stopped into the store for a personal appearance. Free photographs of the stars were given away at Sattler's, as well as a chance to win one of 25 tickets to see *The Four Poster* or a weekend trip to Prudhomme's Garden Centre Theatre in Vineland Station, Ontario, Canada, where Coca and Donovan were currently appearing. (535)

June 1960

Hugh O'Brian Is Mobbed at Sattler's

Television and movie star Hugh O'Brian was mobbed by 3,000 fans during a personal appearance at Sattler's. Known for his role of playing Marshal Wyatt Earp, this former U.S. Marine was a local born in Rochester. After a 30-minute autograph-signing session, O'Brian's fans swamped the rear of the store and flooded into the parking lot. In order to leave the store and return to his car parked in the Sattler's lot, it was necessary for O'Brian to be escorted by 4 U.S. Marines. O'Brian appeared in the movies: *The Life and Legend of Wyatt Earp, Come Fly with Me, Love Has Many Faces, Ten Little Indians, Cruise Into Terror, Night Friends, Wyatt: Return to Tombstone,* and many more. (594,595)

September 1960

Hell to Eternity

World War II, June 1944: Private First Class Guy Gabaldon, an 18-year-old Marine, was a scout for the Intelligence Unit during an attack on Saipan. He single-handedly captured over 1,000 Japanese soldiers and was awarded the Navy Cross Medal.

There was a personal appearance and book-signing session with Guy Gabaldon at Sattler's. If you purchased a copy of the book, *Hell to Eternity,* you not only received an autographed copy at Sattler's, but also received passes to see the movie *Hell to Eternity* at the Basil's Lafayette Theater. *Hell to Eternity* is a movie based on the war story of Guy Gabaldon. (536, 537)

October 1960

Polish Cultural Treasure at Sattler's

Reproductions of the manuscripts and papers of Polish composer and pianist Frederic Chopin were exhibited on the main floor at Sattler's. A mini Polish Folk Festival took place in front of 998, and it included the Chopin Singing Society's Male Chorus, Villa Maria Alumnae Choir and the Merry Tatra Dancers. All for your enjoyment at Sattler's! (538)

November 1960

Santa Claus Parade Sponsored by Sattler's

Those Santa Claus Parades that came down Broadway were magical! There were movie stars, singing stars, local celebrities, circus animals, balloons, floats, clowns, marching bands and SANTA! It warms the hearts to bring back those fond memories on Broadway, as that was the happening place to be. Sattler's sponsored the Broadway Santa Claus Parade for many wonder-filled years for wide-eyed children of all ages.

Getting ready for the Santa Claus Parade was no small feat. In October 1960, Sattler's announced a yearly contest to entice a beautiful young woman to become Sattler's Ice Queen: "In 25 words or less tell us why you want to be Sattler's Ice Queen." The Ice Queen in 1960 was crowned at the opening night of the Ice Capades in Memorial Auditorium on November 1st. The reigning winner in 1960 was Miss Penny Martin from Walden Avenue, who was a senior at Immaculate Heart of Mary Academy. Sure she won some lovely prizes: a trip for two to

Bermuda, a weekend stay in Ellicottville during its winter carnival and a night at the Town Casino, but her most important job as Sattler's Ice Queen was to ride with her court on the Ice Queen Float and reign over the 13th annual Santa Claus Parade.

The Santa Claus Parade had become the official start of the Christmas shopping season in Buffalo. In 1960, it began the morning of November 12th along Broadway, from Memorial Drive past Sattler's to Fox Street. In front of Sattler's, there was a reviewing stand where WBEN's TV and radio personality Mike Mearian was the master of ceremonies. He was joined by city of Buffalo dignitaries and Sattler's store executives. There was a bandstand opposite Sattler's reviewing stand where the Grand Island Band began playing at 9:00 A.M. The weather was cool this November morning, but snow-free, and the parade began at 9:15 A.M. sharp!

The first Broadway Santa Claus Parade was in 1948, and in 1960 there were over 100,000 people lining Broadway to view the parade. Troops of Boy Scouts collected canned goods from the crowds of parade-goers for a Thanksgiving and Christmas food collection that was distributed to the needy by the Salvation Army. The food collection was a success, with over 3 tons of food donated.

In 1960, the Santa Claus Parade featured the theme of fairy tales, with more than 40 balloons and storybook floats. Some of the themed balloons included: Three Little Kittens, Cinderella, Sleeping Beauty, Prince Charming, Little Boy Blue, The Old Woman in the Shoe and Old King Coal. There were many marching units and bands in the parade, and they included a 95-piece marching band from the University of Buffalo that was complete with a drum major and majorettes. Other bands and marching units were: Bishop Timon High Caballeros, Adam Plewacki Post Color Guard, Sheriff's Mounted Division, Melodies Drum Corps, Buffalo Crossing Guards, 40 and 8 Locomotive and Box Car, Big Tree Volunteer Firemen's Drum Corps, Rescue Drum Corps, Lockettes Girls Drum Corps, the Lockport Blazers Drum Corps, as well as equipment from the Buffalo Fire Department.

In addition, recording and TV star Tony Bennett appeared in the parade! Sattler's Ice Queen, Miss Penny Martin, and Mr. Universe, Bruce Randall, joined the celebration and waved to the crowds. Mr. Universe had won his title in London, England and was a world champion weightlifter. But, as you may suspect, the man himself - Santa Claus - appeared in a sleigh complete with reindeer and stole the show.

The festivities didn't end at the conclusion of the parade, as parade goers continued to enjoy their day with a trip to Sattler's. Toyland was on the third floor at Sattler's, and if you entered Lollipop Land in Toyland you not only received a free lollipop, but you could get your picture taken with Santa Claus! There were times that year when you might have to wait a few minutes to have your picture taken with Santa because he might be busy answering his phone. Sattler's had set up a mobile phone on the second floor of the store, where one of the Sattler's Charm School graduates invited children to spend some time on the phone talking to Santa himself! (539-548)

April 1961

Popular Nite Club Singing Star

Meet Miss Roberta Sherwood in person at Sattler's! She performed in the main window at 998 on a Wednesday afternoon. There were 500 autographed pictures of Miss Sherwood given away. At the time, she was appearing at Harry Altman's Town Casino. Known for her movie role as the maid in *The Courtship of Eddie's Father,* she also appeared in the shows of *Joey Bishop, Lucy, Tennessee Ernie Ford* and *Donna Reed*. Roberta recorded 19 record albums, mostly with Decca Records. (549, 550)

May 1961

Dad's Trip to Paris

"In 25 words or less you need to complete the statement, 'My Dad Is The World's Greatest Because...' Nothing to buy. Just get an entry blank to fill out and deposit it into the blue barrels in the Men's Department."

Winner of the Sattlerama Holiday Father's Day Contest was Kenneth R. Mikos, 787 Seventh Street, Buffalo, NY.

Another drawing for a free trip for two to Paris was open to all Sattler's customers. You were to fill out the Sattlerama entry blank and drop it off at Sattler's. The winner of that Paris trip for two went to John Lacks of 75 Westfield Road, Eggertsville, NY. (551, 552)

May 1961

"Say It with Flags"

On May 5th, 1961, Commander Alan Shepard, Jr. became the first American in space. He flew 116 miles above the earth on the spacecraft Mercury, and his flight lasted about fifteen minutes. The flight was a great source of pride for Americans. With Armed Forces Day and Memorial Day just a few days away, the Courier Express and WEBR Radio teamed up to encourage people to fly the American flag. The goal of the campaign was to have an additional 10,000 new flags flying in the Buffalo area by Memorial Day. Sattler's joined in on the campaign, supplying 2,000 flags - with flagpoles and mounting brackets - at their 998 store for distribution. "We are very pleased with the opportunity to back up this most important idea, not only because we want to salute Memorial Day, but because we feel that every American should fly the flag on every official occasion throughout the year," said Sattler's President Aaron Rabow. (603-607, 613)

"Say It With Flags"
On Memorial Day

Join the Say It With Flags Campaign, sponsored by The Courier-Express and WEBR. Salute this nation's heritage and its future . . . fly your own flag on Memorial Day and every legal and national holiday thereafter.

Memorial Day is dedicated to heroes, heroic sacrifices and historical memories. This year, Western New Yorkers will be flying flags also to signify their pride in the history-making space flight of Astronaut Alan B. Shepard Jr.

Display Your Patriotism!

June 1961

Debbie Reynolds' Gown on Display in 998's Window

"Complete in 25 words or less the statement: 'I would like to be married in the replica of the wedding gown worn by Debbie Reynolds in *The Pleasure of His Company* because...' The winner will receive a size 9 wedding gown replica."

Winner of Sattler's Sattlerama Debbie Reynolds' Wedding Gown Contest was Hilda Mae Cotton of Broadway in Alden, New York. (553-556) Hilda said that she was shopping in Sattler's with her grandmother when she noticed the contest for the wedding gown. She quickly filled out her contest application while she was in the store. She can't remember just what she said in her 25-word statement, but she does remember that she was shocked when the mail came with a notice that she had won the replica of Debbie Reynold's wedding gown and veil!

At 17, Hilda was not ready to get married. When she married a few years later, she did not use the dress that she won at Sattler's. However, she did go back to Sattler's to buy the gown in which she walked down the aisle, before enjoying 48 ½ years of marriage with her husband Richard.

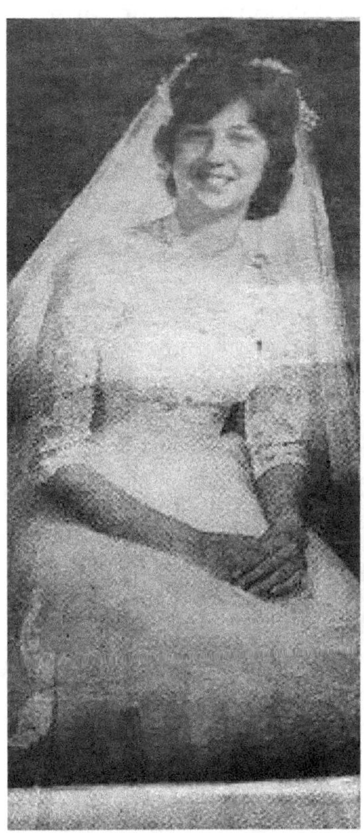

"The floor-length gown is designed with three layers of net over a satin skirt. The bodice is of fine embroidered net. A floor-length veil falls from a headband of lily-of-the-valley and is waist length in front." (612)

Bride photograph courtesy of the Alden Advertiser.

On the right is a photograph of Hilda Mae with the wedding gown she won from Sattler's in 1961.

Photograph courtesy of David Voorhees.

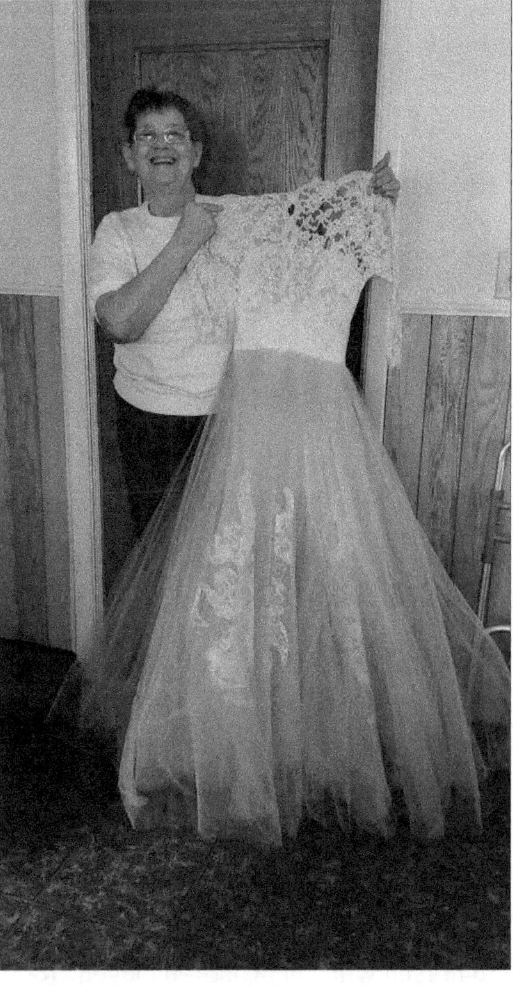

June 1961

All-American Game at the Old Rockpile

Sattler's President, Aaron Rabow, announced, "Four All-American football players will appear at Sattler's to participate in the public drawing for 10 personally autographed footballs." Those players are: Al Vanderbush, Joe Bellino, Tom Brown and Dan LaRose.

"Sattler's purchased $15,000 worth of reserved seat tickets to support the All-American ball game. Sattler's is supporting this civic enterprise, which will put Buffalo on the map as the sports center of America," said Rabow. The All-American Game was played at War Memorial Stadium from 1961-1965. (610,611)

October 1961

Meet Aunt Jemima

Christmas breakfast came early at Sattler's, and it was served by Aunt Jemima! Sattler's started their Christmas events a little early, as Santa's Workshop Float, from North Pole, NY was on display in front of 998. When finished checking out the Christmas float, you could stop at Sattler's parking lot where a free breakfast was being served up by Aunt Jemima herself. That's right! A free breakfast of Aunt Jemima Pancakes, Tang Breakfast Drink, Boscul Coffee and Log Cabin Syrup. And a free balloon and lollipops for the kids! (557)

November 1961

Recognize Anyone?

(608)

May 1962

Mother's Day Party at Sattler's

Sattler's invited 500 mothers as guests for a Mother's Day Dinner Party at the Glen Park Casino to enjoy a dinner of filet mignon and a huge Mother's Day cake. If you filled out an entry blank at Sattler's and your name was drawn as a winner, you enjoyed an afternoon with one of your children, compliments of Sattler's. Sattler's also provided amusement rides for the kids so that Mom could enjoy a few minutes to herself while her children played. (609)

October 1962

Fire-Sire and Spanner

Sattler's had another contest in October of 1962. The contest was conducted jointly by Sattler's and the Buffalo Fire Department to help promote Fire Prevention Week. Two 6-week old Dalmatian pups needed names, and you could come see them in the window at Sattler's!

The contest was for children under the age of 16. The winner of the Name that Dog Contest received one of the Dalmatian pups, while the other was given to the firehouse in the winner's neighborhood. That pup would be used as the station mascot.

The winning name chosen was "Fire-Sire" and the winning entry was from Nigel J. Houenstein of Doyal Ave. The other Dalmatian pup went to Engine 35 on the corner of Clinton and Bailey .

Nigel recalled that the day to pick up his puppy began with a visit to Buffalo City Hall. His next stop was to the main headquarters of the Buffalo Fire Department, where the two Dalmation puppies were being kept. Nigel was given first pick of the two pups. He recalled that his mother urged him to select the puppy with the patch on his eye, and that's what he did. When the dog came home with Nigel, the name Fire-Sire didn't last. "Mom started calling him Pumpkin," said Nigel. Pumpkin quickly became a loving member of the household, and years later a new baby in the family was charmed by Pumpkin's gentle disposition, as the baby would hold his bottle in one hand and twirl Pumpkin's ear with the other. Pumpkin lived a good long life, about 12 or 13 years.

The Dalmation that went to Engine 35 was named Spanner, after the spanner wrench to tighten and loosen fire hose connections. Spanner became part of the one-dog, forty-four man fire unit at Engine 35. As a rookie, Spanner learned that the fireman's pole was not his friend. It only took one lesson to learn that. One day he attempted to follow the men down the fire pole to access the main floor of the station house. Spanner landed on the concrete floor below. He soon recovered and learned to use the stairs.

When an alarm sounded at the station and the front door of the pumper truck was open, Spanner was the first to hop aboard and man his post. He was the friendly greeter at the station and was a welcome sight to the children who visited on their way home from school. His stealthy ability to sneak over to the Clinton Farmers' Market, across the street from the fire station, and visit with vendors and marketgoers usually insured him at least an apple to bring home for a snack. He also earned top honors for bravery and for doing his job at fire scenes, as he once kept a drunkard at a fire scene pinned in place until the unruly man was escorted away by the police. However, when it came to the first crash of thunder he would seek the comfort of the lap of his nearest fire station family member. Spanner died a hero's death as he preceded the firefighters into the remains of a burned building. Spanner stepped on a live electrical wire and died, sparing the possibility that one of the firemen could have suffered that same fate. (558-560)

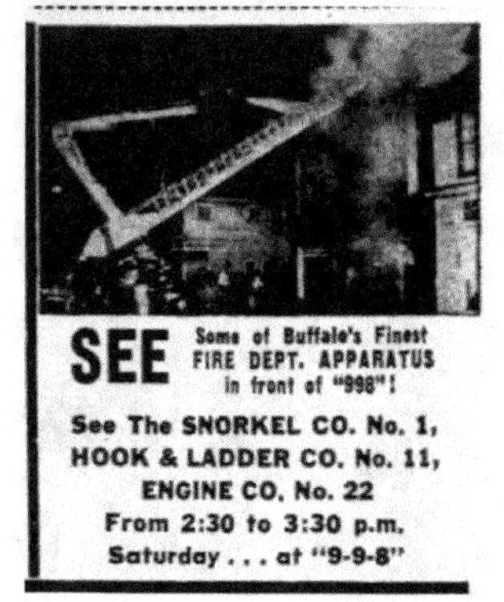

February 1963

Aaron Rabow Retires

It was the end of an era. What a wonderful leader Aaron Rabow was. Employees were truly saddened to see him retire. Mr. Rabow joined Sattler's in 1927 as a buyer for women's wear. By 1931, he was the store's merchandise manager; in 1941, he became vice president; and in 1948 he became executive vice president of Sattler's. In 1953, when Charles Hahn sold Sattler's and the store was purchased by Irving Levick, Mr. Rabow was appointed as the store's president. In 1963, the employees of Sattler's said goodbye to a father figure who was kind, compassionate and caring. Mr. Rabow was truly the heart and soul of Sattler's for so many years, and he was one of the reasons that employees felt that Sattler's was family. (561-563)

Photograph courtesy of the Voorhees Family.

February 1963

New President at Sattler's

Ralph Wilcove was announced as the new president of Sattler's, having started at Sattler's in 1947. In 1950 he was appointed as assistant comptroller, in 1956 as vice president and comptroller, and in 1959 as treasurer of the store. In 1961, Wilcove was made the executive vice president. (561-563)

Photograph courtesy of the Voorhees Family.

January 1964

75th Diamond Jubilee Dinner Dance

Sattler's was 75 years young, and the employees celebrated at the 33rd annual Sattler's Social Club Dinner Dance with the presentation of service awards. The dinner dance took place at Kleinhans Music Hall. The program began in Kleinhans' main auditorium with the official closure of the 1963 Club administration by the president of the Club, Irene Luczak, along with treasurer of the Club, Grace Harrison. Next was an introduction of the 1964 Sattler's Social Club candidates and the announcement of the election results for the officers, followed by the presentation of service awards. After the service awards were presented, all of the Club members proceeded to the Mary Seton Room for dinner and dancing.

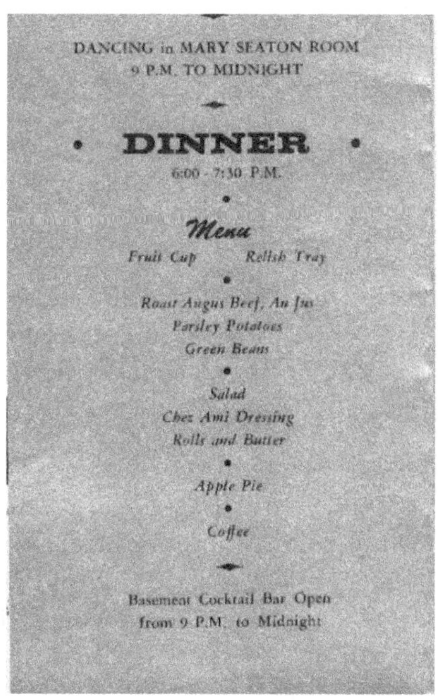

DANCING in MARY SEATON ROOM
9 P.M. TO MIDNIGHT

DINNER
6:00 - 7:30 P.M.

Menu

Fruit Cup *Relish Tray*

Roast Angus Beef, Au Jus
Parsley Potatoes
Green Beans

Salad
Chez Ami Dressing
Rolls and Butter

Apple Pie

Coffee

Basement Cocktail Bar Open
from 9 P.M. to Midnight

Don't Give a Voice to Those Who Don't Deserve To Be Heard

In the late 1970's, Sattler's was acquired by United Department Stores. The stories that I've been told by former employees about working at Sattler's during its final years, including how they were treated by management, are unworthy of being included in this book. The people of Buffalo who worked, shopped and built Sattler's to the fine store it was deserve to remember the store as a place where there was fellowship, a caring staff, and owners who supported and nurtured a company for the people of the city they loved. Long live the memories of all Sattlerites!

"It Happened at Sattler's"

Over the last 35 years I have become the owner of boxes of archives and photos related to Sattler's. I have dug through offices and family members' homes looking for Sattler's memorabilia. I have made hundreds of phone calls and interviewed hundreds of people. Hardly a day goes by when I don't discover an interesting tidbit about Sattler's Department Store or something about a Sattler family relative. I am sure there are so many more stories out there, and that is what I would love to share as it becomes available.

If you have information you would like to share about Sattler's, please go to *The Sattler's Diary* Facebook page and share it with everyone. If you recognize someone in a photo from the book and can put a name to a face, that would be a wonderful. If you see a contest that was written about in the book and you are willing to share information about one of the winners, thank you. If you worked at Sattler's or have fond memories of an employee or a special moment at Sattler's, we welcome you to share it with us.

The information that you are about to read is out of chronological order. I did it that way because it enables me to end with one of my favorite parts of this book, **YOUR STORIES**!

As an introduction to those stories, here are the details of a contest called "It Happened at Sattler's," which took place in February of 1959: In 100 words or less, you were to write about a unique shopping experience that you had at Sattler's. Winners received a $10 merchandise gift certificate.

This is what was written in the newspaper on February 22, 1959: "Thanks to the thousands of friends who wrote to tell us of their truly interesting, humorous and unique experiences while shopping at Sattler's. Sorry we couldn't give every one of you a prize, but we're mighty proud of the nice things you wrote - and we'll keep trying to make Sattler's an interesting and thrifty store to shop!"

Winners:

Mrs. Arthur Griffin, 441 Wabash Ave., Kenmore
Mrs. Clare Holinski, 302 North Ogden St.
Mrs. Albert Hulin, 79 Bissell Ave., Depew

Mrs. Clarence Machemer, Sr., 88 N. Buffalo Rd. Orchard Pk.
Mrs. Edward Drdul, 126 Longnecker St.
Mrs. Irene R. Joyce, 80 Victory Ave., Lackawanna
Mrs. Marie Stroka, 170 Prospect Ave.
Mrs. Carol Bonnas, 77 Coit St.
Mrs. Soren Nielsen, 1332 Union Rd., W. Seneca
Mrs. T.V. O'Connor, 167 Peach St.
(564-567)

Unfortunately, I don't have the winning stories from 1959. However, I've been fortunate to hear so many fond memories about Sattler's Department Store, and about the Sattler, Hahn, Rabow and Cornelius families, that I thought I would end with the memories that have been told to me. Sattler's may be gone, but the joy of its memories will remain in the hearts of Buffalonians.

What Are Your Memories of Sattler's?

The following are memories and stories of Sattler's that were told to me by Buffalonians.

Oh, Christmas Tree!

This is a story told by the great-grandson of John G. Sattler, Charlie Hahn. It is about his grandparents, Charles Hahn, former president of Sattler's, and his wife Marion Sattler Hahn. On Christmas Eve back in the 1930's, Charles Hahn went out on his lunch hour to buy a Christmas tree. He tied it to the top of his car and went back to work at the store. At the end of the day, the employees had a Christmas party and boozed it up a bit.

When Charles Hahn left the store, it was late in the evening so he drove home. On entering the house, his wife told him that the kids were in bed and she asked him to bring in the Christmas tree. When Charles went back to the car, there was no Christmas tree! Mr. Hahn and Marion got back in the car and took his route back to the store, hoping that the tree fell off the car on his way home or perhaps in the parking lot at Sattler's.

Unfortunately, there was no Christmas tree to be found, and it was so late that no one was selling Christmas trees at that hour. You might have guessed that this couple was not about to disappoint their two young children by letting them wake up on Christmas morning with no tree! Since Mr. Hahn had the store keys, he unlocked the store, and both he and Marion took a tree out of the front window at Sattler's, untrimmed it and took it home. At home they re-trimmed the tree, wrapped the presents, and then went to bed. Twenty minutes after the Hahns were in bed, their children, Jack and Jill, woke up and shouted that Santa had come. Christmas was a merry one for Charles and Marion Hahn's children!

Grandpa Loved to Travel

Mr. Sattler loved to travel. He visited his relatives in Germany and traveled throughout Europe. He would go to Florida and the West Coast, and traveled across the country. His thoughts of home and family were never far away, as is seen in the copy of these personal letters between him and his grandson, Jack.

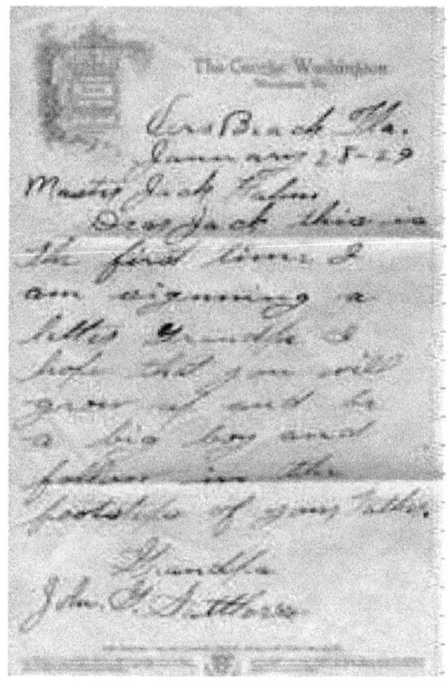

Vero Beach Fla.
January 28-29
Master Jack Hahn
Dear Jack this is the first time I am signing a letter Grandpa I hope that you will grow up and be a big boy and follow in the footsteps of your father.
Grandpa
John G. Sattler

Vero Beach, Fla.
January 28-29

Master Jack Hahn

Dear Jack this is the first time I am signning {sic} a letter Grandpa. I hope that you will grow up and be a big boy and follow in the footsteps of your father.

Grandpa
John G. Sattler

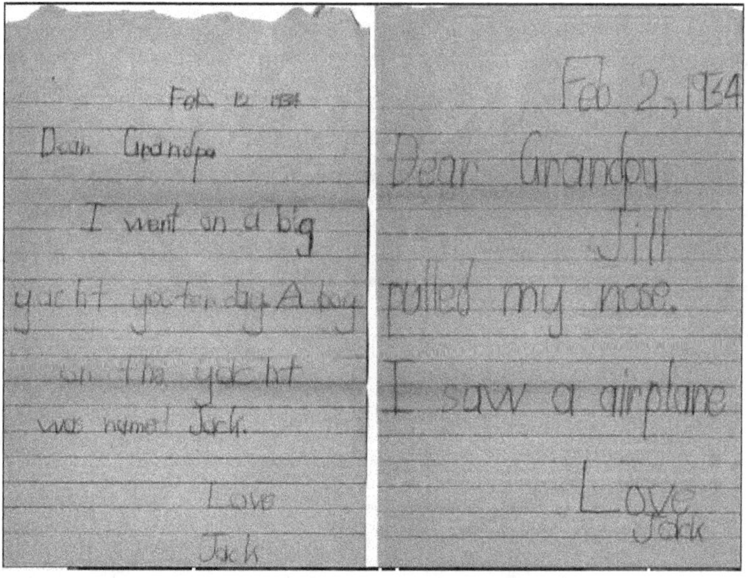

Feb 12 1934
Dear Grandpa
I went on a big yacht yesterday A boy on the yacht was named Jack.
Love
Jack

Feb 2, 1934
Dear Grandpa
Jill pulled my nose.
I saw a airplane
Love
Jack

These letters are courtesy of the Hahn Family

Feb. 12, 1934

Dear Grandpa

I went on a big yacht yesterday. A boy on the yacht was named Jack.

Love
Jack

Feb 2, 1934

Dear Grandpa

Jill pulled my nose yesterday. I saw a {sic} airplane.

Love
Jack

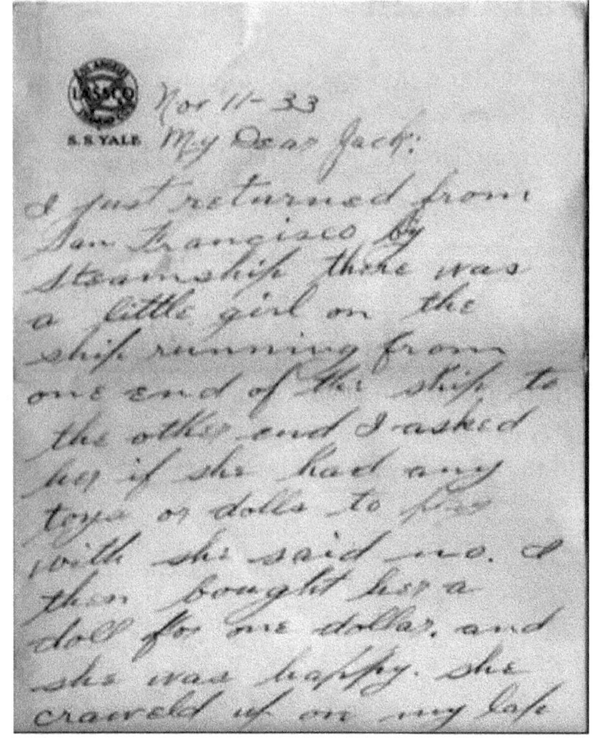

S.S. YALE

Nov 11-33
My Dear Jack:
I just returned from
San Francisco by
Steamship there was
a little girl on the
ship running from
one end of the ship to
the other end and I asked
her if she had any
toys or dolls to play
with she said no. I
then bought her a
doll for one dollar, and
she was happy. she
crawled up on my lap

and thanked me for
the doll. the little girl
was 4 years old. we
started on the ship at
5 O clock in the evening
from San Francisco at
11 O.Clock the next
morning we landed
in Los angeles about
450 miles this trip with
the state room two
meals and evening
entertamment of dancing
music singing cost $9.00
this ocean trip was
fine. I wish you was
with me Jack.
Best wishes to
you all GranDad.

This letter is courtesy of the Hahn Family.

Nov 11-33

My Dear Jack:

I just returned from San Francisco by Steamship. There was a little girl on the ship running from one end of the ship to the other end. I asked her if she had any toys or dolls to play with. She said, "No." I then bought her a doll for one dollar and she was happy. She crawled up on my lap and thanked me for the doll. The little girl was 4 years old. We started on the ship at 5 o'clock in the evening from San Francisco, at 11 o'clock the next morning we landed in Los Angeles about 450 miles. This trip with the state room two meals and evening entertainment of dancing, music, singing cost $9.00. This ocean trip was fine. I wish you was {sic} with me Jack.

Best wishes to you all
GranDad

Aug. 30-32
Mrs. G. Luippold

Dear Cousin,

I received a letter from Julia stating that you are not well. I hope that you have fully recovered when I return. If convenient, I would like to call on you and tell you what I saw at the former home of the Sattler's at Grasellenbach, if you prefer calling at my home I would be pleased to have you come and bring Mr. and Mrs. Macker and their family. With best wishes for a speedy recovery,

Your cousin
John G. Sattler

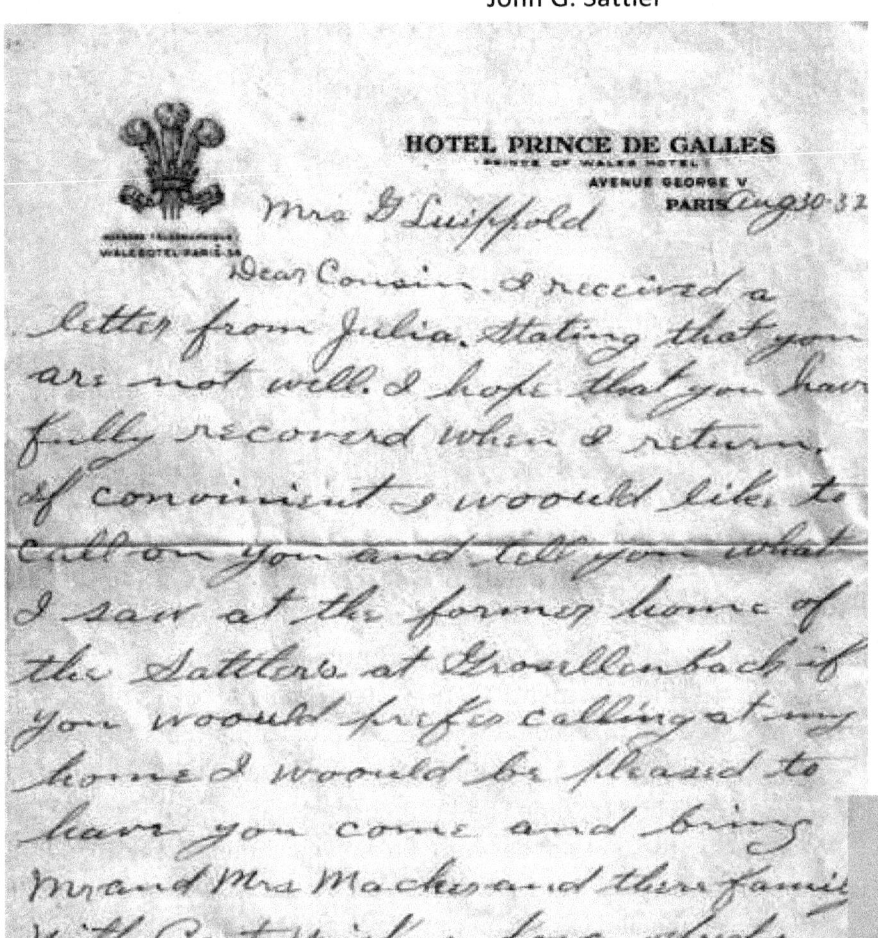

HOTEL PRINCE DE GALLES
PRINCE OF WALES HOTEL
AVENUE GEORGE V
PARIS Aug 30-32

Mrs G Luippold

Dear Cousin I received a letter from Julia stating that you are not well. I hope that you have fully recoverd when I return. If convinient I would like to call on you and tell you what I saw at the former home of the Sattlers at Grosellenbach if you would prefer calling at my home I would be pleased to have you come and bring Mr and Mrs Mackes and their family With Best Wishes for a speedy recovery. Your Cousin
John G Sattler

This letter is to John G. Sattler's cousin, Gertrude Habberman Luippold, who lived in Buffalo.

This letter and the photo are courtesy of Adam D. Gibbons.

Gertrude Habberman Luippold

~~~~~

Jim K. was living on Johnson Street in Buffalo when this happened to him: "I was standing in line one time at a counter in the basement of Sattler's where they sold all the food. The line to be served was really long. A man came up and stood at the counter but not in line. He was just staring and staring at the goods that were being sold. After a while, a woman tells him 'You can stand there until your ass drops off, get in line!'"

~~~~~

Sharon R., a former Sattler's employee who worked at the Boulevard Mall store, remembers 998 fondly, particularly that: "Sattler's had the most delicious real French custard."

~~~~~

Mary Anne S. of 1024 Lovejoy had her first chocolate ice cream cone at Sattler's. She remembers when they sold cottage cheese at 3 pounds for $1.

~~~~~

Betty, a patron at the Happy Swallow restaurant on Fillmore Street, remembers when she would shop in the basement for tub butter and ice cream waffle cookies.

~~~~~

Photograph courtesy of the Voorhees Family.

Ann O., who lived on Rother Street, remembers: "On Saturday we did our weekly shopping at Sattler's. But we would go there at least twice a week. There were many, many counters in Sattler's grocery department in the basement. There were counters for everything. For coffee, all kinds of coffee and butter, tub butter, all the different types of butter and wonderful soft custard. The first time I had soft custard was at Sattler's. And the donuts that were baked and coming down the rollers. My mother would give me .50 cents and I could go and get a paper carton and fill it with pickles or olives. During the wintertime they had small samples of Lipton Chicken Noodle Soup. That was great on those cold days in winter. When I was a teenager I would go there with my girlfriends at Christmas time and watch the kids visiting Santa. They had a car on tracks for kids to ride while waiting for Santa."
~~~~~

"Cool and Crisp as a Lettuce Leaf"

Jill, granddaughter of John G. Sattler recalls: "My grandfather would stand outside the store to greet customers. When I came to visit him at the store, I would ask him why his head was so bumpy. He would take me in his office that was on the first floor of 998. His office was very accessible to anyone who wanted to speak with him. He was a very tall man and he had a big wooden desk and he always kept hard candy in the left desk drawer for me.

I would go and sit on the lap of the switchboard operator, Julia, and I would be allowed to plug in the switchboard cables to the extension connection. The best thing was that I was allowed to make announcements at the store over their intercom system. One of my favorite announcements that I remember was 'Buy the new spring hats; they are cool and crisp as a lettuce leaf.' I really loved the switchboard operator; she was always so kind."

Animals in the Parking Lot at Sattler's

Bert H., curator of Waterfront Memories and More Museum said: "Sattler's had tents and animals in their parking lot. I would prefer to be in the parking lot to look at the animals or fish or whatever they had going on rather than being in the store. The kids shopping in the store were very well behaved."

Stockings

For those of you who don't remember, there were shortages of different commodities during WWII and one of them was silk. Since silk primarily came from Japan, it was a restricted commodity. Silk was used by the armed forces for parachutes and for the powder bags of naval guns. Nylon was commonly used in different manufacturing processes to support the military, such as strengthening parachute lines and tire rubber. As a result, B. F. Goodrich had an ad in 1943 that stated, "We Borrowed Their (women's) 'Nylons' to Make Tires for the Navy." (568)

Monica K. remembers: "During World War II the hosiery department was in the back of the store, and what huge lines there would be to get stockings!"

Bing Crosby at Sattler's

Mrs. Eleanor S., who is 96 years old and lived on Wilson Street many years ago, walked with her two boys to shop at Sattler's because of all the great bargains on jewelry and clothes. "I bought lots and lots and lots of clothes at Sattler's. They had good bargains. I still got those clothes and I wear them. I wash them in Woolite and hang them up, don't iron them. Yeah, I still wear them. I remember the car giveaways, but I never won nothing at Sattler's." She also said "Bing Crosby came to Sattler's; it was in the summertime."

Shoe Wars

Joseph K.: "I would wait with my wagon at the Broadway Market while my mother would be shopping at Sattler's. One time they had a tightrope walker. The line was stretched from the Broadway Market to Sattler's.

"You could go up to the third floor of Sattler's, and they had a barrel that was filled with marbles. You got a handful of marbles for a nickel.

"There was a machine, when you got off the escalator on the third floor; you would put a penny in and when you stand on it, it would shake. It was supposed to help your tired feet.

"They had the best fried bologna sandwiches.

"In the women's dress department, in the back in the corner, there was a rack with blue dresses with polka dots on them. That is where all the old ladies got their dresses from.

"I remember the shoe wars. There would be a huge pile of shoes on a table and all of the shoes would be left shoes. It you found a shoe you liked you would go to the clerk and ask the clerk to get that shoe's mate."

~~~~~

Joan S. recalls: "'Penny Sales' - Buy a pair of shoes and get the next pair for a penny. Most of the shoes were odd sizes or very narrow widths." **Photograph courtesy of the Voorhees Family.**

Free Snacks

A resident at Seneca Manor stated: "They gave out free samples all the time. If you were waiting at the butcher shop, the butcher would give the kids a hotdog while they waited."

What Did He Say?

Anonymous: "Sattler's had a talking parrot in their pet department. The parrot had a nasty habit of swearing. Rumor has it that the night watchman was teaching the bird some new words."

Easter Windows

Mrs. W.: "I remember the baby chicks and rabbits in the window at Easter. The smell of the roasting peanuts when you walked in the door and the orange juice machine in Sattler's basement."
~~~~~

Time to Pack Your Bags

Barb: "When I was 7, a clerk at Sattler's was demonstrating the proper way to pack a suitcase. How you would first button a man's shirt and then roll the clothing so it wouldn't wrinkle. Who would think that something you learned at 7 would stay with you like that? I also remember the clerks demonstrating how to dye your Easter eggs so you could get a swirl design on them.

"At 4 years old, I got lost at Sattler's. I only lived 2 doors down on Broadway so I knew my way home, but the people at Sattler's had to announce my mother's name over the public announce system and my mom was embarrassed and wondered how I could have gotten lost."

Barb's mother, Dorothy, recalls: "Sattler's was a short walk from our home on Fillmore, and we would go on Saturdays, pulling the coaster wagon. And those barrels of cookies, maybe 50 varieties. You could buy anything you needed at Sattler's."

I Still Have That Silver Dollar

Mary Ann worked at 998 in Accommodations. She won a spelling contest at Sattler's and the prize was a 1921 silver dollar. "Mr. Rabow came around the store early in the morning before the store was open. He asked the employees how to spell an unusual word, and I was the first employee to get the spelling correct." Mary Ann is proud to tell you that she still has that silver dollar.

Mary Ann loved the Sattler's Social Club, where she and the people in her department dressed up as Sattler's paper bags, got up on the stage, and sang.

She recollects a story of the time that the man who ran the shoe department took the cash register out of the store for repairs. Mr. Rabow, the president of Sattler's at the time, came up to her when she worked in Accommodations and asked her how she knew that this man would bring back the cash register. (She had no idea that he was the president of Sattler's at the time). She gave Mr. Rabow the man's name, his employee number and the place he worked. Then she said she got a bit annoyed with him and asked, "And who are you?" He answered her very kindly and the next day she was given the assistant manager job in Accommodations.

She also said she loved it when the employees had parades in the store. "Everyone would be dressed up and the parade would be for the employees. During every holiday, the store was always decorated and everyone received something. Some of us got an extra week's pay. And even if it was your first week working at the store, you would at least get a box of candy."

Mary Ann loved to work at Sattler's; "I actually looked forward to going to work," she said. She was offered a job at the telephone company and turned it down, as she couldn't imagine leaving her Sattler's family.

There's a Riot in the Dress Department

Marcia of Coit Street was only 4 or 5 years old at the time, but she still remembers holding on to the back of her mother's dress when an employee from Sattler's dress department would come out and throw an armful of house dresses on a table. Then all hell would break loose, as a mob of women grabbed for anything they could. Arms and bodies everywhere, all struggling, reaching for that prize dress. Once someone got a dress, she would check it out for the correct color and size. If the dress wasn't what she wanted, she would toss it back on the table and try again for another grab. "It was chaos."

"Growing up on the East Side, there were only little grocery stores in the neighborhood. When Sattler's opened their grocery department in the basement, it changed everything. You would shop between the Broadway Market and Sattler's for all your groceries."

Time for Parents To Shop

A common practice was to go to Sattler's with one's mom and dad, perhaps just a few times a year. That was especially true for families who lived on the west or north side of Buffalo. Christmas and Easter were times when entire families hopped on a bus or trolley and visited Sattler's. How times have changed!

~~~~~

Michael L. recalls that he must have been about 7 when his parents would go to Sattler's. He would be dropped off in the record department and be thrilled to spend the entire day there. "I was a big Beatles fan."

~~~~~

An anonymous friend said, "My parents would take the kids into Sattler's at Christmastime. When they walked through the front door, they would tell the kids, 'Go'."

~~~~~

Another unnamed former shopper told a story of her uncle who would take his 2-year-old to Sattler's. Once he got there, he would drop the 2-year-old in a crib that was on display and then go shopping.

~~~~~

Smoking Behind the Barn

Another story was told to me by Julian Rabow, son of Aaron Rabow, who was vice president of Sattler's at the time. This was about his great friendship with Jack Hahn, who happened to be Mr. Sattler's grandson. It seemed that the Rabow family and John G. Sattler lived directly across the street from each other on Ivyhurst, in the new suburb of Eggertsville. Jack and Julian were typical boys for the time. They would climb John Sattler's barn, chase his chickens, and roughhouse like boys do. Sometimes the two would get into trouble together.

It just so happened that Jack and Julian could not be found one evening after they were outside playing for quite a long time. Julian Rabow remembers: "We were boys about 10 or 12 years old. Several radio stations were informed to broadcast information about a missing person's alert. Everyone was in a panic.

We were hiding out behind Mr. Sattler's horse barn smoking cigarettes. We had lost track of time and it was getting dark and we realized that we needed to be getting home." Julian added, "Neither Mr. Hahn nor my father killed us, but I am sure that the thought had crossed their minds."(569)

Puttin' on Your 288's?

Sheila O. lived on Colvin Avenue at the time. Her mom needed a pair of winter boots, so she hopped on the bus and went down to Sattler's. She came home with the ugliest pair of boots. "They were the heavy rubber, ankle high black boots with gray fur around the top. We thought they were SO UGLY. We kiddingly referred to them as the '288's.' They were ugly, but they were warm."

Don't Forget the Duck for Czarnina

Sandy B. worked at Sattler's in the 1970's. She loved Sattler's and remembers that "the atmosphere was magical. They sold everything at Sattler's, from the fanciest wedding gowns to the simplest items. Employees were happy. If you worked at Sattler's you were family and you were never left out." She talked about the butcher shop in the basement and reminded me of the live chickens and ducks that they sold. They needed the ducks so that people could make czarnina, a classic Polish duck soup. She still has one of Sattler's Jingle Bears.

Sattler's Ball Teams

Above is a photo of Sattler's women's softball team from an unknown time period. Below is a photo of Sattler's men's baseball team from an unknown time period. Photographs courtesy of Michael Stark's Family.

Sattler's Softball Team 1979 Champs

Photograph courtesy of Sandy Boczar.

Back row, left to right: Don Jackson, Tony Marquese, Paul Hybicki, Mike Genau, Karl Leonard, Doug Pagano, Lance Lazewski.

Front Row: Carleen Thomas, Linda Finkley, Elaine Stolarski, Sandy Boczar, Milton Smith.

Joan was a team player at Sattler's. Literally! She played for Sattler's Women's Softball Team. When Joan tried out for the team, her boyfriend told her to take a position as far out in the field as she could, because Joan had never played baseball before. After the tryout was over, Joan was happy to report that she was the team's catcher. Joan's boyfriend's response was, "You're going to get killed."

Jimmy Durante Visited 998

I was told by both Robert Cornelius and Julian Rabow that Jimmy Durante visited 998. It was on May 5th, 1942 that Jimmy Durante came to Sattler's to introduce Borden's famous cow, Elsie. Durante was there to help with the promotion and sale of war bonds and war stamps.

Julian Rabow happened to be Jimmy Durante's ride to the airport, and Julian recalled that Jimmy Durante was a joy to have in the car, as he was cracking jokes all the way to the airport.

Every Thursday We Went to Sattler's

Dorothy M. told me that every Thursday she made a trip to Sattler's. She would go to the basement to seek out all the food vendors, and there was even a buttermilk stand. She would buy small barrels full of fish, and her mother would soak the fish for several days before the fish could be used. She remembers that taffy at the candy stand was in big blocks, and it had to be chipped off for a customer to get the amount desired. Dorothy also bought colored cigarettes for her friends, and she recalls that the cigarettes came in packs with different colors of rolling papers that surrounded the tobacco. (570)

Peanut Butter by the Metal Pailful

Kathy remembers her dad in the 1940's going to Sattler's to buy metal pailfuls of peanut butter. The peanut oil would pool on the top of the peanut butter and they would have to stir it in.

Wages of $.32 an Hour in 1942

Florence from Smith Street worked at Sattler's when she was 17 years old in 1942, earning 32 cents an hour. She also remembers her father buying pails of peanut butter and cottage cheese with chives from Sattler's.

Sattler's Accounting Department

Standing, left to right: Mary Ellen Kavanagh, Helen Mikolajczak, Charles Ott (department manager in the credit office), Helen Szymczak, Ann Delgato. Seated, left to right: Sophia Lach, Edna Zollitsch, Regina Kardach, Madeline LoBue, Theresa Borzillieri and Florance Lafter. **Photograph courtesy of Michael Stark.**

A Family Affair

Ellyn remembers that her entire family worked at 998. Her father Thomas worked in the office part time, and her mother, Lillian, was a sales clerk in the 1920's. Then the three children followed suit: Robert and Ellyn were office workers, while Marilyn worked behind the cookie counter.

The telephone wires were abuzz as Ellyn reminisced with siblings Robert and Marilyn. The story was that Robert was tasked with reading the store's cash registers after the store closed. In order to read all of them in a timely manner, he used roller skates to get from register to register.

Before Ellyn worked at Sattler's, you might have seen her as a small child sitting patiently on those green chairs in the shoe department waiting for her mother. If she was well behaved, she would get a treat of the ever-famous Sattler's vanilla custard that was served in the basement at Sattler's. She remembers the orange juice machine where "orange juice came out of real oranges."

When Ellyn was older she worked in the office. Her memories include readying the weekend sales reports, which were called "Flash Reports." (571)

Remember the Cisco Kid

Ed remembers that the Cisco Kid visited Sattler's back in 1958 or 1959. And if you entered the front right entrance at 998, the watch repairman, fixing watches, was the first thing you saw. Ed would visit the stamp dealer in the basement, and his grandmother bought him his Lionel Train pieces at Sattler's. "If you were lucky enough to be at Sattler's during Eastertime, you could see the demonstrations of the lady who was 'whirling eggs' by the escalators. And don't forget those 10-cent ice cream cones." Ed remembers that the store was also known as 'Sot-lar-a'" when using Buffalo's East Side slang. (572)

Just 14 Years Old

Alice was 14 years old when she started to work at Sattler's in 1947. She worked in the basement at the meat market for Ralph Kushner and Sye Benatovich. She remembers that the animals used by the meat market were corralled inside the basement by the loading docks.

Alice's son John remembers how very hard it was to find a parking spot. John would be in the car with his dad scouting out people walking through the lot. They would look for someone who had keys in his or her hand, as they were pretty sure that person would be leaving and they could grab that parking spot. A small score during those busy times while visiting Sattler's!

Chickens on the Trolley

Mrs. Pat Q. lived on Seminole Parkway and she would take the trolley to Fillmore, where she would transfer and ride to the big front doors of Sattler's. It was actually the trolley ride home that brought back those memories of Sattler's. "Women would be sitting on the trolley holding live chickens that they bought at Sattler's."

Fish Fry

A person who wants to remain anonymous said, "It was the late 1940's when I would go to Sattler's with my Grandma Minnie. She would buy a fish fry at Sattler's. She would not eat it until it was cold and then she would eat it on the bus on the way home."

Buy Gold!

"I was about 20 years old, living on Fox Street," said Sandra. "I would walk to Genesee Street and then hitchhike to Sattler's and meet my girlfriend there. We would go to the jewelry department. My girlfriend told me, 'Gold is the way to invest your money.' So I bought a gold pinky ring and another gold ring. Years later, I sold the rings and I did make a profit."

999 Broadway

999 Broadway is the address of the Broadway Market. "I have a kiosk at the Broadway Market and sell red wine under the label of 999 Broadway. I decided it was a good idea to make a white wine. That white wine is labeled 998 Broadway," said Carl S.

The Freshest in Town

A family friend of one vendor told me, "In the basement of Sattler's there was the orange juice stand that was run by Howard Lewkowitz. A machine to squeeze the oranges made the freshest juice in the city. Mr. Lewkowitz also had a popcorn machine and sold candy at his stand."

Interview with Sisters of Mercy

I spent an interesting afternoon with a few of the Sisters of Mercy at the Abbott Road convent:

M.A. "Where did you grow up?"

Sr. Peggy "I grew up on Hubble and went to Holy Family. My mother was a widow and we were very poor and we did our shopping at Sattler's. We took two buses to get there. We transferred at the National Aniline, then went down to Sattler's. We did it every Friday. And we did grocery shopping and the reason was because the groceries were cheaper."

M.A. "Is there anything specific you would buy at Sattler's?"

Sr. Peggy "Oh yes, in the middle of Sattler's, where the groceries were, there were cookies that were a special every week. And they were piled like... the counter was maybe here (she showed that the counter was about 3 feet off the ground and made us understand that there were tall piles of boxed cookies on the counter), but piled all around her (the clerk) were the boxes of cookies, but you bought them by the pound and whatever they were, they were cheap. And whatever that cookie was (chocolate, coconut, etc.) we bought it. A pound. It didn't matter if we liked them or not, my mother would buy a pound of those cookies. And I remember anxiously trying to wonder what the cookie would be this week."

M. A. "Now my grandmother, the same thing. She used to buy the cookies too. They were 2 cents a pound."

Sr. Peggy "Something like that, they were cheap."

M.A. "But she would buy the broken ones for half price."

Sr. Peggy "Yeah, I don't think we did that, but I don't think it would have mattered to us whether they were broken or not. ….but then now when I think about it, it was my brother, my sister and I. I was the youngest….. but then we lugged all those groceries back on the bus and then transferred. And transfers were 2 cents. And then come all the way home. In later years, I remember having the little wire cart, the cart with two wheels and it folded up. I remember taking that on the bus."

M.A. "Do you remember when you went in Sattler's and you went in the grocery department what the counters were, what did they sell? Do you remember any specifically? What did they sell, other than at the cookie counter, and what year are we talking about here?"

Sr. Peggy "In the food do you mean?"

M.A. "Yes."

Sr. Peggy "Well, I was in grammar school, so it was before I was 12. So, I graduated from Holy Family in the 50's, probably 52 to 56. And they probably did it before they took me because they were older."

M.A. "So do you remember any of the other counters? The meat counter, the candies…?"

Sr. Peggy "The meat market, the counter was white, slanted glass with porcelain around the edges. And I remember all the other counters, because we did all our grocery shopping there. And we lugged this home on the bus because there was no place around here to go grocery shopping but the A&P on South Park, but that was more expensive than Sattler's so we went to Sattler's. And I remember it was kind of an adventure out of the neighborhood. Because when we went there it was crowded. And there would be a lot of people down there doing their grocery shopping. You know, the cans would be piled up. Like cans of stuff would be piled up. It was always neatly piled up. And it seemed to me, each little place had a counter, like just a counter for those cookies. There wasn't a checkout. So if you went over there you would check out there and pay there and pay there and pay there."

M.A. "So you paid at each counter."

Sr. Peggy "That's what I remember. I think we paid 2 cents for those cookies at the cookie counter. Then went over to the meat market and paid there."

M.A. "When you went over to the meat counter and say, if you bought a chicken, was it a live chicken?"

Sr. Peggy "No, they were in packages. Well actually, they were wrapped in paper; there was no plastic yet. If you wanted two chicken legs they were wrapped up in paper."

M.A. "Do you remember anyone famous who came to Sattler's or any of the gimmicks they had?"

Sr. Peggy "Yes, gimmicks and we remember the jingle, 'Sattler's 9-9-8 Broadway.'

"And I have one more memory of Sattler's. They sold everything there. I got my confirmation dress there. And it was the most expensive thing I ever had. And probably the newest thing I ever had because I had all hand-me-downs. And I can picture it to this day; it was mint green, sort of nylon over an underskirt. It had white flocks on it and rhinestones and pearls. And I cut off the price tag; it was in my scrapbook which I don't have anymore. I put the price tag in my scrapbook; it was $13.98. (Gasps) That was huge. I think that was the first thing I ever had that was new."

M.A. "Do you have a picture of yourself in that dress?"

Sr. Peggy "No, I don't....... I remember it was green and the price tag was green with perforations around the edges with a little string around the edge, and I scotch-taped it in my scrapbook because it was the most expensive thing I had.

"And the first new coat I ever had I was in 8th grade. And they came in coat boxes, big coat boxes, you didn't take them home on a hanger. And every time I wore it, I took it off and I put it into the box. And my mother kept saying 'Peggy? It will get dusty on that rack there.' I was so excited because it was new and it was pretty. I'd button it up and fold it and put it in the box every time I wore it. But this confirmation dress was even before that. That was the first thing I ever remembered."

M.A. "Were you in 6th grade?"

Sr. Peggy "Yes I was in 6th grade; Sister Mary Caritas taught me in 6th grade." (Sister Mary Caritas is sitting across from us.)

Sr. Caritas "How did you get there? Taxi? Streetcar?"

Sr. Peggy "To Sattler's? No, on the bus."

M.A. "And Sister, where did you live?"

Sr. Caritas "I lived on Sheffield in two different houses."

M.A. "And what do you remember?"(Looking at Sr. Caritas.)

Sr. Caritas "I'm fascinated because she (Sr. Peggy) is restoring back my remembrance. I just remember going with my older sister Eleanora and she used to take me places. She would take me and she would say 'you could have candy or go to the show; you couldn't do both.' "

Sister Peggy "So what would you take, candy or the show?"

Sr. Caritas "Candy, I didn't care much about the show. My sister was a clothes freak; you know she loved having new clothes. And I never gave clothes a thought."

M.A. "Do you remember what you shopped for at Sattler's?"

Sr. Caritas "We just walked around, see what there was. I don't quite remember it as clearly as they do."

Sr. Peggy "Do you remember anything Josepha?"

Sr. Josepha "Yeah, I remember a lot. I lived at St. Stephen's on Elk Street in the 60's. I didn't come from the city. I entered the Sisters of Mercy in 1943, so I've been a Sister of Mercy for 75 years." My connection with Sattler's was, I lived at St. Stephen's on Elk street with Sister Mary Derkin. Sister Derkin has lived there her whole life. And on every Saturday, or almost every Saturday we would get on the bus and go to Sattler's. I don't think they still had the trolley system. I'm pretty sure they didn't. But anyway that's my story about St. Stephen's."

M.A. "How many of the sisters were at St. Stephen's?"

Sr. Josepha "Then probably six or seven."

M.A. "So did you and Sister Derkin go shopping for food?"

Sr. Josepha "Well for the house and for school."

M.A. "You would go shopping for, for the school? What would you buy for the school?"

Sr. Josepha "The school supplies for the beginning of the year. "

M.A. "You would buy them at Sattler's?"

Sr. Josepha "You would get bargains you know and get decorations for the school."

Sister Caritas "I remember you used to buy sheets of paper, not a tablet, but like 6 sheets of paper. "

M.A. "You bought it by the sheet?"

Sr. Caritas "Yeah."

Sr. Josepha "But my big story about Sattler's is the curtains. We had these big windows, so you bought off the bolt. And when you took them down you never washed them and put them back up. You took them down and then threw them out, because we lived right in the middle of the industry. If the Aniline didn't get ya' the steel plant did. They would get the curtains. So twice a year we would take the curtains down and throw them out and we bought the material at Sattler's off the bolt."

Sr. Peggy "So who sewed them?"

Sr. Josepha "Katherine did, I did. We lived right in the middle of the... depending how the wind was blowin'" (being interrupted by Sr. Peggy).

Sr. Peggy "That's right; when we took the bus we transferred at the National Aniline on Lee Street and it smelled terrible."

Sr. Josepha "Well we took the bus on Smith Street, we just went over on a Saturday and went shopping. We would always end up in yard goods too, because we make our habits. I had a 28 waistline then and it took 6 yards of material and they had everything from serge to poplin. And you bought your dresser scarves and pillowcases there for embroidering. Everybody had embroidered pillowcases in those days. Those are my stories."

After a brief pause, Sr. Josepha continued by saying, "The radio, the radio was what we would listen to in those days and every 20 minutes they would have, 'Come on down to Sattler's'; they would have a commercial. "

(In comes a sister on her scooter)

M.A. "Sister Joan! My 7th and 8th grade teacher!"

Sr. Joan "I remember going to Sattler's as a little girl. Every week I went shopping to Sattler's with my father."

M.A. "Where did you grow up?"

Sr. Joan "St. Monica area. I grew up on Babcock. The one thing I remember about Sattler's is the way they use to pile their shoes. There were these big tables; the shoes were attached together with a string and you had to find your shoes. Whatever size you wanted.

We went to Sattler's at night; it was such a treat to go there. It was overwhelmingly packed with people everywhere. We would go as if we were on a mission."

M.A. "It was a pleasure to spend the time with all of you. I thank you for the stories and for my education."

After-Christmas Strategy for the Thrifty Shopper

Kevin B.'s mom waited until after Christmas to get the real bargains. It seemed Kevin's mom really wanted a new nativity set. "So we would go to Sattler's the day after Christmas. Mom had a plan. When you get to where the nativity sets are, she said to 'grab the baby Jesus,' because no one will buy a nativity set without baby Jesus.

"My father also worked for Sattler's. He was from an outside company and he was hired to refinish the scratched and dented appliances that came into Sattler's appliance department."

~~~~

"I lived on Sweeney Street and my sister lived on C Street. We would walk to Sattler's. One day my sister took her two young boys to Sattler's in a stroller; the boys sat one behind the other in the stroller. We often went just to walk around in the store. When my sister went to take the two boys out of the stroller after she returned home, she found two pink little girls' outfits in the stroller with the boys. The kids must have taken them off the shelf when she wasn't looking."
~~~~

~~~~~

Paul from Fulton Street mentioned his memories: "Next to the elevators they had soft serve ice cream. The first time we took our kids to see Santa in 1972-1973 was at Sattler's. And in 1963-64 I would buy my Modra Indian tunic/shirts at Sattler's."

A Three-Day Cry

Kathy grew up on Sherman and Sycamore Street. She tells of "waiting in the long lines with food ration stamps when I was going to buy butter at Sattler's. You had to take the RIC Street Cars to get there. At Christmastime there were so many people trying to get into the store that you couldn't even walk on the sidewalks on Broadway."

I asked Kathy if she ever worked at Sattler's. At first Kathy said no, but then she said, "Actually, yes I did work at Sattler's, I was hired for 2 or 3 days to peel onions in Sattler's kitchen."

Kathy also fondly remembers the profile silhouettes that were made for you at Sattler's.

Coming in by Bus from the Country

Betty came from the "country" (Lakeview, NY) with her parents by bus to buy furniture or clothing when there was a big sale. Most people didn't have cars in those days, so they took the trolley or buses, walked or hitchhiked. Transporting things home would be done by public transportation, baby buggy, bikes or wagons. To see a family march out of a store carrying a dresser, loading it on their wagon and pulling it home was common. Balancing two bags of groceries on the handlebars of a bike was normal. People used two-wheel wire carts or baby buggies to transport their food home. And don't be standing too close to the lady who just bought a duck, or you might just get nipped!

Thursday Evenings at Sattler's

Chris told of how her father would take her family in the car from South Ogden and Clinton on Thursday evenings. "We would go to buy meat downstairs in the basement. Dad would always treat us to a hot dog with kraut and soft serve ice cream."
~~~~~

Part of Me Was Buried with the Store

Debbie remembers being only a small girl from William Street when she first went to Sattler's. She said she didn't go often, but the bells in the basement always intrigued her. The bells she spoke of were the "call bells" that were used to alert store managers that their assistance was needed by someone in the store. Like so many people, Debbie had delicious memories of Sattler's soft serve ice cream and Christmas memories of Santa in the store. The best memory is her dad taking her to Sattler's to get her first bra. It was an experience she will always cherish, as Debbie was close to her father. Neither Debbie nor her dad knew what to expect and she admits that the event was a bit bewildering for a young girl with her father. However, with the help of those knowledgeable Sattler's foundation experts Debbie remembers the event was a happy one. Debbie's final memory of Sattler's was a bit sad. When 998 was being demolished, Debbie went to the demolition site and picked up a brick from the store. In the process of getting that brick, Debbie lost her keys in the rubble of bricks. She tells me, "When they tore down Sattler's, I left a bit of myself there" to be buried with the store.

A Surprise Trip with Dad

Gordon G. remembers, as a young boy, how his father told him he needed to get into the car to take a ride with him. They ended up at Sattler's where the *Ralston Rocket* was being displayed in the parking lot. The rocket was being towed by a truck with the memorable red and white checkerboard of the Ralston Company. He recalls how excited he was as he walked through the spaceship. Gordon possesses a wealth of knowledge about the *Ralston Rocket*, and he gave me a wonderful history of how the rocket was made by Standard Carriage Works out of Los Angeles, California. The company actually made two rockets for Ralston. There was the rocket which traveled the country, the one that visited Sattler's in 1953 and a duplicate *Ralston Rocket* that was a bit smaller, weighing in at 5 tons. The smaller rocket was used in a Name the Planet Contest, which was won by Ricky Walker of Washington, Illinois. Ricky kept the clubhouse version of the *Ralston Rocket* in his yard for several years, eventually selling it after the novelty wore off.

One Ton of Butter Is Missing

Photograph is courtesy of the Voorhees Family.

I was told that a one-ton tub of butter was ordered and specially made for Sattler's. This was to be another one of Sattler's huge eye-catching promotions to bring people into the store. However, the butter which was sent by railcar did arrive in Buffalo but never made it to 998 Broadway for the targeted promotion date. By mistake, the one ton of Morning Bloom Butter was sent to Buffalo, Wyoming.

Memories of Gibson Street Girls

Ruth, in the early 1950's, worked at the Butter Counter. "It was a big counter and many people worked there. The butter was on the counter in big chunks, which would be cut with enormous knives for customers.

"I worked from Thanksgiving to Christmas and they were so good to their employees. I remember that even though I only worked temporary over the holidays, I received a Christmas gift from the store; I think it was handkerchiefs.

"We lived on Gibson Street, across from the parking lot. In the winter, Sattler's was not open on Wednesdays, so they closed the gate to the parking lot which was facing Gibson. Then we would go over to Sattler's and ice skate in their lot."

~~~~~

Terri lived at 69 Gibson St., and her mother bought her wedding dress at Sattler's for under $100. "You could buy everything there." Terri's children also used to ice skate in Sattler's parking lot.

Back to the Shoes

Helen lived on the Street of Demond in Downtown Buffalo. The street is no longer there. Helen's father, Edward Cheney, was a civil engineer and he installed the escalators at 998. Helen went to Bishop McMahon High School and she had to wear a certain type of black shoes that were sold only at Sattler's. She remembers how her older sister took her to Sattler's to buy those shoes. Helen also knew someone who won a TV at the store.

~~~~~

During the Depression, Eileen lived on Pawnee Parkway and her dad was a policeman. He was paid every two weeks, and Eileen would go with her dad in their car to pick up his pay at the station. If the paycheck was good, she would hope to go to Sattler's for ice cream. Times were tough, so you never knew if there would be enough money for an ice cream treat. She knew that Sattler's was a discount store, not an upper crust store, so she was embarrassed when her parents would come home with bags from Sattler's. She hoped that no one saw her parents bring in "those" bags. However, things changed after she got married and she had to manage the money. Now she took the bus and traveled to Sattler's since she had to be smart with her money. No more embarrassment! She recalled a huge shoe sale at Sattler's where the shoes were 75% off. These were top quality designer shoes. She called her girlfriend, who was the wife of a doctor, and they went shopping. Eileen did buy a pair of shoes, and her friend bought 12 pairs of shoes. Eileen recalled Eddie Cantor and Jimmy Durante at the store.

~~~~~
~~~~~

Anonymous had more memories of those wonderful sponsored Christmas parades down Broadway. She remembered how you could buy ANYTHING in Sattler's; she especially loved the delicious pickles from the pickle barrel and the yummy pizza bread that was sold there.

~~~~~

When Wayne was 8 years old he lived on Fillmore Avenue. He recalls going to Sattler's with his parents and his brother, who was 3 years older than he was. Wayne's parents left Wayne's brother in charge of Wayne while they shopped. The two boys were just outside the main entrance on Broadway, and to stay occupied they decided to slide back and forth on the terrazzo walkway that was just outside the main lobby. As fate would have it, Wayne slipped and took a head dive into the aluminum molding on the outside of the building. A good head gash sent Sattler's employees scurrying to get the boy up to Sattler's emergency medical facility in the store. Soon the parents returned to find blood on the sidewalk and no little Wayne. The concerned parents turned to their-11 year old son, wanting to know what had happened and where Wayne was. Their son said, "I don't know." Wayne was eventually found, and he still has a prominent scar on his forehead. Another childhood battle wound to reminisce about with the family.

Wayne also recalls when Sattler's had one of their big renovations. All the properties on Beck Street that Sattler's needed for expansion were bought by Sattler's, except for one. That one Beck Street resident decided to be a holdout. Sattler's decided to continue their expansion and just build around the holdout's property. Faced with the prospect of being surrounded by Sattler's was not appealing, and so the Beck Street property owner did eventually sell his home to Sattler's.

~~~~~

Mr. and Mrs. Anonymous grew up on Ridgewood Road and Altruria Street in Buffalo, respectively. Both remember the wooden tables piled high with shoes, pairs being wired together. The shoes had color-coded stickers for the different sizes. Mr. Anonymous remembers "big fat ladies after those shoes."

Additionally he said, "When you were a kid you would go downstairs and see this broad expanse where the groceries were."

Mrs. Anonymous recalls shopping for her communion dress there, as Sattler's was the only place her parents went to buy clothes.

~~~~~

Dennis lived on Orleans in the Kensington Bailey Area. He has fond memories of the kraut dogs you could buy in the basement when he and his parents would shop once a month at Sattler's. He also loved the hot peanuts that were sold there. And how his dad would complain about the parking!

~~~~~

Anonymous lived in Snyder and received her first set of dishes for a bridal shower gift from her grandmother. Those dishes were purchased at Sattler's.

~~~~~
~~~~~

Joseph grew up on Northampton Street. When Sattler's closed, he bought all of the remaining Sattler's boxes and bags. A relative who was with Joseph during this interview remarked how gifts were always given in a Sattler's box after that. Joseph went to Sattler's about every two weeks when he was younger. "The parking lot at Sattler's was a nightmare. There were long lines to get into the parking lot; sometimes they were jammed up for two streets and the streets (Beck and Gibson) were one way." Joseph had fond memories of the bargain basement, the meats and sausages. He told me about a friend of his who was an employee at Sattler's. The employee would bring his lunch every day and eat it in the basement of Sattler's. When he was done with his lunch, the man would take a Sattler's bag and put his napkin, lunch bag and the wax paper from his sandwich in the Sattler's bag and leave the bag on a counter. The employee would stand back and watch how long it would take before someone would steal the bag.

~~~~~

Carol worked in the children's department for four years as a floater in the late 1960's. She was a Sattlerite and attended the dances, dinners and picnics held for Social Club members. She stated, "There was always a cash bonus if you were the top seller in your department. I remember I would get coffee and a sandwich in the basement. Everything was sold at individual stands. The food was very good. My dad and my husband worked in the wallpaper and paint department. Dad was there for 25 years and my husband for 10. The two of them were often sent to people's homes to put up the wallpaper or paint. Sattler's did everything for their customers," said Carol. "And my husband also played on Sattler's baseball team."

~~~~~

Bob would deliver pharmaceuticals to Sattler's for the drug store, which was in Sattler's basement. Sattler's drug store was actually run by Lee Drugs. Whenever Bob would go to the basement with his deliveries, he remembered seeing a barrel of pigs' feet.

~~~~~

An anonymous gentleman from Reid Street said his most memorable recollection of Sattler's was their pressed ham. He would take it home and have it on white bread. It was so delicious! He said he doesn't know if they even make pressed ham anymore, and the bread was nothing like the bread they have today. He thinks they also sold musical instruments at Sattler's.

~~~~~

Joan's husband drove her from their home on Strauss Street to Sattler's for work. She worked in women's wear, selling tops and blouses in 1950. She remembers the orange juice machine, the groceries, the sausage and meats, the Christmas parades and especially that they always received money for a Christmas bonus.

Sat-Ken-Ann Lodge

When I was doing some digging in the office of one of Mr. Sattler's great grandchildren, I happened upon a 78 record. It tells the unusual story of how a summer camp named Sat-Ken-Ann Lodge was donated by John G. Sattler. This camp included a 160-acre farm, as well as Mr. Sattler's summer home on the Canadian shore near Chippewa, Ontario. Mrs. John G. Andrews of Kenmore was the chairwoman of this project and the camp director. The camp was set up for children from Kenmore and Tonawanda, who camped for two-week periods in groups of eight or ten.

The recording is marked, "WKBW Program Surprise Package recorded from ABC - dub (duplicate) only portion referring to Sattler's - recorded 10/17/1950." It is a recording of an interview with Mrs. John Andrews, giving her thanks to John G. Sattler for his help in building a children's camp. The recording is very difficult to understand, but nevertheless it was a delight to hear. John G. Sattler was a kind and generous man who gave back to the community he loved. (573)

Mrs. Andrews described how John G. Sattler was a stranger to her, but in a dream she was told to write a letter to him to ask for his help in starting a summer camp. She did write the letter to Mr. Sattler, and he responded by giving her use of his summer home. The camp ran for about 10 years, and over 500 children enjoyed it. (573)

I found a bit more information about money raised by people in the local community to help the camp. In April of 1936, the Kenmore Harmony Chorus presented a play called "Spooky Corner" to help raise $2,000 to pay for equipment and expenses for the children who attended camp. (574) In April of 1938, a concert with an international theme was held at the auditorium of Kenmore High School. The groups participating were: The Bavarian Mannechor, Swiss Mixed Chorus, Ukrainian Singers, Cambrian Male Chorus of Niagara Falls, Negro Choir of Lincoln Memorial Church, Scottish Choral Society and Italian Choral Society. (575) In March of 1939, a new choral group called Triune Choristers of Buffalo, Kenmore and Williamsville held a barn dance, and the proceeds were donated to the Sat-Ken-Ann Lodge. (576)

James Whitmore, Just Another Customer

Rita was a floater for Sattler's in the early 1950's. She was working as a cashier one day when the famous actor James Whitmore came into the men's department to go shopping. He bought several suits while he was there. Whitmore was just one of the neighborhood boys who made it big in Hollywood. But from Hollywood or Buffalo, who can resist a Sattler's bargain?

~~~~~

Florence was from Clair Street. She remembers the butter counter had butter in huge blocks. "They would cut the butter with a string. They had everything at Sattler's. We went down every Saturday. My cousin worked at Sattler's with Santa. She would help put the kids on Santa's lap. Sattler's was so good for Buffalo; they really tried to keep the citizens of the city in jobs. They worked so hard to see that everyone was working. Dad would drive my mother to work and back when she worked at Sattler's.
~~~~~

"Sattler's had good quality dresses, and there was a fine ladies' dress department in the back of the store; that's where my mother worked. When Dad went to pick up Mom, I remember going down to the grocery department, and dad would tell me to run and get in line to buy 2 smoked hams; it must have been a holiday. We had 6 kids, so we needed to buy two. The lines at Sattler's were long and you had to get into them quick or your wait would be so long."

~~~~~

Another Anonymous person recalls that, "I would go with my dad, and when we got there he would say 'run.' We would spend the whole day there. We would go to buy mom's Christmas present, and we always would get a pound of chocolate-covered raisins."

~~~~~

"I bought my first record there; it was Buddy Holly," remembered a person from another interview.

Lackawanna Seniors Remember 998

Bob said, "There was a giant machine there that had two big shiny barrels that would roast the peanuts that would always be going around. When I worked at the Buffalo Forge plant, someone would go down to Sattler's and buy the fresh roasted peanuts, come back and sell them to all the people working at the Buffalo Forge plant. When I was young, I remember going with my parents and seeing a broadcaster from WEBR radio, Lucky Pierre. He was a radio announcer in a glass-enclosed booth conducting a contest or a promotion or such."

~~~~~

"I remember that we would always go to look at the sheets, linens and muslin at Sattler's. Sattler's had the best muslin," said a lady from the Lackawanna Senior Center. "The only time I saw such good quality muslin is when I brought some home from Poland in the 1990's. We would make quilts with the material, 'pierzyna' (comforters) and pillows. We lived on Electric Street in Lackawanna and we would raise the birds and then pluck and skin them, and we used the feathers to make 'pierzyna.'"

~~~~~

Another lady from the Lackawanna Senior Center said "I bought a leather coat and a felt hat at 998, and they were good label names and I still have those clothes; you can take a picture of them if you want."

~~~~~

Karl and Dorothy talked about how their sister, Suzanne, met her husband, Leonard, at the "ham bar," also known as Sattler's meat department. They lived in the Valley on Elk and Euclid Streets and they took the trolley or the bus to get to Sattler's.

~~~~~

Kathy recalls that Sattler's had very fine jewelry.

~~~~~
~~~~~

Joe was a maintenance man in the 1940's and his memories are of the peanut roaster. "It was a big cylinder that tumbled. There was a fire underneath the tumbler, and the smell of roasting peanuts would permeate the air. And one thing I will never forget was that there was a table filled with handkerchiefs that were marked 3 for $1.00. The salesclerk would try to keep the handkerchiefs in neat piles, but the customers would ravage through them, looking for just what they wanted. And perhaps 3 for $1 was a great price for these handkerchiefs that were a mess on the table. But next to this pile of handkerchiefs was another table. Handkerchiefs all boxed up, pretty as can be, and they were 4 handkerchiefs in a box for a dollar."

Little Penny Profits and Big Tom Turnover

Big Tom Turnover and Little Penny Profits were the popular team that appeared during Sattler's Anniversary Sale ads in the late 1940's and early 50's. (591 & 592)

The Whoosh Tubes

Both Hans and Berta reminisced about the tubes in Sattler's. Before the store had cash registers, Sattler's had a tube system. The tubes fascinated Hans and Berta in the 1930's when they were kids. They would go shopping with their parents and the "tube system was on a shiny wire that would whoosh through the store." It worked on a pulley system. "The clerk would put your money for your purchase in the tube, and it would whoosh off and quickly whoosh back with your change and a receipt." Hans and Berta were both fascinated by the tubes, and they said it was much quicker than the checkout system at the stores of today.

~~~~~

Both Joan and her mother from Swinburne Street worked at Sattler's. Joan's mom worked in the deli. It was the first job her mom ever had and she took it to help pay for Joan's wedding. Joan was an office girl at Sattler's, and her primary job was to obtain the previous day's newspaper and record the prior day's weather-how hot it was, how much it snowed, rainfall etc. The statistics were for the sales department so they could plan their sales and buying strategy for the upcoming year. Sattler's had tubes to send messages, money and layaway information throughout the store, and Joan also worked the "tube" in the office.

Steiner's Grocery Store

In the 1930's, Steiner's Grocery Store opened on Elk Street. Gert Steiner had $25 and went to Sattler's, buying $25 worth of goods to open her store. When she sold those products, she took that money, with the profit, and again went back to Sattler's to restock her shelves. She bought and sold Sattler items until she had enough stock to fill her store, and she continued doing so until Steiner's Grocery store closed in 1962. Veronica, from Orlando Street, has fond memories of her grandmother's store, and she also remembers having to go to Sattler's to pick up tub butter that would be sold at Steiner's.

Veronica also had an aunt who was a Dominican Nun in the cloistered convent on Doat St. On weekends, Veronica would take the bus with another of her aunts, Aunt Gen, to bring things to the convent. They would start out by taking the bus from Sage and Seneca Streets to Babcock and Seneca. Her Aunt Gen would get off the bus and go into the Quality Bakery, and the bus would wait for her while she picked up her order. Next they would board the Fillmore bus and go to 998. There they would pick up personal items for the Dominican Sisters. The one thing that was absolutely necessary to pick up was toilet paper, as it seems that the rough paper at the convent was not to the liking of some of the Sisters- "too rough."

~~~~~

Perfect Fit

Sattler's was always prepared to make its customers happy. However, there was a customer who was a frequent shopper in Sattler's Men's Department, but was having a problem with getting just the correct fit for his suits. The problem was quickly solved by the department manager, who lay newspapers on the floor of the men's department and had the gentleman shopper lie on the floor to have his body outline traced on the paper for a pattern. The measurements were made so that the customer had an exact fit, and Sattler's could then tailor his suits on the spot.

"Rudolf the Red-Nosed Reindeer"

A story that is often told during the Christmas season by relatives of the Sattler family is about Jack Hahn, grandson of John G. Sattler. The family remembers when Jack would say, "When I came home from college on winter break, I worked at 998. It was the year that 'Rudolf the Red-Nosed Reindeer,' sung by Gene Autry, came out and I was working in the toy department. A sales representative came into the store with a windup Rudolf the Red-Nosed Reindeer toy and a record player with a recording of 'Rudolf the Red-Nosed Reindeer.' I had to keep winding up all those toys and keep playing that annoying record all day and every day I worked in that department over Christmas vacation. I can't stand that song."

~~~~~

Remember to visit ***The Sattler's Diary* Facebook page,** and add your Sattler's stories and photographs for everyone to enjoy!
~~~~~

SATTLER'S SALUTES

The S. S. Santa Alicia

The first ocean-going American vessel to Call at Port of Buffalo via the new St. Lawrence Seaway!

May 8th

★★★★ *SEE!*

Robert Goulet

Whose voice has thrilled the nation on Screen, Stage, TV and Recordings.

IN PERSON At "998"

Parasol Room Restaurant 2nd Floor

2:30 to 3:30 Thurs., Sept. 14

MEET the INK SPOTS IN PERSON AT SATTLER'S

Appearing At Our Boulevard Mall Store Tomorrow (Tuesday) at 7 p.m. on the Main Floor near Mall Entrance — Appearing at 998 Broadway Wednesday at 7 p.m. in Our Main Floor Record Dept.

(See Them at Harry Altman's Glen Casino, Starting November 13th.)

Footnotes

BEN-*Buffalo Evening News*

BCCP-*Buffalo Common Council Proceedings*

CEX-*Courier-Express*

1 Records from Forest Lawn Cemetery, Buffalo, NY
2 Records from Concordia Cemetery
3 Information from Marilyn Clement, private book
4 Family history from Jack and Jill Hahn
5 BEN 1941-08-25 p. 9
6 Family genealogy, family tree
7 BEN 1898-06-23 p. 5
8 School of Buffalo (call Number) V2 Buff LA 339 B9B33 p. 126
9 1900 Census NY Erie, Buffalo Ward 3, District 0102
10 BEN 1899-12-02 p. 3
11 Buffalo NY Courier 1900 pdf 3021 Old Fulton Postcards
12 Buffalo Review 1900-08-28 p. 2
13 Buffalo NY Morning Express 1900-08-29 p. 7
14 Buffalo Courier 1900-09-08 p. 5
15 Buffalo Express 1900-12-31 p. 5
16 The Illustrated Buffalo Express 1900-08-26 p. 18
17 BEN 1900-08-31 p. 6
18 BEN 1900-02-28 p. 6
19 Buffalo Courier 1901-05-25 p. 5
20 Buffalo Courier 1901-12-23 p.21
21 Buffalo Courier 1900-11-27 p. 5
22 Buffalo Courier 1900-07-29 p. 20
23 Illustrated Buffalo Express 1902-06-08 p. 26
24 Buffalo Courier 1903-08-19 p.
25 BC 1909-08-15 p. 32
26 BEN 1913-09-04 p. 19
27 Recollections from Marilyn Clement
28 BC 1911-12-21 p.14
29 Buffalo Courier 1913-10-15 No page
30 BEN 1915-09-10 p. 5

31 BEN 1915-08-03 p.1
32 Buffalo Courier 1916-02-03 p. 1
33 BC 1917-05-01 p. 4
34 The Evening Leader Corning 1924-06-18 p. 7
35 Recollection from Jack Hahn
36 Recollections from Marilyn Clement
37 Recollections from Jill Hahn Russo 2017-12-17
38 BEN 1925-03-21 p.7
39 BEN 1925-10-29 p. 10
40 BCCP 1926-07-21 p. 1840
41 BCCP 1926-07-21 p. 1841
42 BCCP 1926-07-21 p. 1842
43 BCCP 1926-07-28 p. 1944, 1945, 1946
44 BCCP 1926-09-15 p. 2227
45 BCCP 1926-09-08 p. 2135
46 BCCP 1926-10-27 p. 2546-2548
47 BCCP 1926-11-10 p. 2646
48 BEN 1926-07-08 p. 14
49 BEN 1926-11-08 p. 88
50 BEN 1926-07-01 .p.33
51 BEN 1926-07-08 p. 14
52 BEN 1926-07-17 p. 1
53 BEN 1926-07-24 p. 3
54 BEN 1926 11-26 p. 22
55 BEN 1941-08-25 p. 9
56 BEN Voorhees family history (private files)
57 CEX 1929-08-06 p. 7
58 BEN 1927-03-23 p. 31
59 Buffalo Times 1927-08-24 p.17
60 CEX 1930-05-23 p. 5
61 CEX 1931-04-04 p. 1
62 BEN 1931-05-04 p. 1 Sec. II
63 BEN 1931-08-07 P. 21
64 BEN 1931-08-06 p. 21
65 BEN 1931-09-24 p. 14
66 BEN 1932-10-28 p. 12
67 BEN 1932-07-12 p. 14
68 BEN 1932-09-02 p. 12
69 BEN 1932-09-28 p. 18
70 BEN 1932-09-23 p. 22

71 BEN 1932-09-21 p. 18
72 www.Federalreservehistory.org/essays/bank_holiday_of_1933
73 Dictaphone tape of Charles Hahn to Holly Hahn-Baker
74 Dictaphone tape of Charles Hahn to Holly Hahn-Baker
75 Story told by Jill Hahn Russo in Jacksonville, OR 2019-01-16
76 CEX 1933-03-26 p. 8
77 BEN 1933-07-11 p. 16
78 Family story told by David Voorhees on February 8, 2020
79 Federal Census 1910
80 Geni Search Family of Henry Rabow 1918-03-30
81 Report from Sattler's, private family archives
82 BEN 1933-12-27 p. 12
83 BEN 1934-02-28 p. 16
84 BEN 1934-05-09 p.20
85 BEN 1934-05-22 p. 18
86 BEN 1935-05-29 p. 12
87 BEN 1934-05-23 p. 39
88 BEN 1934-05-23 p. 22
89 BEN 1934-05-16 p. 44
90 1920 United States Federal Census
91 Holy Cross Cemetery
92 Interview with Linda Chludzinski 2018-05-09
93 BEN 1935-11-18 p. 14
94 Interview with Mary Chase Connors 2020-01-20
95 E-mail from Mary Chase Connors 2020-01-22
96 CEX 1936-11-10 p. 19
97 BEN 1934-07-10 p. 16
98 www.ourdocument.gov
99 The Niagara Falls Gazette 1933-07-26 p.13
100 CEX 1935-06-01 p. 20
101 CEX 1933-07-26 p. 1
102 BEN 1934-08-24 p. 16
103 BEN 1934-08-22 p. 16
104 BEN 1934-08-29 p. 14
105 BEN 1935-01-30 p. 23
106 BEN 1935-03-04 p. 25
107 Boston Sunday Advertiser 1936-09-28 p. 3
108 The Philadelphia Inquirer 1954-04-10 p.15
109 The Desert News 1947-05-24 p. 13
110 The Desert News 1947-05-24 p. 16

111 The Desert News 1947-05-31 p. 21
112 The Boston Sunday Advertiser 1936-07-19 p. 15
113 BEN 1935 Old Fulton Postcards PDF 3403
114 Interview with Peggy Szczygiel 2018-05-03
115 1920 United States Federal Census
116 BEN 1935-05-25 p. 3
117 www.wunderground.com/history/airport/kbuf/1935/6/6dailyhistory.html
118 Interview with Linda Chludzinski 2018-05-09
119 BEN 1935-06-03 p. 12
120 BEN 1935-06-07 p. 16
121 BEN 1935-07-15 p. 14
122 BEN 1935-08-29 p. 34
123 BEN 1935-09-18 p. 20
124 Schenectady NY Gazette 1936-06-11 p. 9
125 Schenectady NY Gazette 1935-03-30 p. 17
126 BEN 1935-09-18 p. 19
127 Schenectady NY Gazette 1936-06-09 p. 19
128 Jamestown Evening 1935-04-06 p. 13
129 Modern Mechanic 1931-04
130 Utica Observer-Dispatch 1932-04-24 p. 1
131 Rochester Times Union 1932-11-12 p. 2
132 BEN 1935-09-18 p. 19
133 BEN 1935-09-18 p. 19
134 BEN 1935-09-18 p. 20
135 BEN 1935-10-16 p. 17
136 BEN 1935-10-25 p. 24
137 BEN 1935-11-01 p. 22
138 BEN 1935-11-08 p. 23
139 BEN 1935-11-15 p. 20
140 BEN 1935-11-01 p. 22
141 BEN 1935-10-21 p. 14
142 BEN 1935-11-18 p. 14
143 CEX 1935-12-25 p. 27
144 BEN 1936-01-31 p. 25
145 BEN 1936-02-06 p. 18
146 BEN 1936-06-15 p. 14
147 Interview with Linda Chludzinski 2018-05-09
148 Interview with Dr. Larry Beahan on 2018-005-13
149 BEN 1936-03-07 p. 8
150 CEX 1934-02-19 p.12

151 BEN 1933-01-31 p. 10
152 BEN 1936-02-05 p. 29
153 BEN 1936-03-07 p. 1
154 BEN 1936-03-11 p. 18
155 CEX 1936-04-19 p. L 5
156 www.trainweb.org/wnyrhs/blizzard1945.htm
157 BEN 1936-07-08 p. 15
158 CEX 1936-07-06 p. 11
159 CEX 1936-07-02 p. 1
160 Tonawanda, The Evening News North Tonawanda 1936-07-09 p. 10
161 CEX 1936-07-03 p. 8
162 BEN 1947-09-03 p. 24
163 BEN 1938-10-24 p. 14
164 CEX 1936-06-21 p. 03
165 CEX 1936-06-26 p. 16
166 CEX 1936-07-16 p. 6
167 BC 1936-07-01 p. 16
168 CEX 1936-07-10 p. 12
169 CEX 1936-07-17 p. 7
170 BEN 1936-08-24 p. 14
171 BEN 1936-09-11 p. 22
172 BEN 1936-09-09 p. 18
173 BEN 1936-09-14 p. 14
174 BEN 1937-09-25 p. 22
175 BEN 1936-09-25 p. 22
176 BEN 1935-09-18 p. 20
177 Decatur Herald 1948-12-23 p. 3
178 Decatur Daily Review 1960-04-04 p. 18.
179 BEN 1938-10-06 p. 14
180 The Yale Scientific Monthly 1912-19 No. 4
181 You tube "What is a Playograph?" http://www.theaudiopedia.com
182 http://en.wikipedia.org/wiki/playoghaph
183 www.citylab.com/design/2014/10/how-did-baseball-fans-watch-the-world-series-before-tv/381863/
184 BEN 1936-12-04 p. 23
185 BEN 1936-11-18 p. 21
186 BEN 1936-12-03 p. 21
187 BEN 1936-12-30 p. 12
188 Interview with Robert Cornelius 2018-03-28
189 BEN 1962-11-08 p. 32 Sec. III

190 BEN 1937-05-17 p. 14
191 BEN 1952-10-28 p. 22
192 CEX 1961-05-07 p. 26
193 BEN 1940-02-12 p.10
194 BEN 1949-05-03 p. 22
195 CEX 1939-01-20 p. 9 T
196 BEN 1954-04-19 p. 16
197 BEN 1937-02-10 p. 18
198 BEN 1949-04-06 p. 53 Sec. 5
199 BEN 1950-05-10 p. 28
200 Broadway Arsenal https www.preservationready.org/building/201broadway
201 CEX 1937-03-30 p. 24
202 CEX 1937-09-14 p. 1
203 CEX 1938-08-21 p. 1
204 BEN 1938-09-08 p. 5
205 BEN 1941-08-25 p. 1
206 BEN 1941-08-26 p. 22
207 CEX 1938-05-26 p. 9
208 Erie County Hall, record of deeds
209 BEN 1939-03-14 p. 12
210 BCEX 1939-03-14 p. 5
211 www.trainweb.org/wnyrhs/blizzard1945.htm
212 Interview on 2018-04-10 with Martha M.
213 CEX 1939-03-17 p. 23
214 BEN 1939-04-04 p. 28
215 CEX 1939-10-05 p. 11
216 CEX 1939-09-03 p. 5 T
217 BEN 1939-09-01 p.32
218 BEN 1939-09-13 p. 3
219 BEN 1939 11-18 p. 7
220 BEN 1939-10-04 p. 11
221 Interview with Mrs. Lalli in her home 2019-02-19
222 Interview with Mrs. Lalli by phone 2019-01-15
223 Interview with Mrs. Lalli by phone 2019-02-21
224 CEX 1939-11-11 p. 1
225 BEN 1940-01-20 p. 12
226 CEX 1940-05-17 p. 6
227 CEX 1940-07-23 p. 8
228 BEN 1940-11-18 p. 7
229 BEN 1941-01-08 p. 16

230 Interview with Esther Kaufman, Pittsburgh, PA 2019-01-29

231 Interview with Hans Spielberger 2019-07-23

232 BEN 1941-01-11 p. 18

233 CEX 1941-02-05 p. 4

234 Rochester Times Union 1941-04-18 p.10 A

235 CEX 1942-08-23 p. 8

236 BEN 1941-04-23 p. 22

237 CEX 1941-04-06 p. 7 Sec. VI

238 https://www.waymarking.com/waymarks/WM2D5Z_Buffalo_Masonic_Consistory_Buffalo_NY

239 British Pathe 1941-03-24 Media URN38573 Film 1109.46, Canister 41/24 Sort Number 41/024

240 CEX 1941-04-20 p. 13 Sec. IV

241 BEN 1941-04-21 p. 14

242 BEN 1941-07-08 p. 10

243 BEN 1941-07-24 p. 15

244 BEN 1941-08-27 p. 40

245 CEX 1941-08-26 p. 22

246 BEN 1941-08-26 p.12

247 BEN 1941-09-12 p. 29 Sec. III

248 BEN 1941-09-05 p. 43

249 BEN 1941-11-07 p. 50

250 https://www.loc.gov/item/today-in-history/december-07

251 CEX 1941-10-25 p. 7

252 Sattlerite 1951-01-23 p. 8

253 CEX 1941-11-23 p. 4 Sec. 5

254 CEX 1941-01-10 p. 8

255 CEX 1942-03-12 p. 23

256 CEX 1942-03-01 p. 4

257 www.imdb.com/name/nm0443000

258 CEX 1942-04-09 p. 25

259 CEX 1942-04-05 p. 3 Sec. V

260 Albany Times Union 1940-08-25 p. 18

261 Lancasterfarming.com 2012-06-23

262 BEN 1942-05-05 p. 8

263 Niagara Falls Gazette 1942-02-25 p. 11

264 CEX 1942-06-25 p. 11

265 Genesee County Express & Advertiser 1942-09 p. 12

266 www.sarahsundin.com

267 www.eresource.nibgov.sq-Malayancampaign

268 www.ww2db.com
269 www.americaslibrary.gov/jb/wwii.jb-wwii-pearlhar.1
270 BEN 1942-06-30 p. 3
271 BEN 1942-06-27 p. 9
272 CEX 1942-07-01 p. 24
273 CEX 1942-07-01 p. 19
274 CEX 1942-06-29 p. 18
275 CEX 1942-07-01 p. 5
276 CEX 1942-07-01 p. 2
277 CEX 1942-06-30 p. 11
278 BEN 1942-06-30 p. 2
279 BEN 1942-07-01 p. 25
280 CEX 1942-07-18 p. 9
281 BEN 1942-06-02 p. 10
282 Interview with Mary Benatovich 2019-04-03
283 NY Times 1942-08-24
284 Monterey County's North Coast and Coastal Valleys by Margaret Cloves p. 85
285 Oakland Tribune 1942-07-27 p. 13
286 CEX 1942-12-06 p. 15
287 CEX 1943-04-24 p. 14
288 BEN 1943-07-23 p. 24
289 Jamestown Post-Journal 1943-07-31 p. 3
290 BEN 1943-11-04 p. 18
291 BEN 1945-12-07 p. 41
292 BEN 1944-12-15 p. 42
293 BEN 1944-11-24 p. 41
294 BEN 1944-11-28 p. 22
295 BEN 1944-12-29 p. 18
296 CEX 1945-02-06 p. 18
297 Captain John W. Lovell and Army Transportation Journal, April, 1945 p. 16, 41
298 www.trainweb.org/wnyrhs/blizzard1945.htm
299 BEN 1945-03-29 p. 12
300 CEX 1945-03-30
301 BEN 1945-04-12 p. 9
302 Syracuse Herald 1945-05-14 p.7
303 Interview with Bob Cornelius March 2017
304 South Side Sentinel 1928-07-06
305 Interview with Shirley Kessler 2019-07-13
306 Philadelphia PA Inquirer 1924 pdf 4254 Old Fulton Postcards
307 New York Telegram Evening Mail 1924-04-05 p. 22

308 BEN 1947-12-06 p. 3
309 BCEX 1948-12-04 p. 22
310 Tonawanda Evening News 1950-01-05 p. 8
311 CEX 1950-01-07 p. 17
312 CEX 1950-08-31 p. 19
313 BEN 1953-10-29 p. 41 Sec. III
314 BEN 1945-07-28 p. 3
315 BEN 1941-09-05 p. 43
316 BEN 1945-12-07 p. 42
317 BEN 1945-12-07 p. 41
318 BEN 1946-06-15 p. 5
319 BCEX 1946-06-17 p. 5
320 BEN 1937-08-02 Sec. II p. 1
321 CEX 1937-01-24 p. 1
322 CEX 1937-09-05 p. 1
323 CEX 1937-10-17 P. 1
324 CEX 1939-08-06 p. 1
325 CEX 1941-05-29 p. 7
326 CEX 1942-09-29 p. 11
327 CEX 1950-06-12 p. 22
328 CEX 1951-06-16 p. 26
329 BEN 1937-09-03 Sec. II p. 1
330 BEN 1939-06-01 p. 17
331 BEN 1939-06-05 p. 1
332 BEN 1946-06-15 p. 4
333 BEN 1947-08-03 p. 40
334 BEN 1948-06-04 p. 19
335 BEN 1949-no date p. 44
336 BEN 1956-07-14 p. 8
337 BEN 1957-08-26 Sec. II p. 21
338 BEN 1962-06-26 p. 22
339 Interview with Charles D. Hahn, March 13, 2018
340 Interview with Jill Hahn Russo, July 2012
341 BEN 1946-10-03 p. 32
342 BEN 1946-10-17 p. 31
343 The 9-9-8 cornerstone history "paper from Sattler's reunion"
344 BEN 1947-01-10 p. 34
345 CEX 1947-01-28 p. 7
346 BEN 1947-10-10 p. 21
347 BEN 1947-10-24 p. 19

348 BEN 1947-10-03 p. 19
349 BEN 1947-11-14 p. 12
350 BEN 1947-09-26 p. 22
351 CEX 1964-10-14 p. 10
352 BEN 1966 -02-27 p. 19 A
353 CEX 1965-05-18 p. 25
354 CEX 1965-03-07 p. 19 A
355 CEX 1965-03-28 P. 11 A
356 BEN 1948-01-24 p. 6
357 BEN 1948-02-05 p 12
358 CEX 1961-03-05 p. 11
359 BEN 1947-10-17 p. 18
360 BEN 1947-11-07 p. 13
361 Interview with Robert Cornelius 2018-03-28
362 BEN 1947-11-07 p. 12
363 BEN 1949-09-08 p. 12
364 BEN 1948-09-11 p. 6
365 CEX 1948-09-08 p. 12
366 CEX 1949-09-12 p. 2 B
367 Pintrest-Dayalee 1948-09
368 BEN 1948-09-23 p. 6
369 www.revoly.com/page/eddiepolo
370 www.imdb.com/name/nmo689737/bio
371 www.cyranos.ch/sppolo-e.htm
372 BEN 1949-01-12 p. 46
373 CEX 1949-01-11 p. 7
374 Interview with Jack Hahn and notes from Jack Hahn
375 Letter from Jay Rabow
376 BEN 1949-03-02 p. 24
377 BEN 1949-03-01 p.18
378 CEX 1949-03-01 p. 16
379 Letter from Julian Rabow E-Mail
380 Speech read by Jack Hahn at the Saturn Club
381 BEN 1949-05-18 p. 30
382 BEN 1949-05-19 p. 40
383 BEN 1949-05-17 p. 30
384 BEN 1949-05-18 p. 49
385 BEN 1949-05-28 p. 6
386 BEN 1949-05-16 p. 30
387 BEN 1949-05-21 p. 6

388 www.oldtimeradiodownloads.com-truthorconsequences
389 www.radiogoldindex.com-truthorconcequences
390 Notes and interview with Jack Hahn
391 BEN 1949-05-04 Sec. 4 p45
392 BEN 1949-05-07 p. 5
393 BEN 1949-05-07 p. 5
394 BEN 1949-05-03 p. 22
395 BEN 1949-05-04 p. 30
396 BEN 1949 no date p. 44
397 CEX 1949-08-20 p. 18
398 Candywrapperarchive.com
399 CEX 1949-09-08 p. 12
400 BEN 1949-09-01 p. 22
401 CEX 1949-09-09 p. 9
402 BEN 1949-10-15 p. 12
403 BEN 1949-09-30 p. 23
404 BEN 1949-09-23 p. 22
405 Interview with Jack Hahn
406 Interview with Bob Cornelius March 2017
407 CEX 1949-11-08 p. 17
408 BEN 1949-11-08 p. 18
409 BEN 1952-10-18 p, 22
410 BEN 1950-02-21 p. 22
411 www.horsefame.tripod.com/francis.html
412 BEN 1950-04-07 p. 12
413 BEN 1950-05-10 p.28
414 www.city-buffalo.com/mayor/home/leadership/citystatsandfacts/historyofmayors
415 BEN 1950-05-10 p. 71
416 BEN 1950-05-10 p. 28
417 CEX 1950-08-20 p. 10 A
418 CEX 1950-09-16 p. 25 A
419 CEX 1950-09-14 p. 14
420 BEN 1950-09-11 p. 18
421 CEX 1950-09-10 p. 15 A
422 CEX 1950 -09-08 p. 11
423 BEN 1950-09-18 p. 14
424 BEN 1950-09-17 p. 23 A
425 CEX 1950-08-27 p. 2 D
426 CEX 1950-09-14 p. 47

427 Interview with Alan Sticklen 2019-04-27
428 www.at;asobscira.com
429 BCEX 1950-12-26 p. 10
430 CEX 1950-10-01 p. 20 AA
431 CEX 1950-09-13 p. 15
432 CEX 1950-10-01 p. 14 A
433 CEX 1950-10-01 p.20 A
434 CEX 1950-10-24 p. 3
435 CEX 1950-10-26 p. 18
436 CEX 1950-10-12 p. 14-A
437 BEN 1950-10-09 p. 18
438 E-mail 2018-03-01 Julian Rabow
439 BEN 1950-11-05 p. 30
440 BEN 1950-11-08 p. 57 Sec. 5
441 BEN 1950-11-08 p. 30
442 The Sattlerite 1951-01 p. 2
443 Private letter from Julian Rabow
444 E-mail 2018-03-01 Julian Rabow
445 BEN 1951-02-21 p. 32
446 www.quotes.net/quote/41324
447 BEN 1951-04-06 p. 1 number Sec. III
448 Interview with Michael Siuta 2018-05-06 about Mayor Mruk
449 BEN 1951-04-07 p. 4
450 BEN 1951-05-03 p. 73
451 BEN 1951-05-11 p. 22
452 BEN 1951-05-02 p. 30
453 BEN 1951-05-02 p. 30
454 BEN 1951-05-10 p. 26
455 BEN 1962-10-12 p. 22
456 www.burchfieldpenny.org-search"porterfield"
457 BEN 1958-11-17 p. 25
458 CEX 1941-01-12 p. 5 Sec. V
459 CEX 1951-11-18 p. 29 A
460 The Sattlerite Vol. 21 No. 1
461 CEX 1952-03-05 p. 13
462 CEX 1952-03-04 p. 1
463 CEX 1952-03-04 p. 10
464 CEX 1952-03-18 p. 13
465 The Evening News of the Tonawandas 1952-03-05 p. 1
466 BEN 1952-07-31 p. 32

467 BEN 1952-08-02 p. 8
468 BEN 1958-11-07 p. 20 Sec. II
469 Interview with Mary Ann Anonymous at New York Bar Exam 2019-02-27
470 Pittsburgh Press Republican 1953-07-01 p. 15
471 BEN 1953-06-29 p. 1
472 BEN 1961-06-07 p. 42 Sec II
473 BEN 1953-06-10 p. 26 Sec. II
474 BEN 1953-09-09 p. 34 Sec. II
475 http://www.solarguard.com/ralrckpn.htm
476 BEN 1954-07-22 p. 31 Sec. III
477 BEN 1954-08-31 p. 16
478 BEN 1954-09-20 p. 18
479 BEN 1954-09-14 p. 28 Sec. II
480 BEN 1954-09-17 p. 25 Sec. II
481 CEX 1954-06-27 p. 25 A
482 CEX 1954-09-12 p. 5 B
483 Voorhees Family Private Archives
484 BEN 1955-06-17 p. 8 Sec. I
485 BEN 1955-06-29 p. 61 Sec. IV
486 Voorhees Family Private Archives
487 BEN 1955-09-14 Sec II p. 33
488 BEN 1955-10-26 p. 88 Sec. VI
489 BEN 1955-10-25 p. 41 Sec. IV
490 BEN 1956-01-25 p. 63 Sec. IV
491 E-mail 2018-03-01 Julian Rabow
492 BEN 1956-08-21 p. 22
493 www.imdb.com The Helen Morgan Story
494 Interview with Greg Guest of Georgia Pacific by phone 2019-02-19
495 Lockport NY Union Sun Journal 1958-08-20 p. 12
496 Randolph NY Register 1958-08-22 p. 2
497 Binghamton NY Press 1958-08-31 p. 11 A
498 Jamestown NY Post Journal 1958-08-15 p. 10
499 CEX 1958-08-17 p. 18
500 CEX 1958-08-17 p. 21 A
501 BEN 1958-09-15 p. 15
502 BEN 1958-09-12 p. Sec. II
503 CEX 1958-07-13 p. 15 A
504 BEN 1958-11-19 p. 33 Sec. II
505 BEN 1958-11-28 p. 24 Sec. II
506 Alone Across the Top of the World by Dave Irwin

507 BEN 1959-01-08 p. 20
508 BEN 1959-01-12 p. 27
509 CEX 1959-01-12 p. 8
510 BEN 1959-01-12 p. 18
511 CEX 1959-02-05 p. 22
512 Philadelphia Inquirer 1960-02-05 p. 14
513 CEX 1959-04-11 p. 4
514 CEX 1959-03-15 p. 18 A
515 Phone call with daughter of Lynda Bannister, January 2019
516 CEX 1959-10-18 p. 19 A
517 BEN 1959-10-21 p. 34 Sec. II
518 BEN 1959-10-21 p. 34 Sec. II
519 BEN 1959-10-16 p. 21 Sec II
520 BEN 1959-10-17 p. 6 C
521 BEN 1959-11-04 p. 41 Sec. II
522 Wikipedia Lee Meriwether
523 BEN 1959-12-04 p. 34 Sec. II
524 BEN 1959-12-03 p. 32 Sec II
525 BEN 1960-03-25 p. 22
526 BEN 1960-03-26 p. C-5
527 BEN 1960-03-31 p. Sec. III-47
528 CEX 1960-03-26 p. 28
529 CEX 1960-03-31 p. 6
530 CEX 1960-03-27 p. 20-A
531 BEN 1960-03-24 p. Sec. III-29
532 CEX 1960-05-21 p. 7
533 BEN 1960-05-19 p. 30 Sec. II
534 CEX 1960-06-26 p. 21 A
535 BEN 1960-06-15 p. 36 Sec. II
536 CEX 1960-09-18 p. 13
537 BEN 1960-11-10 p. 31 Sec. II
537 http://hispanicmedalofhonorsociety.org/R4_gabaldon.html
538 BEN 1960-10-11 p. 36 Sec. II
539 CEX 1960-11-13 p. 34-A
540 CEX 1960-11-12 p. 28
541 BEN 1960-10-13 p. 36 Sec. II
542 CEX 1960-11-10 p. 39
543 BEN 1960-11-08 p. 23
544 BEN 1960-11-11 p. 27 Sec III
545 BEN 1960-10-27 p. 38 Sec. III

547 CEX 1960-11-17 p. 29
548 BEN 1960-11-11 p. Sec. III-21
549 BEN 1961-04-04 p. 18
550 https://en.wikipedia.org/wiki/Roberta_Sherwood
551 CEX 1961-05-31 p. 28
552 BEN 1953-06-10 p. 26 Sec. II
553 BEN 1961-06-11 p. 22
554 CEX 1961-06-04 p. 23
555 BEN 1961-06-14 p 34 Sec II
556 CEX 1961-07-02 p. 6
557 BEN 1961-09-29 p. 13
558 CEX 1969-12-08 p. 20
559 BEN 1962-10-05 p. 46 Sec. VI
560 BEN 1962-10-11 p. 39
561 CEX 1962-11-11 p. 31 A
562 CEX 1962-11-11 p. 31 A
563 BEN 1962-11-10 p. 3 A
564 CEX 1959-02-22 p. 18 A
565 BEN 1959-02-06 p. 16
566 BEN 1959-02-06 p. 16
567 CEX 1959-02-22 p. 18-A
568 1943 Goodrich tire ad
569 Letter from Jay Rabow
570 Interview with Dorothy Mozg 2019-05-24
571 Interviews with Ellyn Fay Maloney 2019-06-13 and 2019-06-16
572 Interview with Ed Czuba 2019-06-13
573 WKBW Program “Surprise Package” recorded from ABC 10/17/1950
574 BEN 1936-04-27 p. 5
575 CEX 1938-03-30 p. 11
576 www.revoly.com/page/eddiepolo
577 The Philadelphia Inquirer 1951-02-06 p. 8
578 The Boston American 1936-07-02 p. 11
579 The Boston American 1936-07-21 p. 6
580 Malta Migration.com
581 St. Joseph Press 1941-02-13 p. 3
582 The Boston Sunday Advertiser 1938-07-05 p. 6 D
583 Reading Eagle 1951-05-15 p. 11
584 The Boston American 1936-07-02 p. 11
585 BEN 1935-03-09 p. 6
586 The Boston Sunday Advertiser 1936-06-28 p. 6 ME

587 Find a Grave, Philip Taylor of Lawtons, NY
588 CEX 1941-11-15 p. 9
589 BEN 1941-11-12 p. 29 Sec. 3
590 BEN 1936-06-15 p. 14
591 CEX 1948-1015 p. 10
592 BEN 1948-10-16 p. 7
593 CEX 1959-02-26 p. 29
594 CEX 1960-06-24 p. 8
595 IMDb Hugh O'Brian Biography
596 The Plain Speaker, Hazleton, PA 1933-04-24- p. 7
597 CEX 1936-07-09 p. 1
598 Tonawanda Evening News 07-09-1936 p. 3
599 Tonawanda Evening News 07-09-1936 p. 10
600 New York State Death Index July, 1936
601 Noorden Passenger Log 1903-06-07
602 North Tonawanda, NY 07-10-1936 p. 3
603 CEX 1961-05-19 p. 10
604 CEX 1961-05-16 p. 16
605 CEX 1961-05-29 p. 3
606 CEX 1961-05-13 p. 6
607 CEX 1961-05-15 p. 15
608 BEN 1961-11-29 p. 36 Sec. II
609 BEN 1962-05-01 p. 18
610 CEX 1961-06-02 p. 16
611 proballresearchers.org>archives>Coffin Corner
612 Alden Advertiser 1961-07-20 p. 5
613 CEX 1961-05-18 p. 30
614 sarahsundin.com World War II War Bonds

Interviews listed alphabetically by last name

Joseph Alfieri
Anonymous
Kathy Anonymous
Joan Bryk Bartkowiak
Mary Benatovich
Ruth Janulewicz Boczar
Sandy Boczar
Hilda Mae Cotton Braun
Sheila O'Shea Brodnick
Betty, patron at the Happy Swallow
Veronica Steiner Canfield
Dianne Catlin
Orrin Catlin
Dennis Clark
Robert Cornelius
Eileen Hauptman Courtade
Ed Czuba
Sr. Patricia Donovan
Charlotte Eckborg Driscol
Brad Fisher
Florence of Smith Street
Robert Fay
Sandra Braun Fundalinski
Adam D. Gibbins
Joan Schork Gloss
Sr. Peggy Gorman
Joe Guercio
Gordon Green
Betty Greening
Charles D. Hahn (Son of Charles J. Hahn, grandson of Charles Hahn, great grandson of John G. Sattler)
Charles J. Hahn (Son of Charles and Marion Sattler Hahn, grandson of John G. Sattler)
Kathy Hay
Wayne Herr
Nigel J. Houenstein
Bert Hyde
Paul Johnson
Sr. Joan Klein
Florence Klimtzak Kogut
Dorothy Komisarek

Michelle Kraft
James Krause
Joseph Krause
Henry "Cowboy" Kusmierczuik
Monica Kwiatkowski
Rita Bernhard Landgraff
Joyce Leviolette
Alice Lewindowski
Mary Ann Bracickowska Lewandowski
Michael Losi
Helen Lawandus
Dorothy M
Carol Skowron Maliewicz
Ellyn Fay Maloney
Martha L. Marmion
Connie Stark Moffit
Ann Olzak
Rosemary Leo Potter
Pat Quinlavin
Carolyn Poloncarz
Sr. Caritas Quinn
Julian Rabow
Bob Rosen
Sharon Rudy
Jill Hahn Russo (Daughter of Charles and Marion Sattler Hahn, granddaughter of John G. Sattler)
Marcia Saramce
Chris Sarna
Joan Scahil
Mary Ann Schuster
Residents of Seneca Manor
Anna Siuta
Marian Siuta
Dorothy Slifka
Karl Slifka
Kathy Spencer
Hans Spielberger
Terri Stefanski
Joseph Steffan
Bob Stone
Sr. Diane Swanson
Mrs. Szefler
Sylvi Taylor
Debbie Tilmon

Sr. Mary Joseffa Timmins
Barb Trabold
David B. Voorhees, Jr. (Son of Jill Hahn Russo, grandson of Charles Hahn, great grandson of John G. Sattler)
Mrs. Walzak
Doris Sholtez Wodzinski
Marilyn Fay Zubler

www.ingramcontent.com/pod-product-compliance
Lightning Source LLC
LaVergne TN
LVHW080319110826
845155LV00026B/161